Childhood Denied

We dedicate this book to the memory of Earl Noblet.

Childhood Denied

Ending the Nightmare
of Child Abuse and Neglect

Kathleen Kelley Reardon, PhD

University of Southern California, Marshall School of Business

Christopher T. Noblet, MA, MBA

Los Angeles • London • New Delhi • Singapore • Washington DC

For information:

SAGE Publications, Inc.
2455 Teller Road
Thousand Oaks,
   California 91320
E-mail: order@sagepub.com

SAGE Publications India Pvt. Ltd.
B 1/I 1 Mohan Cooperative
   Industrial Area
Mathura Road, New Delhi 110 044
India

SAGE Publications Ltd.
1 Oliver's Yard
55 City Road
London EC1Y 1SP
United Kingdom

SAGE Publications Asia-Pacific Pte. Ltd.
33 Pekin Street #02-01
Far East Square
Singapore 048763

Printed in the United States of America

Library of Congress Cataloging-in-Publication Data

Reardon, Kathleen Kelley.
Childhood denied: ending the nightmare of child abuse and neglect/Kathleen Kelley Reardon, Christopher T. Noblet.
   p. cm.
Includes bibliographical references and index.
ISBN 978-1-4129-3976-8 (cloth)
ISBN 978-1-4129-3977-5 (pbk.)
   1. Child abuse—United States. 2. Child abuse—Government policy—United States. 3. Abused children—Government policy—United States. 4. Child abuse—United States—Prevention. I. Noblet, Christopher T. II. Title.

HV6626.52R43 2009
362.760973—dc22   2008022448

This book is printed on acid-free paper.

08 09 10 11 12   10 9 8 7 6 5 4 3 2 1

Acquisitions Editor:	Kassie Graves
Editorial Assistant:	Veronica K. Novak
Typesetter:	C&M Digitals (P) Ltd.
Cover Designer:	Candice Harman
Marketing Manager:	Carmel Schrire

Contents

Foreword

These Are Our Kids as Well as Theirs

By Peter Samuelson, president, and Sherry Quirk,
vice-chair, co-founders of First Star, www.firststar.org

Whether Republican or Democrat, conservative or liberal, Americans should surely support unanimously, vigorously, and with a whole heart the well-being of all our children. . . . after all, they are the only future we have. Yet First Star's distinguished child welfare experts tell us repeatedly and clearly that threats just as scary as those of Homeland Security endanger the safety and future of many American children: right here, right now: abuse, neglect, and the real perils of our nation's broken-down child welfare and foster care systems. The National Child Abuse and Neglect Data System determined that in FY 2006 an estimated 3.6 million children in the 50 states, the District of Columbia, and Puerto Rico received investigations by child protective service agencies. Of those, approximately 905,000 children were determined to be victims of child abuse or neglect and 1,530 died. Appallingly, more than three-quarters of these deaths were of children under the age of four.

Many more maltreated children die an emotional death and suffer unimaginable stress, severe anxiety, depression, and low self-esteem that blight their prospects for a happy, productive life. Half the adult males in our prisons were abused or neglected as children. . . . what does that cost us? Thousands of abused kids think about or attempt suicide. More than three-quarters of a million children (799,000) experienced foster care in 2006. Worse, in many cases it is the government that places these children in harm's way, while claiming to protect them through foster care. The dictionary defines *foster* as "to bring up, nurture, promote the growth and development of, nurse or cherish." Foster care should always provide security and protection from an unsafe home. Unfortunately, in many cases it is even worse. And too many children become stuck in perpetual foster care motion: moved repeatedly from house to house and never finding permanency. Both children and society pay a heavy price for this unstable, precarious reality. The federal government sets standards to protect children and find safe, permanent homes for them. Yet not one state has fully complied. According to UNICEF, in 2007 the United States ranked number 20 of the 21 wealthiest First World nations by multiple measures of child welfare. . . . How can that be? Abused children have no lobbyists, don't vote, and thus have no real voice to protest. In two-thirds of the country, proceedings are shrouded in secrecy, even after the child dies.

Hello, America: this is happening on our watch! William Gray (D-PA), former majority whip and chairman of the House Budget Committee, who serves as vice chair of the nonpartisan Pew Commission on Children in Foster Care, noted, "the foster care system is in disrepair. Every state has now failed the federal foster care reviews and we've seen far too many news stories of children missing from the system or injured while in care." The commission released far-reaching recommendations to overhaul the nation's foster care system. Formulated by leading experts, these recommendations represent intensive analysis and interviews with professionals, parents, and children. Commission Chairman Bill Frenzel (R-MN) said in 2004 that these recommendations include "greater accountability by both child welfare agencies and courts; giving states a flexible, reliable source of federal funding, new options and incentives to seek safety and permanence for children in foster care and helping courts secure the tools, information and training needed to fulfill their responsibilities to children." What is not to like here?

Much of this work to put children first involves changing their status as chattel or property under our legal system. How can it be right that in half the country a man who beats a dog goes to jail but one who beats his child the same way is not prosecuted?

First Star (www.firststar.org), the charity we founded in 1999, is working day and night right now on three critical issues for children: to guarantee abused children in all 50 states the right to their own, competent attorney during court proceedings where their future is held in the balance; to eliminate legal and regulatory barriers that prevent those children's advocates from exchanging information vital to keeping them out of dangerous situations; and to shine the light of day where bureaucracy is hidden in shadows away from public scrutiny and accountability. First Star and the Children's Advocacy Institute of the University of San Diego recently sponsored the fifth bipartisan Congressional Roundtable on Children on Capitol Hill, presenting a detailed analysis of State policies in concealing or revealing systemic failure after the death of a child from abuse or neglect. We gave grades of A through F to each State. Regrettably, despite Federal mandates to the contrary, 20 States received grades of C– or below. Ten received an F.

> We hope and pray as an American Mom and an American Dad that we will finally prioritize the rights of our children. Likewise, we hope every member of Congress, Republicans and Democrats alike, will join First Star in reforming the current child welfare and foster care systems. Their disrepair poses a high threat to our nation and to the safety and happiness of our nation's most vulnerable children. Let's nurture these kids and give them a fair chance for healthy and bright futures. What better investment can we make? If we don't do this, who are we? And if not now, when?

Note: Film producer and media executive Peter Samuelson *(Wilde, Tom & Viv, Arlington Road, Revenge of the Nerds)* has founded four significant charities: Starlight (1982), Starbright (1990), First Star (1999), and Everyone Deserves a Roof (2005). He teaches entrepreneurial philanthropy and is at work on a book, *Giving a Damn.* Peter lives in Holmby Hills with his wife Saryl and four children and may be reached at peter@samuelson.la.

Attorney Sherry Quirk is a partner at Schiff Hardin, LLC in Washington, DC, and has a long history of child advocacy.

Foreword

By Robert C. Fellmeth

This work addresses a special population. These more than 500,000 children have been abused, molested, or severely neglected. They have been removed from their parents. Many of their parents have been adjudicated as unfit, and the state has supplanted their authority. These children of the state now have a court, social workers, and foster care providers serving as their parents. As the pages to follow document, their prospects are not promising, for the state has been itself a neglectful parent. In a democracy, we are the state. So, dear reader, peruse these pages with special care, for they concern your children. When you hear religious zealots talk of Christ and sanctimoniously pray and invoke their special relationship with God, ask whether they know about the information in this work, and whether it comports with the Sermon on the Mount. When the political left responds reflexively to the Service Employees International Union (SEIU), ask how a child subject to constantly changing faces—social workers (represented by SEIU), judges, attorneys, foster care placements—are really served by simply more desks for the pieces of paper who become these children to the social service establishment. When you hear our public officials on the right talk about family values, ask them how they are doing with this group. They are used to talking about how the children of our nation are the children of us all, but they do not seem to fully grasp the obvious and profound difference here—these children are not ours in a cosmic or theoretical sense; they are literally and legally "our children." So how much is this group of self-indulgent rationalizers investing in them?

These children need three things. First, we need to have fewer of them—as few as possible. So where do they come from? They come from extreme poverty, from paternal abandonment, from meth addiction. But we have seen our unwed birth rate climb from 8% to 20% to 30% and now to 37%—with nary a comment from the politically correct and relentlessly adult-centric media. For African American children the unwed birth rate is almost 70%. These are not the children of celebrities. The census data about them are stark. These children live well below the poverty line, and the median income for married couple families exceeds $55,000. It is not merely a 50% gain for our children. When they have two committed parents, it is a factor of more than 400%. Absent fathers are paying child support at a rate under $70 per month per child. But we do not talk about it. Here is a revolutionary idea that this book implicitly endorses—every child has a need to be cared for by at least two people dedicated to his or her welfare and future. Maybe there will be a divorce; maybe there will be disease or death or other misfortune. But at least we postulate the attempt is worthy of praise and, indeed, of expectation.

Having changed the social ethic, we rightly follow with parenting education in our schools. Most of these children will become parents. Isn't it necessary to teach them how to protect and nurture a child—information about contraception and prenatal care, and about how children develop—how to avoid sudden infant death and brain injury from shaking a baby, and a hundred other lessons? How is such education less important than a literature course or trigonometry? I do not know about you, but I haven't used cosine or tangent formulas ever—in the 45 years since I took the course. We need not devote even an entire course to this subject—just brief modules interspersed periodically in grades 9 through 12. We do not do it.

Second, these children need a parent, preferably two parents. They need to be adopted or given guardians who have a commitment to them one on one. Every child needs to feel that there is someone who cares, someone who will stay up all night worrying if something goes wrong. The child needs the example, even needs someone to rebel against during the phased insanity of adolescence. Psychologists have a word for what happens when children lack that anchor: detachment syndrome. These foster children tell us how much it means to have a home—not an institution but a personal home. If relatives are not able to adopt, the next best bet is the family foster care provider. These families volunteer to take children into their homes. They are reviewed, licensed, and here is what happens wonderfully often—they bond. These parents are the source of most non-kin adoptions for these foster children.

But the supply of foster care families is in decline, and adoptions are increasingly rare. In fact, many states now simply label children past the cute stage of infancy as unadoptable. States need to stop shortchanging these future parents by paying them at least the out-of-pocket costs of care so that their introduction to a child is not conditioned on sacrifice of their pension or self-sufficiency. We now pay these families consistently

30% to 50% below the out-of-pocket cost of care. Family placements are down, and adoptions are down. Instead of four or five couples competing for each child—as should be the case—we have suspicious Uncle Ned getting them because there is no other choice, or we have siblings split, and we have too many, far too many, going into institutional group homes. The real irony is that we pay those folks about eight times what we pay families to care for the children, not 8% more or 80% more, but 800% more. Increasing compensation for families who provide the care would result in more family placements, more adoptions, and much lower cost. Why, then, is this happening in so many states? Is it because state legislators failed to comprehend simple addition and subtraction skills? It seems more likely the product of group homes financing lobbyists in state capitals, leaving family foster care providers—and the children who should be in their care—dispersed, unorganized, and bereft of campaign contribution power.

Third, these children need to be more visible. Their plight as outlined in this book is only possible because in most states their situation, status, conditions, and even the judicial proceedings deciding their fate are locked in confidentiality. Allegedly, this is to protect them. Actually, it is to protect the social service establishment that—with some notable exceptions—cares for them very badly. It would be possible to allow a court to seal a proceeding or a child on petition without burying an entire system in secrecy. Ironically, most states even hide information when a child dies from child abuse or neglect—both those who are in private hands and those under their own jurisdiction. Few states (New Hampshire and Nevada) have defensible state laws ensuring disclosure of the causes of those deaths.

Note: Robert C. Fellmeth is Price Professor of Public Interest Law at the University of San Diego School of Law, author of *Child Rights and Remedies* (Clarity Press, 2002, 2006), and Director of the Children's Advocacy Institute.

Foreword

By Charles D. Gill

"These are the times that try men's souls."

—Thomas Paine

Thoughts on the Present State of American Affairs

"In the following pages, I offer nothing more than simple facts, plain arguments and common sense; and have no other preliminaries to settle with the reader, other than that he will divest himself of prejudice and prepossession, and suffer his reason and his feelings to determine for themselves that he will put on, or rather that he will not put off, the true character of a man, and generously enlarge his views beyond the present day."

—Thomas Paine

I give a standing ovation to the foregoing remarks, efforts, and thoughts of my esteemed colleagues, Peter Samuelson, Sherry Quirk, Professor Robert C. Fellmeth, and, of course, the sensitive first author of this important book, Professor Kathleen Kelley Reardon and her able co-author Christopher T. Noblet.

We all come from different backgrounds and experiences on the issue of the mistreatment of America's only national treasure, her children. As the only one of us to actually sentence child abusers, hear their testimony, see the photographs of their abuse, and hear the testimony of witnesses to that abuse as well as the many professionals who analyze these cases, I am perhaps more militant and aggressive then my colleagues on this issue.

Twenty-five years on the bench is a great teacher.

As the first neighbor lawyer in the Nation on the so-called "war on poverty," I long ago discovered that we have been naive in fighting wars on poverty, drugs, and child abuse. All are doomed to failure.

The real war we should be fighting is the war on the poverty of values ensured not by the usual social worker "needs" of children but rather by a transition to the "rights" of children. One hundred and ninety-three nations in the world recognize the "rights" of Children in the United Nations Convention on the Rights of the Child created under and with the input of President Ronald Reagan.

There are only two nations in the world who have not signed on to this "Magna Carta" for children: Somalia, a nation without a recognized government, and the United States, a government that does not recognize children as rights-bearing citizens. Yet there is virtual silence from our political leaders and even traditional children's "needs" organizations. Many are in my view one thousand shards of glass that are insular, shortsighted, and even vain.

Because of this book, I hope the entire political spectrum of Americans, left, right, and center might consider the following courses of action:

1. The original U.S. Constitution had three genetic defects. It excluded women, African Americans, and children. The first two defects have been cured by amendments. Groups such as the American Academy of Pediatrics and American Association of School Administrators (18,000 school superintendents) support an amendment for children as have scores of other countries. We need to support this.

2. Every child shall have a trained and independent lawyer represent him or her whenever that child's life or liberty is at stake in a court or agency.

3. Every judge in a child's case shall be educated on the developmental levels and words of children.

4. All courtrooms deciding issues concerning children's issues shall be open, unless it is clearly established that it is not in the child's best interest to do so. The judge and the child's lawyer shall state in writing why the court proceeding is closed.

5. All schools shall have mandatory parenting courses.

6. Each state shall have an omsbudsman overseeing its protection agency.

7. The United States should ratify the UN Convention on the Rights of the Child.

   "The sun never shined on a cause of greater worth."

   —Thomas Paine

Note: Connecticut Superior Court Judge Charles D. Gill is a tireless advocate for the rights of children.

Preface

Childhood Denied was written to advance the advocacy of those who work with children to protect them from abuse and neglect. It takes the issues Peter Samuelson and Sherry Quirk describe in the first foreword and conveys them in language our lawmakers and people in positions to make a difference can more easily comprehend. We must take what experts tell us about the plight of children harmed each day because of a dysfunctional system and their inability to protest with votes and bring it into the light of day. We are not the first to attempt this; we hope to be the last required to do so. This book is a wake-up call to those in government who can assure that children at risk for abuse and neglect are protected, their lives saved. Otherwise, we don't deserve to call ourselves civilized.

The very idea of allowing the nightmare of child abuse to continue, hardly abated, is appalling. Surely no one thinks of himself or herself as belonging to any group that does this. But as you read what experts have to say, hear the voices of vulnerable children at risk, learn how long this tragedy has been going on, and understand how a few good people pressuring those in the right places could turn it around, you will wonder why so many children suffer so much on our doorsteps. You will read the impressive, relentless efforts by those in the media who've tried to open our eyes and our hearts and provoke us to action. They and child advocates everywhere keep banging at the door of change with success here and there but the travesty mushrooms around them. They need our help. This book is a call to provide it.

We attempt here to educate not by reviewing all the research and writings out there but by highlighting some of the efforts that clearly articulate the nature of the problem, why it continues, and much of what we must do now to make significant changes. We need to make them for children like Frankie, one of the first children Kathleen met during research for this book. That's what we need—to have children who've been victimized by abusers and neglected and those at risk for the same on our minds until we provide them the protection and love they, like all children, so richly deserve.

Today I Met Frankie

I didn't want to write a book about the treatment of children in our society without first getting to know some of those whose lives have been characterized by what Thoreau would term quiet desperation. It would be irresponsible to recommend that children be removed from dangerous homes without also knowing where they can be placed, what they need, whom they need, and how to get it for them.

So my journey and this book started at a facility outside of Los Angeles that houses what have come to be known as level 12 children. These are often children who could not make it in foster homes. The mission of this facility is to protect and care for such children until they can be placed in foster care, returned to their homes, or adopted.

Not long after my arrival, I was invited to lunch in the same room in which several young children were eating pizza. We sat at a table near the window some six yards from the curious eyes of mostly six- and seven-year-olds. We were served a lovely meal of chicken, rice, and vegetables. As we were commenting on the delicious fare, a little boy escorted by the cook approached our table. He stopped next to Minister Tim, a gentle man at the head of our table. "Frankie wants to tell you something," the cook said smiling. "Go ahead, Frankie," he urged.

Frankie stood a little more than three feet tall. He had light brown hair cut in a slight Dutch-boy fashion. His cheeks were full, accenting his blue eyes that matched his T-shirt. He glanced around the table. A sheepish smile crept across his face. His eyes glistened, possibly in anticipation of his effect on us. "What makes you so special?" he challenged, pointing at one of the plates and then looking directly into Tim's amused eyes. We broke into laughter. Frankie was delighted but he stayed with his mission and awaited an answer. "We have guests today," Tim said, composing himself. "so we're having a special lunch." Frankie nodded, accepting the explanation. "Why don't you say hello," Tim suggested. Frankie turned to me, paused, then proceeded slowly closer. He paused a second time to gaze momentarily into my eyes and study my face. He then walked over to me. As he approached I wondered: Should I shake his hand? Will I frighten him? I noticed his small right hand move as if he were wondering the same thing. I cautiously reached out. He readily met my hand with a firm shake and a broad welcoming smile. I could feel my heart as I held that small hand. I hoped against hope that this same hand had not been used to protect him from abuse. That this adorable little boy was the exception to the rule for level 12 children—those who are supposedly high risk in foster care, rejects even of a system that itself often deserves rejection. As he moved away to lean against the wall next to me, I could tell that he wanted to talk more. "How old are you?" I asked. "I'm six," he said. "But," he added, looking around to be sure he had everyone's attention, "tomorrow is my birthday." We chimed in with Ohs and Ahs. "Will you be six tomorrow or seven?" I asked. "I'll be seven," Frankie told us with delight. "And do you know what I want?" he asked. I shook my head. "I really want a remote control car." "My goodness," I said. "That would be wonderful." Frankie nodded again, looking at each of us, no doubt hoping that among this group there would be someone who could appreciate and respond to his heartfelt hope.

This was not a broken child. Frankie did not look like the children we all hear about, the ones we shouldn't adopt because they're too far gone. He could be any boy on the playground of any school. Here was hope in a disarming package. There was no sign of what he must have endured to be there on this day. He was just an adorable boy who was about to become seven with just one dream, that of a remote control car. For that moment, at least, he was safe, comfortable, and captivating. If someone had said, "We are looking for a home for Frankie," I would have been hard pressed to not take him in my arms and do whatever I could to make the rest of his dreams come true. But as I was to learn, Frankie's life was more complex than that. The ties binding him to the system were too durable for such a simple solution and perhaps for any solution other than frequent change due to frequent failure not of Frankie's making.

After reasonable assurances that his birthday would not be forgotten, six-year-old soon to be seven-year-old Frankie bid us farewell. He waved to each of us and smiled once more. "Bye, Frankie," we called as he left in the company of a little girl named Samantha who had joined him. "Have a happy birthday," I said. Frankie turned back to look at me. He smiled, turned away and walked back into his daily life, having left an indelible mark on mine.

Acknowledgments

We are grateful to many people, especially those with First Star, who have helped us comprehend and express the issues preventing children at risk for abuse and neglect from receiving the protection they deserve— the protection we adults owe to them but so often fail to deliver.

We especially wish to thank Peter Samuelson for believing in this project, in fact nudging us into it in his inimitable, subtle way, from start to finish. Peter's dedication to improving the lives of children through Starlight, Starbright, and, with Sherry Quirk, First Star has been nothing short of remarkable. He is truly a man who has given back many times over and continues to do so everyday.

We'd like to thank several people at First Star: Debbie Sams for her work in connecting us to experts, working with us in the early stages on key concepts, and helping in many other ways. Erika Germer and Whytni Kermodle Frederick worked diligently on permissions, sending us articles and contacting experts in advance of interviews. Amy Harfeld became First Star Executive Director in time to be there for us in coordinating the tying up of loose ends and keeping us informed of First Star research.

Our thanks, too, to Connie Noblet, who interviewed Darlene Allen of Adoption Rhode Island and shared with us not only what was said in the interview but also what she learned about challenges in our quest to better protect children.

We're grateful to Kassie Graves, editor at SAGE Publications, who has been there in every way, as has Veronica Novak. Also at SAGE, we'd like to thank Kristen Gibson, Laureen Gleason, Helen Glenn Court, and Carmel Schrire.

1

Keepers of the Plan

Child abuse and neglect are like dancing with a bear.[1] The trouble is, we've been doing far too much sitting down. The bear takes over and then we're surprised at how bad things have gotten. Too little has been done at the federal and state levels to get a grip on this bear and to make it follow our lead.

Why are conditions so bad? What keeps us from protecting the most vulnerable among us? Blair Sadler, president and CEO of Children's Hospital and Health Center of San Diego, applauded the excellent studies on child abuse conducted in recent years, but observed that "they have not served as an effective catalyst to galvanize a nationally coordinated action agenda."[2] What he terms a *national call to action* was the purpose of a compendium of articles in a special issue of the international journal *Child Abuse and Neglect*.[3] Sadler described the situation then as it might still be described today: "The field of child abuse remains fragmented, disjointed, and largely ineffective at the national level."[4] This is certainly not from an absence of effort on the part of extraordinary people whose work lives and volunteer hours have been devoted to the advancement of child protection in the United States and throughout the world. Yet, the issue receives sporadic attention by governments around the world and continues to be the stuff of frustrating conversations among those closest to the child abuse and neglect issue.

In this chapter, we examine the definitions of child abuse and neglect and look at a potentially unifying view, what types need immediate focus, why it continues (resistance, poverty, fear), and what issues need to be addressed immediately. The goal is not simplistic solutions, because they are destined to fail. The challenge is too great. But we can't throw up our hands and simply say that no one can get their arms around this issue and thus our only hope is to make small inroads. We need a sustained effort with a number of approaches.

This is a huge goal if the past is any indication of the future. As Bob Herbert of the *New York Times* reminded us, "every few months some horrifying child abuse case elbows its way onto the front pages, and there is a general outcry." But then, silence. "And then the story subsides," Herbert wrote, "and we behave as if this murderous abuse of helpless children trapped in the torture chambers of their own homes has somehow subsided with it. But child abuse is a hideous, widespread and chronic problem across the country. And despite the sensational cases that periodically grab the headlines, it doesn't get nearly enough attention."[5]

Kathleen's work in preventive medicine has largely involved the use of persuasion protocols to change health habits; therefore, we're inclined to look at child abuse and neglect as an issue in need of a message that galvanizes people to action—especially those with the power to make change. Over the past several decades, this has proven an extremely tall order and is unlikely to be achieved with a single book, but it is certainly part of the reason for writing one. What's needed desperately is a message that gets through to all people who care about children at risk, about the extent to which we've tuned out their voices and the many ways in which each of us can help protect the most vulnerable among us. To do this, we need to explore what stands in the way—why abused and neglected children are abused and neglected again by people meant to care for them and who could change their lives for the better. We need to explore what has been done well and what needs to be done better and give everyone who cares about children the opportunity to participate. We could argue about who is the best expert, and there would be many candidates, but our time is best used allowing such experts to continue their excellent work and using their expertise to get the horror of child abuse and neglect the attention it so richly deserves.

To this end the authors have collaborated with First Star.

First Star's Vision

First Star envisions a future in which all of America's abused and neglected children have a right to be heard and protected by the systems and laws entrusted with their care, and in which these systems are transparent and accountable and receive the resources necessary to ensure positive outcomes for the children they serve.

First Star engages in reform that is systemically focused, synergistic, collaborative, entrepreneurial, bold, non-partisan, and expert-driven.

First Star's Mission

First Star's mission is to strengthen the rights and improve the lives of America's abused and neglected children by illuminating the child welfare system's worst failures and igniting reform to correct them.

First Star fulfills its mission through an integrated approach that combines research, public awareness, advocacy, and policy reform.

This book presents the messages of child abuse experts and practitioners affiliated with First Star, as well as many affiliated with other key organizations devoted to improving protection for children at risk. This book uses an accessible format, one intended to break through— to galvanize a nationally coordinated agenda and make the difference. Blair Sadler has steadfastly argued that changes must be made if children at risk are to be protected and cherished. It is through First Star's work that the authors came to this subject and with First Star's encouragement and help that this book was written.

First Star is clear in its mission statement, as we are in this book, that the issue of child abuse and neglect requires a team effort to derive excellent, workable solutions from people of all political affiliations. Children belong to no political party. As we discuss in Chapter 8 regarding the politics of child abuse, we must come together to find ways to better serve these children. This of course is the main reason for writing this book, followed by making understanding of the issue accessible to those who can make a difference. To do so sometimes requires extrapolating from the findings of science and social science. We do that with great care and with an eye toward balance in presenting prevalent views.

Organizations Devoted to Helping Children at Risk

Alliance for Children and Families www.alliance1.org

American Bar Association Center on Children and the Law www.abanet.org/child

American Professional Society on the Abuse of Children www.apsac.org

American Public Human Services Association www.aphasa.org

Chadwick Center for Children and Families www.chadwickcenter.org

Chapin Hall Center for Children www.chapinhall.org

Child Abuse Prevention Network www.child-abuse.com

Childhelp www.childhelp.org

Child Relief and You www.cry.org

Children Now www.childrennow.org

Children's Advocacy Institute www.caichildlaw.org

Children's Defense Fund www.cdf.org

The Children's Partnership www.childrenspartnership.org

Children's Rights Council www.gocrc.com

Children's Rights Division of Human Rights Watch www.hrw.org/children

Child Welfare League of America www.cwla.org

Defense for Children International www.dci-is.org

Every Child Matters www.everychildmatters.org

First Star www.firststar.org

International Bureau for Children's Rights www.ibcr.org

Kempe Children's Center www.kempecenter.org

National Association of Counsel for Children www.naccchildlaw.org

National Center for Youth Law www.youthlaw.org

National Center on Child Fatality Review www.ican-ncfr.org

National Children's Advocacy Center www.nationalcac.org

National Child's Rights Alliance www.youthrights.net

National Citizen's Review Panels www.uky.edu/SocialWork/crp

National Foster Parent Association www.nfpainc.org

National MCH Center for Death Review www.childdeathreview.org

Prevent Child Abuse America www.preventchildabuse.org

Robert F. Kennedy Memorial Center for Human Rights www.rfkmemorial.org

Save the Children www.childrennow.org

United Nations Children's Fund (UNICEF) www.unicef.org

Voices for America's Children www.voices.org

To achieve the objectives of First Star and other organizations devoted to protecting children at risk for abuse and neglect, we need what Dr. David Chadwick, director emeritus of the Center for Child Protection at Children's Hospital San Diego, called *keepers of the plan*. These are people who don't give up as unrelenting advocates for children. He argued that we may need another century to adequately wage and win the child abuse and neglect fight—a bottom-up rather than top-down insistence that violence against children end—as no president or prime minister, king or dictator has ever called for a shunning of violence. He explained the need for sustained, long-term focus:

> To be effective, we require keepers of a plan who will devote many decades of their lives to the effort. The keepers will keep the message alive. It will take sweat and tears. These keepers must recruit successors with similar dedication. Who, among you, are the keepers? Who will be willing to step forward and work tirelessly to keep the message alive?[6]

In this book you meet a number of keepers of the plan, those famous and those toiling away behind the scenes to benefit children who suffer daily at the hands of people they should be able to trust. These people don't seek recognition, but they receive it here because their work is what protects children from unspeakable terror. Theirs are the voices, the helping hands, and the protective arms that reach out and make a difference in the lives of suffering children who desperately need our help.

We also explore programs that have worked and those that have not—and benefit by learning from both. Any effort on behalf of children at risk for abuse and neglect with good intentions is of value. Solutions in this struggle do not derive from exact science, but from successful and even failed efforts by people driven by good intentions.

What Is Abuse and Neglect?

Chadwick argued that part of escalating attention and finding solutions involves defining child abuse and neglect in ways that have credibility.[7] We need good and consistent definitions and good and consistent remedies. We need to move beyond a divergence of views about what needs to be done. We must stop allowing confusion between significant abuse and a loving parent becoming frightened and lightly slapping a child who ran into a busy street. The latter is not best practice, but lumping it in with the horrors abused children face daily threatens to diminish the credibility of those who endeavor to save children from the worst practices in child rearing and abusiveness. It generates debates that hold up progress and play on fears of parents who think, "One mistake and I may lose custody of my child."

Peter Samuelson, co-founder of First Star, explained the distinction in this way:

> At First Star, we have our hands full living in an altogether darker and more awful place than the gray area where a loving and good parent disciplines their child for running into the road. At the Grossman Burn Institute, I was shown a photograph of an 8-year-old girl who'd been deliberately burned by her parent with cigarettes. She had over 100 burns all over her body. If ever we have finished helping these kids whose lives are being totally blighted by fear, violence, molestation and neglect, then we'll look at some of the gray areas. I look forward to that day. But right now we are helping kids escape total blackness of heart, of spirit, of destiny. No sane human being could ever defend the wrongs against children that First Star is addressing.[8]

This book, then, isn't about children who experience what would be considered questionable parental practices—a rare rap to the hand, for example, by a parent who is tired or overwrought. Darker gray areas might include spanking a child who is rude or physically aggressive. Here again, we would argue that these do not fall into the category of best practices for parental discipline. Child psychologists focus on that area and provide alternatives forms. It is not our primary focus, because the goal of this book is to help children whose future development—and lives—are in danger, children who suffer intensely or regularly from abuse and neglect.

Let's be quite clear here. It is not that the authors of this book, experts, and First Star don't care about gray area parental practices (especially those further along the continuum toward abuse), but rather that the conditions of child abuse and neglect are so serious and so extensive that focus must first and foremost be targeted squarely on preventing discipline practices and harm that can truly ruin children's lives. At the same time, we need to look into when prevention efforts must be undertaken to ensure that less egregious types of child maltreatment are not overlooked and thus allowed to escalate into more perilous forms. We need to keep our priorities straight when it comes to defining abuse and neglect or the credibility to which Dr. Chadwick referred will not be achieved and people who must listen will not. We must bear in mind that whether physical punishment should ever be inflicted on a child is a very important issue for child development experts and that there is wonderful research in that area. But we endeavor here to separate, as clearly as possible, mild to moderately questionable parental discipline practices from abuse and neglect—the kind all people who care about children, whether Republican, Democrat, Libertarian, Green, Independent, or otherwise, can agree must stop now.

We need to first deal with the most awful dereliction of the duty that is owed to every child.

Clarity of focus in this book and for First Star is also important because of the undercurrent of fear among some parents that because they are not perfect someone may come and take their child away, that their moment outside the area of best practice as a parent will cost them dearly in this regard. We are fully aware of the difficulties faced by people who endeavor to raise children under less than ideal circumstances and will review many of those circumstances. This is not a book by or for those who are oblivious to the plight of people who face stress in their lives. Most people under financial, social, and emotional stress also care deeply about children; they want to ensure that they do not move along the continuum from constructive child discipline to abusive forms. More support is needed for prevention programs to aid such persons when they find help necessary.

From Good Practices to Abuse and Neglect

The continuum that follows depicts the range of child disciplinary practices from constructive to clearly abusive. As mentioned, even good parents and caregivers can move into the gray area. Unless they slip further along the continuum when they do so, their parenting may not be ideal but neither is it abusive. First Star encourages all those who work with children to provide constructive guidance and discipline and to focus their efforts on reducing the numbers of children subjected to abuse.

As difficult as it is, we do need to put issues in context. We need to look at how well we're meeting children's needs. We can't stop child

Child Discipline Continuum

abuse, but we can do more for children in foster care. We can certainly reduce child abuse and neglect and do more for children who have suffered. We also need to address the problem of children who reach 18 and age out of foster care. Would a good parent force a child out of the house, especially one with significant special needs, just because that child reaches a certain age? Such teenagers have nowhere to come home to. More than 40% of children who age out report being homeless at some point after leaving foster care.[9] Isn't this a kind of neglect? We do need to remove children from harmful and potentially harmful situations, but we need to be very careful in determining what those situations are and whether prevention and intervention measures will work. We need to be sure not only that we focus our attention on protecting children from harm, but also that we don't then fail them in other significant ways.

Clarice Walker, former commissioner of social services for the District of Columbia and emeritus professor at Howard University, proposed that considerable caution is required when removing children from their homes. But, she added, "we must ask the question whether there are times when a parent can't take care of a child. And there are." As she told me, "we have to err on the side of safety." Walker proposed one temporary though imperfect solution in which the conditions of an at-risk child are monitored by a responsible, observant relative (kinship care), at least until adequate observation by the child welfare system is possible. This is certainly better than one visit by a social worker to substantiate abuse after which follow-up is delayed or inadequate. "You can't expect the system to have all the answers," Walker said, "but the child needs to be protected until we have the answers we need."[10]

As will become evident in the chapters that follow, there is no one solution to child abuse and neglect because there is no single category into which all cases neatly fit. Clarice Walker cited four primary reasons for continued abuse.

The first reason is poverty. When people are unable to manage their own private issues, they become the subjects of public intervention.

Also, homelessness has become the reality for many families. "Lack of housing and housing opportunities separates families. There are huge waiting lists for adequate housing, which causes stress and causes some people to give up," Walker explained. And housing people during the day at shelters and after school facilities but having them leave at night is not a solution. It's erratic and doesn't promote the kind of privacy Walker believes people need to deal with problems. "Substantial numbers of children come into the system from families experiencing inadequate resources."

The second reason is substance abuse. Here again is a problem that creates cycles of abuse. Children raised around drugs are likely to be negatively affected by that environment both physically and emotionally. They pass these issues onto their own children, often in the same form.

The third reason is mental illness of those caring for children. Walker pointed to the 2005 case of a woman who threw her three young children off a bridge.

The fourth reason is severe disabilities of children beyond the management abilities and resources of families.

Many adults who abuse and neglect children do so because they have lost the ability to manage their own lives, let alone care for children. Those children then abuse their children and the cycle continues. To save one child from abuse now is to probably save dozens or more down the line as well.

Preventing a cycle of abuse and neglect requires a strong federal role in determining what needs to be done, Walker suggested, but "management of programs must be left to the states." To this Peter Samuelson added that we must ask, as would senior executives at FedEx: Why are money and programs reaching some states and counties faster than others? Business success depends on asking this kind of question; so, too, does the safety of children at risk:

The Federal Express people sit every Monday morning in Memphis and ask why last week's stats show it took longer to deliver an envelope in Cleveland than in Cincinnati. But a states' rights orientation in the U.S. with regard to child protection has resulted in 2,200 individual jurisdictions determining how to deal with child abuse and neglect. They tend not to talk to each other as they keep their bureaucracy conveniently secret. The kids can't sue for damages (courtesy of the

DeShaney ruling) and they don't vote or lobby. The children's' opinions and their pain are often not heard, and in our system if you aren't heard you don't count. This balkanized 2,200 sets of rules is absurdly inefficient: right there you see a big reason why our stats compare so badly with so many other First World nations. They have central coordination: when they get it right, it gets right everywhere. We instead have pockets of best practice totally ignored by the black hole of inept procedure down the road. If Federal Express can learn the lessons of locality A to help determine best practice in locality B, is it really too much to ask that we treat the kids as well as the boxes?[11]

As will become evident, laws and how they are implemented from state to state vary significantly. This is part of the unevenness of attention that children at risk suffer. Even definitions of the best interests of the child vary widely. How well a child at risk is protected depends, to a large extent, on the state in which he or she resides. This is why we need to look seriously at more consistency across states. This is likely to be provided only if the federal government steps up and takes the lead, perhaps later returning greater prerogatives to states with demonstrated readiness to take them on. We'll look more closely at the debate over this and some possible solutions in the course of this book.

Efforts at Defining Abuse and Neglect

Having looked at some of the complexities involved in defining child abuse, let's start with some working definitions. Child abuse and neglect is defined, according to the Child Abuse Prevention and Treatment Act (CAPTA), at a minimum as

- any recent act or failure to act on the part of a parent or caretaker, which results in death, serious physical or emotional harm, sexual abuse or exploitation, or
- an act or failure to act, which presents an imminent risk of serious harm.

CAPTA defines child sexual abuse as

- the employment, use, persuasion, inducement, enticement, or coercion of any child to engage in, or assist any other person to engage in, any sexually explicit conduct or simulation of such conduct for the purpose of producing a visual depiction of such conduct.

- the rape, and in cases of caretaker or familial relationships, statutory rape, molestation, prostitution, or other form of sexual exploitation of children, or incest with children.[12]

Elaboration on Child Maltreatment

The definition of child maltreatment varies from state to state. All states but one define the four major categories of maltreatment that are specifically discussed in CAPTA: neglect, physical abuse, sexual abuse, and emotional abuse. Many states also include other types of maltreatment such as abandonment, medical neglect, lack of supervision, and risk of harm.

First Star defines child maltreatment to include physical abuse, sexual abuse, emotional abuse, physical neglect, educational neglect, and emotional neglect. A child subjected to abuse, neglect, or withheld medical treatment is maltreated regardless of an absence of intent to harm.

For many years, child welfare professionals and researchers have discussed the benefits of clear and consistent definitions of child abuse and neglect. It is widely agreed that consistent definitions will greatly improve the effectiveness of reporting systems, research, and policy planning and hence the services provided to children. With this in mind, First Star offers the following working definitions of the various types of abuse and neglect:

- Physical abuse includes but is not limited to inflicting or attempting to inflict harm on a child's person by hitting, kicking, burning, choking, suffocating, dropping, throwing, shaking, or holding the child under water. It is not necessary for the abuser to intend to cause the child pain or injury for the child to be physically abused. Bruising, bleeding (internally or externally), scarring, or other manifestations of abuse need not appear for the child to have been physically abused.

- Sexual abuse includes but is not limited to "the employment, use, persuasion, inducement, enticement, or coercion of any child to engage in, or assist any other person to engage in, any sexually explicit conduct or simulation of such conduct for the purpose of producing a visual depiction of such conduct; or the rape, and in cases of caretaker or interfamilial relationships, statutory rape, molestation, prostitution, or other form of sexual exploitation of children, or incest with children."[13] Sexual conduct includes but is not limited to inappropriate touching of the breasts, buttocks, penis, or vagina with any body part (including oral contact), inappropriate kissing, sexually explicit talk, and intercourse. It is not necessary for the abuser to use force in the commission of the acts for the child to be sexually abused.

- Emotional abuse includes but is not limited to psychological, verbal, and mental abuse, and may involve extreme forms of punishment (including periods of isolation, force-feeding, or making the child perform acts of violence on animals or other people), berating, belittling, shaming, or such acts that cause or are known to cause mental, emotional, cognitive or behavioral disorders. It is not necessary for the abuser to intend to cause the child emotional harm, or for the child to manifest symptoms of emotional abuse for the child to be or have been emotionally abused.

- Neglect includes but is not limited to basic failure to provide for the child. First Star recognizes that any assessment of neglect must recognize the effects of poverty on a caregiver's ability to provide the child's basic necessities.

- Physical neglect includes but is not limited to failure or refusal to prevent the child from ingesting harmful substances (including medication, alcohol, drugs, pesticides, and cleaners), desertion, abandonment, insufficient monitoring and supervision, failure or refusal to seek or provide health care, or withholding medically indicated treatment where, in the qualified medical judgment of the child's treating health care provider or providers, such treatment would effectively improve the child's condition.

- Educational neglect includes but is not limited to failure or refusal to enroll a school-aged child in school or to otherwise provide a substantial and appropriate education, failure or refusal to ensure the child's classroom attendance, and failure to follow the child's educational progress to ensure that special needs (including alternative education to address learning difficulties) are met.

- Emotional neglect includes but is not limited to failure or refusal to provide the child with regular nurturing and affection, failure or refusal to keep the child from witnessing potentially traumatic events within the home (including domestic violence or sexually explicit conduct), and failure or refusal to address the child's psychological needs (including services and health care). It is not necessary for the caregiver to believe that his or her action or inaction constitutes neglect for the child to be neglected.[14]

The issue of intentionality is critical in the determination of abuse. First Star stipulates that the intention to harm a child is not required for abuse to be present. The definition just given specifies that intentionality need not necessarily be present, but courts in some states require intentionality. The difficulty, of course, is that intention to harm a child is deniable. Who really knows what is going on in the mind of a person who harms a child? If the child is severely or repeatedly abused in one of the many ways described, most advocates for children (and anyone who cares about children) believe that the question of intention is far less relevant than the safety of the child in determining protective action.

Despite these definitions and other efforts to establish clarity as to what constitutes child abuse and neglect, Jill Elaine Hasday's work on *The Canon of Family Law* indicates that in many states parents retain the right to physically discipline their children even in ways that might be considered in the gray area of the aforementioned continuum. Hasday explained that though courts do now stress the best interests of the child,

> The law of parenthood has changed over time, and the emergence, since the middle of the nineteenth century, of child custody cases purporting to apply a "best interests of the child" standard is a significant development. But the canonical story of the demise of common law property norms importantly misdescribes family law and its governing principles. It overstates the changes that have occurred in family law over time. Here too, there is substantial evidence within family law to support an excluded counter-narrative: the story of the persistence of common law property norms in the law of parenthood. Parents retain substantial elements of many of their common law rights, even where those rights potentially conflict with their children's interests.[15]

With specific regard to corporal punishment parental rights, Hasday wrote:

> Let's turn to the law of corporal punishment, where parents also retain essential elements of their common law rights. At common law, a parent had the right to physically chastise his child. Courts and legal commentators endorsed physical chastisement as a way of securing a child's obedience to his parent's authority, and never required a parent to establish that the chastisement was in the child's best interests. The exact scope of a parent's common law right of correction varied modestly over time, but it was always wide-ranging. By the end of the nineteenth century, a majority of common law courts held that a parent could inflict reasonable or moderate correction on his child, and rarely convicted a parent for exceeding the bounds of reasonableness or moderation. Today, every state still recognizes a parent's authority to impose corporal punishment on his child. At least thirty states and the District of Columbia, for instance, have codified a parent's right to inflict "reasonable" corporal punishment. At least thirteen states have codified a parent's right to impose corporal punishment in slightly different terms.[16]

To these important observations of how slow the progress has been in developing laws that truly protect children at risk, Peter Samuelson added this observation:

> When the Founding Fathers framed the Constitution, they deliberately did not give civil rights to three groups: women, people of color and anyone who hadn't reached their 18th birthday. We've had Suffrage, Emancipation and some progress has been made. For children, the great collective myopia has kept things pretty much status quo for two hundred years: The situation of abused children at law is not far from that of slaves before Emancipation. Remember, when Nat Turner led the first great slave revolt, the law had to be changed to make him responsible so that they could hang him. Kids are still in the legal limbo of that non-person status. They are generally chattel and treated as such. Kids don't vote, they can't sue the government for damages (per DeShaney vs. Winnebago County), they don't send money to Washington nor to their State capital, and most of what happens to abused and neglected kids is kept secret, even when they are killed. So why will anything ever change? Somebody had better start getting angry about this: it is a disgrace for the richest nation in the world to so squander its human capital.[17]

The question of what reasonable corporal punishment is naturally arises. This definition still varies by state.

Hasday concluded that "the canonical story of the demise of common law property norms significantly misrepresents much of family law and its animating principles. Parents have retained (or sometimes expanded upon) important aspects of many of their common law rights, even when those rights are potentially inconsistent with their children's interests."[18] Simply put, what we have come to believe as generally true in family law is indeed not the case. Especially in some states, corporal punishment of children is still entirely legal. So where in the United States a child lives influences the extent to which he or she can legally experience what many experts would consider child abuse or neglect.

Damage Beyond the Visible

If there is one reason for outrage beyond the obvious physical and emotional harm to children who are victims of abuse, it is the long-term effects on the child, the child's children, and therefore society. Research is clear now on the enduring negative effects of abuse and neglect on a child's brain development and function. This story, recounted by Martin Teicher in *Scientific American*, demonstrates the horrors behind the obvious in child abuse:

> In 1994, Boston police were shocked to discover a malnourished four-year-old locked away in a filthy Roxbury apartment, where he lived in dreadfully squalid conditions. Worse, the boy's tiny hands were found to have been horrendously burned. It emerged that his drug-abusing mother had held the child's hands under a steaming-hot faucet to punish him for eating her boyfriend's food, despite her instructions not to do so. The ailing youngster had been given no medical care at all. The disturbing story quickly made national headlines. Later placed in foster care, the boy received skin grafts to help his scarred hands regain their function. But even though the victim's physical wounds were treated, recent research findings indicate that any injuries inflicted to his developing mind may never truly heal.[19]

Research such as that of Teicher and his colleagues at Harvard Medical School and McLean Hospital in Belmont, Massachusetts, reveals a strong link between physical, sexual, and emotional mistreatment of children and the development of psychiatric problems:

> Because childhood abuse occurs during the critical formative time when the brain is being physically sculpted by experience, the impact of severe stress can leave an indelible imprint on its structure and function. Such abuse, it seems, induces a cascade of molecular and neurobiological effects that irreversibly alter neural development.[20]

Teicher explained that the aftermath of child abuse can manifest itself at any age and in a variety of ways. It can appear as depression, anxiety, suicidal thoughts, or posttraumatic stress. Aggression, impulsiveness, delinquency, hyperactivity, and substance abuse are also possible. One of the worst outcomes psychologically is borderline personality disorder, which Teicher described as seeing others in black and white terms, sometimes putting a person on a pedestal then vilifying that person for a perceived slight or betrayal. Those afflicted can also have volcanic outbursts of anger and transient episodes of paranoia or psychosis. They typically have a history of intense, unstable relationships. They feel empty or unsure of their identity, and often try to escape through substance abuse, and experience self-destructive or suicidal impulses.

Research by Seth Pollak of the University of Wisconsin found that failure to receive typical care as a child can disrupt normal development of the child's hormonal systems. This in turn affects their relationships with caregivers. A research control group of 18 four-year-old children raised in orphanages showed lower levels of vasopressin in their urine. Researchers believe that this hormone is necessary for recognizing and responding to familiar others. During an experiment, the children sat on the laps of their birth mother or adoptive mother or an unfamiliar woman to play a computer game. The game directed the children to have various types of physical, playful contact with the adult, such as whispering or tickling each other or patting each other on the head. This type of activity should raise the level of oxytocin, but in the orphanage-raised children this did not occur to the extent that it did in family-raised children. This research suggests that the invisible effects occur not only because of the abuse but also because of the type of protective setting to which many children are moved. Dr. Pollak cautioned, however, that this does not necessarily mean that the children are permanently delayed, but it does open a window of understanding to the biological basis for what happens to children after abuse and could help with treatment design.[21]

The Chadwick Center conducted an extensive investigation into trauma, including that experienced by children who suffer abuse and neglect. The division of trauma into two types is helpful here as it indicates the extent to which single event trauma and repeated trauma elicits disorders and personality changes.

> Lenore Terr suggested two types of trauma. Type I trauma includes trauma reactions as a result of an unanticipated single event, whereas Type II trauma includes trauma reactions as a result of long-term or repeated exposure to extreme external events. Reactions to these types of traumas can be quite different. Type I trauma, or single event trauma, can evoke reactions typical of posttraumatic stress disorder such as re-experiencing the trauma, avoidant behavior, and hyper-arousal. In contrast, children exposed to long-term trauma (Type II) frequently experience fundamental personality changes. These changes are often associated with long-term coping mechanisms such as denial, repression, dissociation, and identification with the aggressor in order to "survive" the ongoing traumatic experiences. In the context of trauma, this reaction is adaptive. However, in the long-term, these methods of coping create maladaptive changes in character and personality.[22]

Among the responses to trauma reported by the Complex Trauma Taskforce in 2003, the Chadwick report includes the following:

- attachment
- boundary problems
- social isolation

- difficulty trusting others
- interpersonal difficulty
- sensorimotor developmental problems
- hypersensitivity to physical contact
- somatization
- increased medical problems
- problems with coordination and balance affect regulation
- problems with emotional regulation
- difficulty describing emotions and internal experiences
- difficulty knowing and describing internal states
- problems with communicating needs
- poor behavioral control
- poor impulse control
- self-destructive behavior
- aggressive behavior
- oppositional behavior
- excessive compliance
- sleep disturbance
- eating disorders
- substance abuse
- reenactment of traumatic past
- pathological self-soothing practices
- difficulty paying attention
- lack of sustained curiosity
- problems processing information
- problems focusing on and completing tasks
- difficulty planning and anticipating
- learning difficulties
- problems with language development and self-concept
- lack of continuous and predictable sense of self
- poor sense of separateness
- disturbance of body image
- low self-esteem
- shame and guilt[23]

The report further explains that "a child's ability to attach and appropriately interact with others influences how they engage in therapy and in other areas of their life. For child trauma and maltreatment victims, attachment patterns are often disrupted because of the traumatic experience or poor relationships associated with the trauma. . . . These attachment patterns have a devastating and long-term effect on subsequent relationships."[24]

In 2008, First Star released the statistics sheet shown in Figure 1.1 that summarizes the damage caused to children by current United States policies. Surely we can do better.

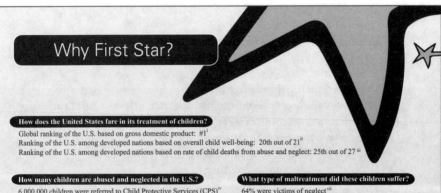

Why First Star?

How does the United States fare in its treatment of children?

Global ranking of the U.S. based on gross domestic product: #1[i]
Ranking of the U.S. among developed nations based on overall child well-being: 20th out of 21[ii]
Ranking of the U.S. among developed nations based on rate of child deaths from abuse and neglect: 25th out of 27[iii]

How many children are abused and neglected in the U.S.?

6,000,000 children were referred to Child Protective Services (CPS)[iv]
3,600,000 children were investigated for maltreatment by CPS[v]
905,000 children were determined to be victims of abuse or neglect[vi]

What type of maltreatment did these children suffer?

64% were victims of neglect[vii]
16% were victims of physical abuse[viii]
9% were victims of sexual abuse[ix]

Which children are at greatest risk for abuse or neglect?

Children under the age of one were 50% more likely to be victims of abuse and neglect[x]
Children with a reported disability were 52% more likely to experience repeated incidents of abuse or neglect[xi]

How many children in the U.S. died from abuse and neglect?

In 2006, there were an estimated 1,530 child fatality victims due to maltreatment in the U.S., or an average of 29 children a week[xii]
78% of children killed were 0-3 years old.[xiii]
Of these, 44% were less than 1 year old[xiv]

How much does child abuse and neglect cost the U.S.?

Annual estimated direct cost of medical care for child abuse and neglect in the U.S.: $33,101,302,133[xv]
Annual estimated direct AND indirect cost of child abuse and neglect in the U.S.: $103,754,017,492[xvi]

What kind of legal assistance is provided for these children?

16 states do not mandate legal representation for children in abuse and neglect proceedings[xvii]
Abused and neglected children in 34 states do not receive the same traditional legal representation received by adults[xviii]

What happens to former foster children?

Number of children in the foster care system: 799,000[xix]
Number of children that aged out of foster care in a year: 26,517[xx]
Percentage of the general population that have a bachelor's degree: 23%[xxi]
Percentage of former foster children that have a bachelor's degree: < 2%[xxii]
Percentage of the general population in jail or prison in 2008: 1%[xxiii]
Percentage of former foster children incarcerated after aging out: Males: 44.6%, Females: 16.4%[xxiv]
Percentage of the general population who experience homelessness over the course of a year: <1%[xxv]
Percentage of former foster children who experience homelessness after aging out of the system: 25%[xxvi]
Prevalence of post-traumatic stress disorder (PTSD) among the general population: 4%[xxvii]
Prevalence of PTSD among Vietnam veterans: 15%[xxviii]
Prevalence of PTSD among former foster children: 25%[xxix]
Percentage of former foster children who reported being unemployed 1 year after aging out: 53%[xxx]
Percentage of former foster children who reported living on food stamps after aging out: 45%[xxxi]

**first
star**
putting children first

Figure 1.1   First Star Fact Sheet

i   WORLD BANK, WORLD DEVELOPMENT INDICATORS DATABASE, TOTAL GDP 2007, at 1 (2008),
     http://siteresources.worldbank.org/DATASTATISTICS/Resources/GDP.pdf (last visited September 11, 2008).

ii   INNOCENTI RESEARCH CENTRE, UNICEF, CHILD POVERTY IN PERSPECTIVE: AN OVERVIEW OF CHILD WELL-BEING IN RICH COUNTRIES 2 (2007)
     (using six categories of child well-being: material well-being, health and safety, educational well-being, family and peer relationships,
     behaviours and risks, subjective well-being).

iii INNOCENTI RESEARCH CENTRE, UNICEF, A LEAGUE TABLE OF CHILD MALTREATMENT DEATHS IN RICH NATIONS 4 (2003).

iv   ADMIN. ON CHILDREN, YOUTH AND FAMILIES (ACYF), U.S. DEP'T OF HEALTH & HUMAN SERVICES., CHILD MALTREATMENT 2006, at xiv
     (2008).

v   Id.

vi   Id.

vii Id. at xv.

viii Id.

ix   Id.

x   Id. at 26-28.

xi   Id. at 30.

xii Id. at 65.

xiii Id.

xiv Id. at 66.

xv   CHING-TUNG WANG, PH.D. & JOHN HOLTON, PH.D., PREVENT CHILD ABUSE AMERICA, TOTAL ESTIMATED COST OF CHILD ABUSE AND
     NEGLECT IN THE UNITED STATES 4 (2007).

xvi Id. at 5.

xvii FIRST STAR, REPORT ON A CHILD'S RIGHT TO COUNSEL 12-13 (2007).

xviii Id. (including D.C.)

xix ADMIN. ON CHILDREN, YOUTH AND FAMILIES (ACYF), U.S. DEP'T OF HEALTH AND HUMAN SERVICES, TRENDS IN FOSTER CARE AND
     ADOPTION—FY 2002-FY 2006, at 1 (2008).

xx   ADMIN. ON CHILDREN, YOUTH AND FAMILIES (ACYF), U.S. DEP'T OF HEALTH AND HUMAN SERVICES, ADOPTION AND FOSTER CARE ANALYSIS
     AND REPORTING SYSTEM REPORT #14, at 4 (2008).

xxi CASEY FAMILY PROGRAMS, THE NORTHWEST FOSTER CARE ALUMNI STUDY, IMPROVING FAMILY FOSTER CARE: FINDINGS FROM THE
     NORTHWEST FOSTER CARE ALUMNI STUDY 2 (2005).

xxii Id.

xxiii THE PEW CENTER ON THE STATES, ONE IN 100: BEHIND BARS IN AMERICA 2008 3 (2008).

xxiv MARK E. COURTNEY ET AL., CHAPIN HALL, MIDWEST EVALUATION OF THE ADULT FUNCTIONING OF FORMER FOSTER YOUTH: OUTCOMES AT
     AGE 21, at 66 (2007) (asking former foster children at age 21 whether they have spent time in jail since their last interview 2 to 3 years ago).

xxv Calculated by dividing the estimated homeless population of the U.S. over the course of a year (1.3 – 2.3 million) by the estimated total
     population in the U.S. (304,364,314). See NAN P. ROMAN & PHYLLIS WOLFE, NATIONAL ALLIANCE TO END HOMELESSNESS, WEB OF FAILURE:
     THE RELATIONSHIP BETWEEN FOSTER CARE AND HOMELESSNESS 4 (1995); THE URBAN INSTITUTE, MILLIONS STILL FACE HOMELESSNESS IN A
     BOOMING ECONOMY, http://www.urban.org/publications/900050.html (2000) (last visited July 2, 2008); U.S. POPClock Projection,
     http://www.census.gov/population/www/popclockus.html (last visited June 17, 2008).

xxvi RONNA COOK ET AL., WESTAT INC., A NATIONAL EVALUATION OF TITLE IV-E FOSTER CARE INDEPENDENT LIVING PROGRAMS FOR YOUTH, at
     4-11 (1991).

xxvii CASEY FAMILY PROGRAMS, supra note xxi, at 32.

xxviii Id. (citing R. A. KULKA ET AL., TRAUMA AND THE VIETNAM WAR GENERATION (Brunner/Mazel) (1990), on current prevalence.)

xxix Id. (incidence in the 12 months prior to the interviews.)

xxx MARK E. COURTNEY ET AL., CHAPIN HALL, MIDWEST EVALUATION OF THE ADULT FUNCTIONING OF FORMER FOSTER YOUTH: OUTCOMES AT
     AGE 19, at 23 (2005).

xxxi MARK E. COURTNEY ET AL., supra note xxiv, at 39 (asking former foster children at age 21 whether they have received food stamps since their
     last interview 2 to 3 years ago).

Figure 1.1 clearly indicates how not getting state-of-the-art care as children leads to problems throughout life, not the least of which is dropping out of high school, low salaries, and higher rates of incarceration.

Variations in Definitions

In 2003, the U.S. Department of Health and Human Services undertook the National Study of Child Protective Services Systems and Reform Efforts. The goal was to identify current practices and improvement efforts in the child protective services system. Seven areas of variation in state child protective services (CPS) policy were identified.

- *Mandatory reporting.* Nearly all states require professionals who work with children (such as social workers, medical personnel, educators, and child daycare providers) to report suspected child maltreatment. However, standards for nonprofessionals and anonymous reporting sources vary.
- *Investigation objectives.* In 31 states, the purpose of an investigation is to determine if child abuse occurred; 18 of these states also included the purpose of determining risk or safety of the child. In the remaining 20 states, the goal is to protect the child or to establish the risk to the child.
- *Standards of evidence.* Relatively high evidentiary standards (preponderance, material, or clear and convincing) are necessary to substantiate abuse in 23 states. In 19 states, lower standards were specified (credible, reasonable, or probable cause). Nine states do not specify a standard of evidence.
- *Types of maltreatment.* Nearly all states define the four major categories specifically discussed in the Child Abuse Prevention and Treatment Act (CAPTA): neglect, physical abuse, sexual abuse, and emotional abuse. Beyond this, state inclusion of other types of maltreatment, such as medical neglect or abandonment, vary significantly.
- *Required timelines.* State policy varies widely both for required response time to referrals and for the completion of investigations.
- *Central registry.* State central registries contain information on perpetrators of child maltreatment. Many state policies allow use of central registries in background and licensing checks, and information can be shared with other agencies on request. The

types of disposition categories (substantiated, indicated, unsubstantiated) included in central registries vary from state to state, as do procedures for accessing information, expunging protocols, and due process requirements.

- *Alternative response.* Alternative responses allow CPS workers to assess the needs of a child without requiring a determination of maltreatment. Parental training may be proposed or more frequent observation required. Just over half of the states have alternative response polices. The policies vary greatly both in purpose and the types of alternative responses available.

Although this study does not place value judgments on differing state practices, it does acknowledge the potential benefits of moving toward parity in state practices. Among these is greater accountability of the CPS system and more equitable treatment for children across the country.[25]

Extent of the Problem Now—Again a Blurred Picture

In addition to parity and clarity in child abuse and neglect definitions, we need to achieve a clear picture of the extent of the problem. Without this, other interest groups better prepared to demonstrate their case are more likely to get limited federal and state attention and support.

The U.S. Department of Health and Human Services has conducted three congressionally mandated National Incidence Studies (NIS) of abuse and neglect. The first was conducted in 1979–1980 and reported in 1981, the second was conducted in 1986–1987 and was published in 1988, and the third was conducted between 1993 and 1995 and was published in 1996. A fourth study, due in 2008, was not yet complete by the publication of this book.

Figure 1.2 is really all we need to see that child maltreatment is a growing problem and that every infinitesimal blip upward reflects the horror some child is living. It's important to note, too, that this chart only pertains to reported cases of child abuse. Consider, for example, the little girl found dead in Las Vegas. Jane Cordova Doe, was named for the apartment complex where her body was found on January 12, 2006. She was between three and four years of age and had died from blunt trauma to her torso. The community mourned and the Reverend David Jimenez of Iglesia Pentecostal de Las Vegas said, "She was just dumped as trash. She's not that. She's a child of God." He added, "This has touched everyone's hearts."[26]

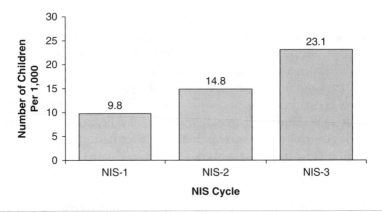

Figure 1.2 National Incidence of Children Harmed or Injured by Abuse or Neglect

Source: *NIS4 Project Summary.*[27]

Consider too the December 2005 revelation that the University of Nevada Las Vegas Center for Business and Economic Research, which compiled data for the Nevada Kids Count Report, decided to omit that category because of "uncovered underreporting problems in Clark County."[28]

The Nevada Department of Human Resources' Division of Child and Family Services found that 114 Clark County child deaths between 2001 and 2004 might have involved maltreatment. That number is more than three times the number of child deaths reported by the Clark County Department of Family Services.

Kids Count is a project of the Annie E. Casey Foundation aimed at tracking trends with state-by-state data. When such data are incorrect, the real picture of how many children suffer and die from child abuse is unclear and actions taken by politicians, child-service providers, school districts, and the media are thereby misguided. The frightening aspect is that Nevada, which has been below the national average in child maltreatment deaths, may just be the tip of the iceberg in terms of incorrect information. Mike Wilden, director of the Nevada Health and Human Rights Department, said that 20 or more deaths found to involve maltreatment would push Nevada over the average, but added, "I doubt we'll be the worst in the nation." The question is whether Nevada is the worst in the nation in misreporting, which could easily mean that far many more children are suffering from abuse and neglect and dying from it than we even know.

NIS4: The Current NIS Study

The NIS design assumes that the maltreated children who are investigated by child protective services (CPS) represent only the tip of the iceberg, so although the NIS estimates include children investigated at CPS they also include maltreated children identified by professionals in a wide range of agencies in representative communities. These professionals, called sentinels, were asked to remain on the lookout for children they believe were maltreated during the study period. Children were evaluated against standardized definitions of abuse and neglect. The data are unduplicated; that is, a given child was counted only once in the study estimates.

The NIS-4 gathered data in a nationally representative sample of 122 counties in the fall of 2005, selected to ensure the necessary mix of geographic regions and of urban and rural areas. The CPS agencies serving these counties were asked to provide data about all children in cases they accept for investigation during the study period, September 4 through December 3, 2005. In addition, professionals working in the same counties in the following types of agencies were asked to serve as NIS-4 sentinels: elementary and secondary public schools; public health departments; public housing authorities; short-stay general and children's hospitals; state, county, and municipal police and sheriff departments; licensed daycare centers; juvenile probation departments; voluntary social services and mental health agencies; and shelters for runaway and homeless youth or victims of domestic violence.

This study sought to be more comprehensive than much previous research. NIS-4 pulled together data from a number of agency sources in each study county. The study began with data from the local child protective services agency (CPS) and incorporated data received from professionals in a number of other community agencies, including the county public health, public housing, and juvenile probation departments, the sheriff or state police, and scientifically selected samples of other agencies, including voluntary social service and mental health agencies, municipal police departments, school, hospitals, daycare centers, and shelters for runaway youth and battered women. The sentinels provided descriptive information on the cases they observed. The study directors thus hoped to obtain a more realistic picture of the extent of child abuse and neglect than those of single agency studies.

In April 2006, the U.S. Department of Health and Human Services reported that in 2004, 830,000 children across the United States were documented victims of abuse or neglect. On any given day, more than a half a million children were in foster care. According to Prevent Child Abuse America, abuse and neglect costs society $258 million every day—nearly $94 billion each year.[29] Its 2001 report estimated the direct costs of intervention as well as those for treatment of the children's related medical and emotional problems, and then added the "indirect costs associated with the long-term consequences of abuse and neglect to both the individual and society at large."

Total Daily Cost of Child Abuse and Neglect in the United States

Direct Costs	Estimated Daily Cost
Health Care System	
Hospitalization	$17,001,082
Chronic Health Problems	$8,186,185
Mental Health Care System	$1,164,686
Child Welfare System	$39,452,054
Law Enforcement	$67,698
Judicial System	$934,725
Total Direct Costs	$66,806,430
Indirect Costs	Estimated Daily Cost
Special Education	$612,624
Mental Health and Health Care	$12,678,455
Juvenile Delinquency	$24,124,086
Lost Productivity to Society	$1,797,260
Adult Criminality	$151,726,027
Total Indirect Costs	$190,938,452
Total Cost	$257,744,882

Source: Fromm 2001.[30]

According to Prevent Child Abuse America, the annual costs are equivalent to $1,461.66 for every family in the United States. The authors cautioned that because "conservative estimates were used, the actual annual cost of child maltreatment in the United States could be higher than $94 billion."

The Unrelenting Cycle of Abuse

As mentioned previously, child abuse often occurs at the hands of people who themselves have been abused. This tendency of victims to replicate the offense on others is one of the more disturbing characteristics of child abuse. When I visited a southern California facility that provided a caring and supportive environment for children who had suffered unspeakable abuse, I learned that every night someone had to be stationed at the end of each hallway to watch for any children attempting to move from one room to another. These monitors, however, weren't watching through the night to keep children from sneaking into a playroom or watching late-night television. Their job was to prevent children who had been sexually abused—and who as a result may have become sexual predators themselves—from harming other children. Peter Samuelson described a similar experience in Ohio:

> I toured a locked facility in Ohio where convicted children are housed: kids who are themselves sexual predators who harmed another child. A very disconcerting place I thought: bars on the windows, child-friendly murals on the walls and teddy bears on the beds. "How many of these children were themselves sexually molested?" I asked the Warden. "Ninety seven, ninety eight percent" he replied. "Kids don't invent this stuff on their own." And so it rolls on. Let's think positive here: save one child and we probably save dozens in the future. Talk about leverage. . . . Let's get this right, or at least apply best practice that demonstrably works elsewhere. And while we're at it, what if we provided the specialized training that the grown-ups through whose hands the kids pass in some enlightened places get to ALL the professionals in every jurisdiction: judges, lawyers, CASA, social workers, teachers, doctors, nurses. . . . Why is there training going on in some places but not in most of the country? You can train to be a television repairperson nationally through distance learning. Are transistors more important than abused children?[31]

The cyclical nature of abuse makes it even more important that we exponentially increase our efforts to eradicate it. Think of how the acts of an irresponsible HIV-positive person can result, years later, in hundreds of new cases. Similarly, abusing only one child can potentially result in harm to hundreds of others through the years. If that one child grows up and raises two, or three, or six more children, and if those children are abused, the potential grows in succeeding generations. Not only are abused children significantly more likely to become abusive themselves, they are also likely to find it difficult to establish and cope with healthy adult relationships.

Indicators of Abuse

Even with consensus on definitions of child abuse and neglect, we need to know the signs of these when we see them. Physical and emotional abuse often occur when parents can't manage stresses, are unable to deal with children, or are very controlling. As mentioned, abusers often were them-selves abused as children and may be in abusive relationships as adults. Alcohol and drug abuse contribute to the problem. Among confirmed cases of child maltreatment, 40% involve the use of alcohol or other drugs.[32]

Emotional abuse can be very hard to identify. Clinicians have testing measures, but caregivers must observe behaviors. Emotionally abused children may nonetheless be quite loyal to their parent, fear retaliation for reporting the abuse, or believe their lot is a normal way of life.[33] Children of alcoholics often have low self-esteem or suffer from anxiety and depression, or both. When parents are heavy drug users, children are caught in a Catch-22. They learn to distrust police, teachers, and aid workers—the very persons who might otherwise help—out of fear that confiding in them will cause harm to the parent.

Indicators of Emotional Abuse

According to Prevent Child Abuse America, behavioral indicators of an emotionally abused child include

- inappropriate behavior that is immature or too mature for the child's age,
- dramatic bedwetting or loss of bowel control (after a child has been trained),
- destructive or antisocial behavior (being constantly withdrawn and sad),
- poor relationships with peers,
- lack of self-confidence,
- unusual fears given child's age (fear of going home, being left alone, specific objects), and
- inability to react with emotion or develop an emotional bond with others.[34]

These are only indicators, and any of the behaviors can also occur in children who aren't being abused. However, changes in the pattern of these behaviors may indicate a problem, and emotional abuse may be considered a reasonable possibility. The likelihood of emotional abuse increases if these indicators coincide with observations of adults publicly blaming and belittling the child, describing the child in negative ways, openly admitting to disliking or hating the child, threatening, withdrawing comfort as a means of discipline, being cold or distant, suffering from alcohol or drug abuse, and having a violent nature.[35] In his book *When Drug Addicts Have Children*, editor Douglas Besharov reported results of an American Enterprise Institute conference on protecting the children of heavy drug users.[36] Drug abuse, as Besharov and Karen Baehler testified, is not a victimless crime but rather—like the cascading and cyclical effects of child abuse—one that affects the user, family members, neighborhood, and community—the hidden victims. Even reductions in the general population's drug use may not stem the tide of drug-related child maltreatment, Besharov and Baehler argued. Frequent, heavy use of drugs coupled with the stresses of deep poverty "will be with us for the foreseeable future." More than 10 years later, their prediction holds.

Again, here is a long-standing problem that remains inadequately addressed. There are preventive measures, in some cases, even solutions available. Why, then, the inertia in responding to the needs of children— like those in homes of drug abusers—at risk? In subsequent chapters we address what can be done to respond more effectively.

When Poverty, Race, and Abuse Collide

There is a very good reason why Clarice Walker placed poverty at the top of her list of reasons why children enter the child welfare system—it is the basis of much of the abuse and neglect they experience.

The third national incidence study showed that U.S. children living below poverty level ($15,000 annual household income) are 22 times more likely to experience observable harm from child maltreatment than those from families with annual incomes above $30,000.[37] The Congressional Research Service echoed this point in a 2005 report: "Disproportionate representation means that when compared to their presence in the overall relevant population, a given racial/ethnic group is over- or under-represented in the specific population of interest. For instance, the 2000 Census shows that African American children make up less than 15% of the overall child population but the most recent data available showed that 27% of the children who entered foster care during FY2003 were African American and that on the last day of FY2003, 35% of the children in foster care were African American."[38] Because minority children are more likely to be poor, they are more likely to be represented in the child welfare system. Experts argue, however, that poverty alone, though a critical component of child abuse, does not fully explain the overrepresentation of minority children.

A variety of studies finds variation in disproportionate representation of children of color across state or county borders. Research in Santa Clara, California, for example, showed that though Latino children constituted 30% of the child population, they made up 52% of the county's child welfare cases. Similarly, in New York in 2003, black children made up about 18% of that child population, but 42% of those entering foster care.[39] A 2004 study of King County, Washington, revealed that though black children made up only 7% of the child population, they accounted for 19% of maltreatment allegation referrals and 23% of the new placements in foster care, and 39% of those who'd been in the system for at least four years.[40] In 2005, the Children's Bureau sponsored an exploratory study of the child welfare system's response to black children.[41] Very few studies have done so and few have looked at the manner in which agencies are responding to the overrepresentation. Nine child welfare agencies were visited to talk with administrators, supervisors, and workers. The general perceptions are summarized here:

• *Poverty.* An overwhelming majority of participants cited poverty and poverty-related circumstances as primary reasons for the overrepresentation of minority children.

• *Visibility.* Minority families are more likely to lack access to resources and so are also more likely to use public services (for example, hospitals and clinics), and to receive public assistance. Their more frequent contact with these systems makes them more visible in terms of the problems they may be experiencing, including abuse and neglect. On this point Clarice Walker remarked, "when you have to go public, it becomes public." In other words, people who are poor are more likely to be unable to deal with the challenges they face in a quiet, private way. Wealthier families can hire resources like therapists and can get help from their family doctor or schools. "Poor families," Walker noted, "are subjected to waiting lists and they are made more stressed until some can't wait anymore."[42]

It may seem odd to suggest that visibility is a factor when we are also calling for more attention to the problem of child abuse and neglect. It is also important, however, to factor in that often families merely need help—help they can't get efficiently and effectively. The system thus forces them to wait and wait until they can wait no longer and the children suffer. Thus, though visibility may cause minority children to be overrepresented, it often stems from the fact that they have not been noticed early enough or provided early enough with programs that could help them avoid the crises that lead to family separation.

- *Overreporting of minority parents for child abuse and neglect.* The study participants believe that the problems of children of minority parents, once again, are more noticeable to schools and medical systems. They and some theorists and researchers argue that this explains some part of the disproportional representation of minority children in the child welfare system.

- *Vulnerability.* Here the issue is related to poverty in terms of the disempowering by undereducation and unemployment. African American communities experiencing few opportunities often become vulnerable to drugs and violence. As the communities become more vulnerable, the report suggests, so do the families.

- *Media pressure* also contributes to overreporting by supervisors and child welfare workers who fear they must bring more children into care to avoid making very public mistakes.

- *Cultural biases in defining abuse and neglect.* Lack of exposure, particularly by staff, can make it difficult for them to see that abuse and neglect may become confused with what is seen within African American culture as discipline. Clearly this is a difficult area. If indeed there are significant differences, we must ask ourselves who is more correct? Where is the line between discipline that is constructive and discipline that is destructive? What this issue does tell us is that it is extremely important that policymakers be familiar with cultural differences and, with those in mind, formulate an agreed-upon definition of abuse and neglect. Then we must do more to inform families of all races of the distinction.

Any serious call for attention to child abuse and neglect must also include, within its primary interests, ways to help families unable to help themselves. In other words, abuse and neglect need to be seen within the contexts in which they occur. Solutions should also be developed with the understanding that people under stress and duress can't always do what they should do, but only what they can do. This is increasingly important in a society with a growing number of single-parent families. We need to be sure that programs do not cavalierly place blame or take actions without considering the context and the influences on those affected. We need to balance caution with common sense, and a determination to protect children but understand cultural differences. We need to be responsive to Clarice Walker's concern for the overrepresentation and not react by ceasing to remove children when necessary, but rather assure ourselves (through quality of training) that it is not simply the visibility and vulnerability of these children that lead us to do too little for them.

Protecting children from abuse and neglect could progress significantly if poverty were both prevented and ended. Some rightly perceive that society's scorn of poverty and the sense that people could easily pull themselves out of it if they only tried keeps children in danger of abuse and neglect. Marion Wright Edelman, founder of the Children's Defense Fund, warned that "it is a dangerously short-sighted nation that fantasizes absolute self-sufficiency as the only correct way of life."[43] She explained that despite our tendency to value complete independence, the government does support everyone, including big businesses. "Chrysler and Lee Iacocca didn't do it alone," she wrote. "Defense contractors don't do it alone. Welfare queens can't hold a candle to corporate kings in raiding the public purse."

Although this may elicit anger among many who prefer to see their successes as due entirely to their own work, the truth is that everyone needs help at some point or another. Edelman pointed out, "but our commitment to help the neediest children has seemed increasingly fragile and ephemeral in recent years. If we want to preserve their futures and our own, we will have to rededicate ourselves to government's side of the partnership, and we will have to do it soon."[44]

Marian Wright Edelman and John McWhorter on *Meet the Press*[45]

These excerpts from the January 15, 2005, *Meet the Press* NBC interview with Marion Wright Edelman and author John McWhorter provide insight into the experiences of black people living in poverty and indicate the extensive challenge before us in terms of reducing the cycle of violence that occurs especially when people suffer the stresses associated with poverty.

Russert: Marian Wright Edelman, you picked up on that very theme in your
            book, *I Can Make a Difference: A Treasury to Inspire Our Children*.
            And then also you are working on a report, which the Kansas City

Star wrote about, and it says that you gave a—excuse me—"a preview to a report on what she called the cradle-to-prison pipeline. She believes the non-level playing field exists for many African American males from the day they're born. A black male born in 2001 has a 1-in-3 chance of ending up in prison. A black girl born the same year has a 1-in-17 chance, she said. 'I want to get a debate going on the cradle-to-prison pipeline, the set of odds that are set in front of our black children. The most dangerous intersection of America is the intersection of race and poverty.'" Explain.

Edelman: Well, we live in the richest nation on Earth and we let a child be born into poverty every 36 seconds. A majority of their parents are working, playing by the rules, cannot get jobs at decent wages that allow them to escape poverty.

We let a child in the world's leading nation on health technology be born without health insurance; 90 percent of those children are born in families where they're working and playing by the rules. Their employers don't cover health care. . . .

Child poverty has been increasing since 2001. A black boy today does have a one-in-three chance of going off to prison. This is a death knell for the black family, for black disempowerment, and we must address it.

And we've got to make sure that every one of our children gets health care, every one of our children gets a strong early education, every one of our children gets education. Eighty percent of black children aren't reading in fourth grade.

And we've got to stop the obscenity of arresting five- and six- and seven-year-old children and then sending children through schools [that] don't educate them, of having zero tolerance policies that start them very early into the juvenile justice system and then to the criminal justice system.

So this poverty which we know how to end and must end, we must do something about it today with a sense of urgency and finish Dr. King's dream. We'd all like to celebrate him, but what we need to do is follow him and to finish what he began.

Russert: When Mr. Cosby says the things he does about young blacks, is it because of poverty, because of racism or is it because of black accountability and discipline?

Edelman: It's a combination of a lot of things, but most young black people are trying to go to school, trying to do right or trying to

(Continued)

(Continued)

live by the rules. They're beating the odds every day. We celebrate them. We train them. And despite violence and despite inner city problems, you know, they're staying in schools, they're going on and they're trying to give back to their community.

There are thousands of black young people who are going to college and who are coming back and getting trained and running freedom schools for their younger sisters and brothers to provide them the mentors and role models and the hope that they were given and we were given in my generation but are trying to give back.

And most people want to work. But we have a problem in this country of poverty and race. The black middle-class did leave ghettos. I'm proud of the Ken Chenaults and I'm proud of Ruth Simpsons, the Browns.

And we've got new leadership, but there is a lot that is going on.

But the key issue here is poverty and race and racial disparities in our school systems, in our health systems, in our criminal justice systems.

You know, black young people still don't have the same chance to succeed, particularly a poor young black person. A young black man who gets pulled into the juvenile justice system is 48 times more likely than a young Latino man is, nine times more likely to be detained for the same drug offense as a white young man.

So we've got to make sure, one, that our children are ready for school and are healthy, have strong families, but we've got to make sure that those families have jobs at decent wages. We've got to make sure that they have schools to teach them to learn because if you can't read in this society, you're not going to succeed. And we've got to make sure that our whole emphasis is not on punishment but on prevention and early intervention.

The only universal child policy in this country that we will guarantee every child is a jail or detention cell after they get into trouble. We will not guarantee them far cheaper health care and far cheaper Head Start and preschool. And we will not guarantee them schools.

In fact, those young people in Chicago are not facing the same kind of educational system. The poorest children get the poorest schools and the poorest neighborhoods, and they're all being plagued by violence. But let me just remind you as Dr. King reminded us in the poor people's campaign that poverty afflicts more whites than blacks, that poverty and teenage pregnancy and violence afflicts more whites than blacks.

What we've got to do is to move beyond that watershed and build across racial movement focused on children that eliminates child poverty in the richest nation on Earth, that stands up to an administration, members of Congress, that would after four massive tax cuts during war give war tax cuts to the rich and cut $40 billion from safety net programs to help these young children, white and black.

That's just wrongheaded. And we are making the wrong choices. And the post-Katrina disaster which we must address, we're spending the life out of our children in a war choice in Iraq and tax cuts for the rich. We need to finish the movement to end poverty and child poverty in America.

With Edelman was John McWhorter, author of *Winning the Race: Beyond the Crisis of Black America*. On the question of where the blame lies, his reply to Tim Russert proposes a shared-responsibility approach to ending poverty among black families, the most highly represented racial group in the child welfare system, and thereby having a potentially significant impact on child abuse and neglect.

Russert: You mentioned strong families.

Let me show what you the National Center for Health Statistics said in terms of births to unmarried mothers.

In the Asian community it's 15 percent; in the white community, 24 percent; Hispanic community, 46 percent; the black community, 69 percent.

Mr. McWhorter, how much of a factor is that in terms of black culture, black society and some of the problems we're talking about?

McWhorter: It's not an absolute that somebody brought up by a single mother is going to have a bad life, but I think that all indications are that it's better for somebody to have two parents.

And more importantly, a great proportion of that 69 percent are women who are not in the best position to give the best life to their children.

We can talk about what the reasons for that are, but again, our history and not just newsreels of Dr. King. It's Chicago. It's poor black Chicago in the 1920s, and people were alarmed that the illegitimacy rate was 15 percent.

Now, what's the difference between then and now? Clearly there are things that happened to our system that made it a lot easier to have children that you aren't necessarily in a position to take care of. You just do what people do, seeing what's going on around you.

(Continued)

(Continued)

This is not the kind of situation that I think Dr. King would have wanted. He's actually on record, I remember in one speech, as saying that the Negro—that was, of course, the terminology of the day—the Negro man does not want to languish on welfare.

Now, of course, you have to have some welfare, but he would have been very surprised to see what was happening to the welfare system with poor black people in mind, precisely when he was assassinated. There are some things that we need to think about. Main thing about King is that one of his legacies, one of the things we should think about with King, is that we can't wait for another one. The problems are different.

The things that Ms. Edelman is talking about are very real and the idea is to fix them now working with local organizations that can help people face-to-face of making the best of the worst.

And so you have the Harlem Children Zone in New York. You have Operation Hope in Los Angeles. You have Eugene Rivers' Ten-Point Coalition in Boston.

These are the things that we need to pay more attention to. Academics need to stop being so professionally pessimistic about race in America and pointing us to these things that are actually making some kind of a difference.

And in general, anyone who tells us what we need to wait for is a second civil rights revolution, whether this is said explicitly or implied, is engaging in a kind of unintended cruelty, because we all know that for better or for worse that revolution isn't going to happen. We have harder, although more concrete, work to do. And it's actually being done. We just need to call more attention to it.

McWhorter's call is critical to responding to children living in poverty who also experience abuse and neglect. Waiting for a second civil rights revolution is indeed cruel when efforts to change children's lives can be undertaken now.

The reason why children are poor, why their families are poor, is not because most of them are lazy or can't help themselves, it's because they need a leg up to do so. Only a country that has lost its way morally allows children to suffer from poverty, abuse, and neglect without taking evident and consistent steps to make it stop. The fondness for capitalism so many of us have does not preclude a love of children and a willingness to give them the help they need to thrive. Children, after all, are our most precious natural resource. They become consumers and voters. Eventually they shape the futures of those who allowed them to linger in an unacceptable past.

As we discuss in Chapter 8, caring for children at risk is not the province of any particular political party. It must concern all of us. We must keep dancing with the bear until we tame the beast. Then, and only then, can we sit down.

Endnotes

1. Derived from Joyce Elders, former surgeon general: "Public health is like dancing with a bear. You get very tired but you can't afford to sit down."

2. Blair Sadler, "The Vision: Why a National Call to Action," *Child Abuse and Neglect* 23, no. 10 (1999): 956.

3. Ibid.

4. Ibid.

5. Bob Herbert, Children in Torment, Editorial, *New York Times*, March 9, 2006.

6. David L. Chadwick, "The Message," *Child Abuse and Neglect* 23, no. 10 (1999): 957.

7. Ibid.

8. http://petersamuelson.blogspot.com

9. Peter J. Pecora, et al., "Assessing the Effects of Foster Care: Early Results from the Casey National Alumni Study" (Seattle: Casey Family Programs, 2003), www.casey.org/NR/rdonlyres/CEFBB1B6-7ED1-440D-925A-E5BAF602294D/128/casey_alumni_study_sum.pdf

10. Clarice Walker, telephone interview, July 2, 2005.

11. http://petersamuelson.blogspot.com

12. http://nccanch.acf.hhs.gov/pubs/factsheets/whatiscan.cfm

13. Child Abuse Prevention and Treatment Act (as amended in 1996, PL104-235).

14. U.S. Department of Health and Human Services, Administration on Children, Youth and Families/Children's Bureau, and Office of the Assistant Secretary for Planning and Evaluation, *National Study of Child Protective Services Systems and Reform Efforts: Review of State CPS Policy* (Washington, DC: Government Printing Office, April 2003); National Research Council, Panel on Child Abuse and Neglect, *Understanding Child Abuse and Neglect*, (Washington, DC: National Academy Press, 1993).

15. Jill Elaine Hasday, "The Canon of Family Law," *Public Law and Legal Theory* Working Paper No. 77 (Chicago: University of Chicago Law School, 2004), 26–27.

16. Ibid., 28.

17. http://petersamuelson.blogspot.com

18. Hasday, "The Canon of Family Law," 32.

19. Martin Teicher, "Scars that Won't Heal: The Neurobiology of Child Abuse," *Scientific American* 286, no. 3 (2002): 1.

20. Ibid., 2.

21. Alison B. Fries, Toni E. Ziegler, Joseph R. Kurian, Steve Jacoris, and Seth D. Pollak, "Early experience in humans is associated with changes in neuropeptides critical for regulating social behavior," Proceedings of the National Academy of Sciences 102(47) (2005): 17237–40.

22. Nichole Taylor, Alicia Gilbert, Gail Mann, and Barbara Ryan, "Assessment Based Treatment for Traumatized Children: A Trauma Assessment Pathway (TAP) Model" (San Diego, CA: Chadwick Center for Children & Families, 2005), www.chadwickcenter.com/Assessment-Based%20Treatment.htm.

23. Alexandra Cook, Margaret Blaustein, Joseph Spinazzola, and Bessel van der Kolk, eds., "Complex Trauma in Children and Adolescents." White paper from the National Child Traumatic Stress Network Complex Trauma Task Force, 2003, 5–7. For more information, go to www.nctsnet.org

24. Taylor, Gilbert, Mann, and Ryan, "Assessment-Based Treatment for Traumatized Children," 35.

25. National Clearinghouse on Child Abuse and Neglect Information, available online at http://nccanch.acf.hhs.gov; U.S. Department of Health and Human Services, *Child Maltreatment 2002* (Washington, DC: U.S. Government Printing Office, 2004); Jane Waldfogel, *The Future of Child Protection: How to Break the Cycle of Abuse and Neglect* (Cambridge, MA: Harvard University Press, 1998), 68; U.S. Department of Health and Human Services, Administration on Children, Youth and Families/Children's Bureau, and Office of the Assistant Secretary for Planning and Evaluation, *National Study of Child Protective Services Systems and Reform Efforts: Review of State CPS Policy* (Washington, DC: Government Printing Office, April 2003).

26. Ken Ritter, "Dead Girl's Remains Go Unclaimed in Las Vegas," Associated Press, 2006.

27. *4th National Incidence Study of Child Abuse and Neglect—NIS4: Project Summary* (Washington, DC: Administration for Children and Families, U.S. Department of Health and Human Services, Westat Inc., and Walter R. McDonald & Associates Inc., 2005). For more information about the study and its progress, see www.NIS4.org.

28. Lisa Kim Bach, "UNLV Report to Omit Abuse Deaths," *Las Vegas Review-Journal*, December 14, 2005.

29. Suzette Fromm, "Annual Cost of Child Maltreatment, Prevent Child Abuse America" (Washington, DC: Child Abuse America, 2001), www.preventchildabuse.org.

30. Suzette Fromm, *Annual Cost of Child Maltreatment* (Washington, DC: Prevent Child Abuse America, 2001).

31. http://petersamuelson.blogspot.com

32. www.preventchildabuse.org

33. "Emotional Abuse & Young Children," Florida Center for Parent Involvement, http://lumpy.fmhi.usf.edu/cfsroot/dares/fcpi/.

34. Ibid.

35. Ibid.

36. Douglas Besharov, ed., *When Drug Addicts Have Children: Reorienting Society's Response* (Washington, DC: Child Welfare League of America, 1994).

37. Andrea J. Sedlak and Diane D. Broadhurst, *The Third National Incidence Study of Child Abuse and Neglect*, NIS-3 (Washington, DC: U.S. Department of Health and Human Services, 1996).

38. Congressional Research Service, Emilie Stoltzfus report to Honorable Charles Rangel, *Race/Ethnicity and Child Welfare* (Washington, DC: Library of Congress, 2005), 1.

39. Ibid., 3.

40. King County Coalition on Racial Disproportionality, *Racial Disproportionality in the Child Welfare System in King County, Washington* (Seattle, WA: King County Coalition on Racial Disproportionality, 2004), executive summary, 1–4, www.hunter.cuny.edu/socwork/nrcfcpp/downloads/King CountyReportonRacialDisproportionalityExecutiveSummary.pdf.

41. U.S. Children's Bureau, "Children of Color in the Child Welfare System: Perspectives from the Child Welfare Community" (Washington, DC: U.S. Department of Health and Human Services, 2005), 1–6, http://nccanch.acf .hbs.gov/pubs/children/execsum.cfm.

42. Clarice Walker, interview, November 23, 2005.

43. Marion Wright Edelman, *The Measure of Our Success* (Boston, MA: Beacon Press, 1992), 90.

44. Marion Wright Edelman, *Families in Peril: An Agenda for Social Change* (Cambridge, MA: Harvard University Press, 1987), 35.

45. www.msnbc.msn.com

2

The Best Interests of the Child

Suppose your wealthy Uncle Max shows up from Palm Beach and, while he is visiting, decides you're doing a lousy job of raising your son. Uncle Max, on the other hand, has the time and money to give little Lawrence a better upbringing than you can—his own room in a grand home, a fine wardrobe, a car when he turns 16, primo dental and health care. And he has more than just material things to offer—he'll give Lawrence all the care, attention, and support he needs, plus an education at elite private schools and great career connections. So Uncle Max goes to court to seek custody of Lawrence.

"It's in the best interests of the child," he and his attorney argue. They go on to prove their argument on just about every point.

Is the judge going to give Uncle Max custody of little Lawrence? No way. It just isn't going to happen.

When Should the State Intervene?

"Children need families—and birth parents are most likely to provide appropriate care and are entitled to raise their children," child advocate Lewis Pitts observed. "Families should not be interfered with just because someone else might 'do a better job.'" If parents have a right to raise their own children, when do "the child's best interests" become paramount? Only in two rare and extraordinary circumstances, Pitts has said:

- where birth parents abuse, neglect, or abandon the child, and
- where the child has had almost no relationship with the birth parents and has been in the custody of others for a long time, and where removal would be traumatic to the child.

In both cases, notions of the child's best interests balance the parents' rights.

Courts are used in balancing competing rights, whether it's the public's right to beach access versus property owners' rights, or freedom of the press versus the right to privacy. In the case of child abuse, neglect, or abandonment, states have affirmed the principle that parental rights must be balanced by the child's best interests, some more clearly than others. In the second instance Pitts cited—the lack of a relationship with biological parents—several states have already recognized the principle through statute or case law.

A Universal Term?

The best interests of the child standard is used almost universally in custody, adoption, and other legal disputes involving today's children. Is there reason to fear, then, that a wealthy uncle—or anyone else—might be able to take a child from his or her parents only because he'd make a better parent, provide more material and emotional support, and offer better opportunities? Even if such benefits would be in the child's best interests, it wouldn't matter—that is, unless the child had been abused, neglected, abandoned, or already in the person's custody for a long time. But what about removals by government? How well based are they, and why are they so inconsistently applied over those 2,200 jurisdictions?

The child's best interests as a concept has slowly evolved since it originated in 18th-century English common law with Lord Mansfield's ruling that a mother should keep her young child after a bankrupt father mistreated both of them. At first merely a contradiction to the accepted notion of children as a father's property, during the 19th century the view arose that mothers were on the whole more nurturing and morally sound than fathers, hence best equipped to guide children's upbringing. By the end of the 20th century, with half of all children winding up under a court's jurisdiction for custody matters (due largely to the rising divorce rate) the weight was no longer so much on either fathers' or mothers' rights as on the state's concept of the best interests of the child.[1]

Chapter 4 contains a fuller historical overview of these matters as well as the concepts of abuse and neglect.

Protecting children from abuse of all kinds is part of the mission of child services, attorneys, and courts—and that's certainly in any child's best interests. Equally important is to find ways to protect children that don't incidentally either cause further abuse or steal their right as children to love and a sense of belonging. To the extent those things do happen—and they do—we can't continue to destroy children in the name of saving them. We can't only rely on foster parents to speak out, at the risk of reprisal, against state systems that are supposed to serve children. We can't afford to fall into hardened ranks of antifamily or bias. We need a more intelligent and sensitive approach to protecting children.

It isn't the concept of best interests that's wrong nearly so much as how we apply it. Many—even most—children aren't served by one-size-fits-all solutions to all or even different types of cases. They are served best by a system that (1) astutely comprehends the factors that impinge on the child's situation and (2) is dedicated to providing the child with both tentative (when necessary) and long-term (whenever possible) solutions that protect him as a whole person—physically, mentally, and emotionally. And the adults who do all this need to be well paid, well trained, and well supported.

The Pioneering Research

Child psychoanalysts Anna Freud, Joseph Goldstein, and Albert J. Solnit (later joined by Sonja Goldstein) began exploring child placement law in 1968 with students at Yale Law School. The resulting series of books, capped with the 1996 publication of *The Best Interests of the Child: The Least Detrimental Alternative,* stands as a landmark contribution to the field. The 1996 volume, which contains an updated version of all three previous books, is highly recommended for anyone interested in what our children face in the child placement system—and for its insights into how children think and what makes an effective parent. The principles that the Goldsteins, Solnit, and Freud elucidated have had international influence but many experts would argue that this has been more in theory than in practice.

The first part of *The Best Interests of the Child* focuses on children already caught up in the legal system as their placements are contested in the wake of various proceedings, including those for abuse, neglect, and abandonment.

The second part looks at why and when a child's relationship with his or her parents (or other primary caregivers) should become a matter of concern for the state. At what point does abuse or neglect justify state intrusion into family privacy, and when should a child have legal counsel?

The third part was developed to help child placement professionals— judges, lawyers, social workers, psychologists, and other experts "recognize and be sensitive to the boundaries of their knowledge and of their authority to act . . . between their personal and professional beliefs, and . . . between the professional and parental roles."[2]

These experts on the mind of the child stressed that their guidelines for dealing with children already in the custody system, due to divorce and separation as well as abuse and neglect, rest on two convictions.

First, a child's need for continuity of care means parents should generally be entitled to raise children as they think best, free of state interference. "So long as a child is a member of a functioning family, the preservation of that family serves her developmental needs," the authors wrote. They prefer minimum state intervention, and restraint in deciding what constitutes a valid reason for intruding on family relationships. "A policy of minimum intervention by the state . . . accords not only with our firm belief as citizens in individual freedom and human dignity, but also with our professional understanding of the intricate developmental processes of childhood."[3] As their thinking advanced over the years— and with the realization that the state too many times places children in worse circumstances than they left—the authors went on to urge that the state should be authorized to intervene in a family "if and only if it can provide the child in jeopardy with a less detrimental alternative."[4]

Second, when intervention by the state is legitimately justified, as in cases of abuse and neglect, the protective shell the family provides for the child has already been broken. At that point, the child's well-being must be the paramount objective—above any other party to the proceedings— and a family must be established for the child as soon as possible. The goal of every child placement is "to assure for each child membership in a family with at least one parent who wants her. It is to assure for each child and her parents an opportunity to maintain, establish or reestablish psychological ties to each other free of further interruption by the state."[5]

Placement, of course, is a thorny problem. When determining what family will be provided—temporarily or for the long term—or reestablished, the best interests of the child in question need to be defined uniquely and comprehensively. Not in an effort to predict everything that might happen down the road for that child in that family, but to ensure that a child-sensitive decision is made—one that is informed by the realities of foster children's lives and that maximizes the likelihood that the child will thrive.

Aiming at the Canon

As mentioned in Chapter 1, Jill Elaine Hasday is among the people who have given considerable thought to this problem of defining best interests. An associate law professor at the University of Minnesota, she believes that just as there is a recognized canon of literature, that is, a recognized list of books that many people think of as the standard, so there is a canon of family law. This canon, Hasday has said, constitutes "the ways of thinking about family law that are widely shared by legal scholars and especially by legal authorities, like legislators and judges." It includes foundational legal sources like cases and statues, as well as archetypal stories and examples. It also "determines what counts as family law, what constitutes a good reason or a convincing argument in a family law debate, what explanations have to be given, and what does not have to be explained. The family law canon operates, moreover, at the level of common sense, powerful enough that its tenets are taken to require no reappraisal."[6]

What does this have to do with defining the best interests of the child? Several critical areas of the system are shaped by what Hasday calls stories—but what we might consider myths.

The first is that common law property norms no longer shape the law of parenthood. This story is reiterated throughout the scholarship, casebooks, and jurisprudence of family law. Here's the story briefly. The law of parenthood has shifted from emphasizing fathers' (and later both parents') property rights over children, toward seeing children as individual persons with interests and rights. Furthermore, that since the mid-19th century, custody decisions have increasingly been based on the best interests of the child.

But this story greatly overstates the interpretation that common law property norms have come to an end in today's family law and its governing principles. According to Hasday, there is substantial evidence in family law to "support an excluded counter-narrative: the story of the persistence of common law property norms in the law of parenthood. Parents retain substantial elements of punishment, rights to control their children's labor, and rights to immunity from tort liability for injuring their children."[7] As Peter Samuelson has noted, "There are many parts of this country where, if a man takes his dog and his child onto the front porch and hits each equally with a stick, he faces more legal jeopardy for the cruelty to the dog. Why is that?"[8]

The Definition Frames Our Reality

Everything we do is influenced by how we frame or define issues and situations. Faced with a potentially fatal disease, one person may see the condition as a challenge, another as a death sentence. How we perceive something is crucial to how we respond. With child protection, if we see our task as removing children from damaging or dangerous situations as soon as possible, we may decide to hire more CPS workers to reach and quickly remove at-risk children, thus serving their best interests. Yet, research indicates that children taken from abusive or neglectful homes often wind up in conditions nearly as bad—sometimes even worse. Simply increasing the number of CPS workers and removing more children from their homes doesn't save lives.[9] And it is much more expensive than helping to make a family function better.

Suppose, instead, we believe that child abuse and neglect indicates a family in crisis—and further, we believe the child's best interests are usually served by keeping the family intact, perhaps after some brief time apart. We risk the grievous error that a child may return home to an embarrassed, angry parent who takes his frustrations out on the child.[10]

If how we respond to child abuse and neglect depends on how we perceive its causes and consequences and how we define solutions, then there are no truly right answers. But there are, indeed, better and worse ones.

When we were writing this book, a seven-year-old child was removed from his father's custody because the father did not realize a lemonade he'd purchased for his son contained alcohol. The father was a 47-year-old tenured professor of classical archaeology at the University of Michigan and had simply bought his son a lemonade during a baseball game. The parents, though, temporarily lost custody of their son when a security guard noticed the little boy drinking "hard lemonade." Even though the emergency room physician found no trace of alcohol in the child's blood and released him, Child Protective Services kept the boy from his parents. When two of his aunts drove from Massachusetts to take custody of the boy, they were denied. The father was also not even allowed back into his home for nearly a week.

Certainly this kind of event is uncommon, but it points to how capricious child protection efforts can be even with the best of intentions.

Complexity is the most common characteristic shared by abuse and neglect cases. Complexity in these situations isn't effectively tackled by simple, reactive responses. Nor is it addressed by delay and confusion. The best way to deal with that kind of complexity is to promote informed responses by people who are expert in the field of child abuse and neglect. We don't mean people—however well-meaning and whether social workers, volunteers, attorneys, or judges—who have been disengaged from actual abused children and their situations, but rather people who are trained to understand the complexities of all forms of abuse, who confront it daily, and who understand the importance of addressing each case for the individual life that is at stake.

Jane Spinak, clinical professor at Columbia Law School and long-time child advocate, believes the term best interests of the child has "tainted the way attorneys and judges look at their jobs." She has pointed out that Goldstein, Solnit, Goldstein, and Freud subtitled the third volume of their trilogy *The Least Detrimental Alternative*. To Spinak, the term best interests of the child is nearly meaningless, being defined differently by whoever uses it. By seeking the child's best interests, we often fail to see what in his or her interests is actually attainable and incorporates his or her circumstances.

Spinak told us of a 12-year-old girl who was removed years ago because her mother couldn't get her to school, couldn't keep the house safe, may have had a mental illness, and generally neglected the child. The girl has undergone many failed placements and longs to live with her mother. Using the concept of the best interests of the child would likely preclude even a consideration of returning the girl to her mother or, at very least, enabling her to visit with her mother more often than currently permitted by the protective state. "No one has even tried to find out if this mother, with assistance, could take care of her now 12-year-old child," Spinak said.

Has the child protection establishment become so enamored with the concept of best interests of the child that it has failed to meet compelling interests? In other words, have we set a goal but given too little regard to the processes by which we try to achieve it? Are we so bent on serving the at-risk child's best interests, that we may fail to see alternate ways to meet many good interests and wind up meeting none at all? Spinak said the term best interests lets many people off the hook by allowing them to make decisions for a child without adequately exploring a host of potential solutions that fall short of some people's notion of the best—but would work best for a child who wants a family. For family has intrinsic value.

The intention to serve a child's best interests is an admirable one. Spinak argued, however, that perhaps it's just a little too admirable and allows people with little or no understanding of a child's real needs and desires, of the circumstances of his or her life, to make a decision and say, "This is in the child's best interests." According to whom? By what standards of decision making? And does the process for determining what is in the best interests of a child do so, not in terms of children like this one, but for this particular child?

What we're saying here is that the best interests of the child is a useful concept when used well, when there is clarity and consistency and understanding. It is not useful to have a concept like this without an excellent process available to ensure that the child's best interests are met. It must be flexible enough to address unusual or extraordinary circumstances, but we shouldn't be treating each case differently according to who is defining best interests of the child. And children in half the country should surely not be at an administrative disadvantage compared to those who live in better trained, funded, supported, and enlightened locations.

The Council for Court Excellence, a civic organization in Washington, DC, visited courts in Illinois, Kentucky, New Jersey, and Arizona that had adopted practices to meet AFSA (Adoption and Safe Families Act) standards. Based on their site visits and other research, the council recommended the following best interest guidelines:

1. Commitment to permanency for children

2. Implementation of the one judge/one family concept

3. Multiyear judicial assignments and prior family law experience

4. Judicial support and teamwork

5. Use of alternative dispute resolution (ADR) techniques throughout the case

6. Collaboration among judges, lawyers, social workers, and other child welfare personnel

7. Improved calendaring practices, including time-specific case calendaring, longer and more substantive hearings and conferences, and fewer continuances

8. Interdisciplinary training on ASFA, court practices, and behavioral sciences

9. Tracking of cases to ensure compliance with ASFA

10. Allocation of sufficient space

It's good to have a list, but this one is procedural, dry, and distant from the needs of children at risk. Spinak suggested that experts develop lists of what we know about how children thrive, and of questions attorneys and judges should ask themselves before determining whether a child's interests will indeed be met. The best interests term itself should be abandoned unless we do a better job of making it meaningful.

People do know a lot about what children need, Spinak told us: "We're just not using what we know." In lieu of using the term best interests of the child, we could use current knowledge. Could it be argued that attempting to master the current knowledge or professional practice is more than most busy people who work with children are willing or able to do? "We don't accept that from our doctors," Spinak asserted. "Why would we accept it from people making decisions about children's lives?"

Yet we do.

This is one area where much more must be done . . . where training is crucial . . . and where old ways of doing things . . . or someone's subjective, personal idea of best interests of the child . . . just aren't good enough. We need to consider how other countries protect children as well and borrow from what works.

In Britain, for example, under the National Health Service (NHS), health visitors go to the home of every newborn baby in the country, and provide follow-up services to those who are at risk.[11] These health visitors are seen as the "eyes and ears of child protective services," Columbia professor Jane Waldfogel reported in her volume *The Future of Child Protection: How to Break the Cycle of Abuse and Neglect.* "Health visitors provide supervision and monitoring for high-risk cases that otherwise might be referred to CPS."

In the 1970s, while the United States was passing mandatory reporting laws, the focus in Britain was on reforming delivery of social services. Social workers were placed in local areas to work more effectively with other service providers, and local social services departments were established. And while, as in the United States, social services began focusing more exclusively on child abuse and neglect cases—in Britain the social services were mandated "to provide preventive services to those at risk, as well as services to those who had already experienced abuse, neglect, or other problems."[12]

From the 1970s to the 1990s, a series of public inquiries in the United Kingdom into child deaths and maltreatment spotlighted and condemned the lack of communication and coordination among agencies that came into contact with at-risk children. Further reviews and research found children being maltreated after being placed in dangerous foster homes or institutions. "There was also research that pointed to the risk that children placed in care, even if they escaped abuse and neglect, would all too often simply drift in a state of emotional limbo, neither returning to their homes nor entering new permanent homes."[13]

The upshot was passage in Britain of the Children Act of 1989, which aimed both to help children who needed protection, and improve the provision of preventive services for children in need (those whose health or development would be in jeopardy without such services, or who were handicapped). The requirements for local authorities were

1. Take steps to identify children in need.

2. "Provide a range and level of services which are appropriate to the needs of children in their area who are in need,"[14] to safeguard and promote their welfare, and—as far as is consistent with that aim—"promote their upbringing by their families."

3. Provide preventive services "to prevent children in the area from suffering neglect and ill-treatment."

4. Provide two specific preventive services: family centers and daycare centers for children in need.

The act emphasized working together both among agencies charged with helping children in need of protection or prevention, and in collaborating with parents. Measures in the act that increased parental rights and responsibilities "were intended not just to safeguard families from overintervention, but also to help CPS work more productively with parents to promote better outcomes for children," Waldfogel explained. "British reformers reasoned that since most children referred to child protective services would remain with their parents, effective intervention would have to involve the parents to be successful in the long run."[15]

You may be surprised by Waldfogel's assessment that provision of Britain's child protective services is much more decentralized than in the

United States. Child protective services, as well as other social and educational services, are administered and delivered by local authorities that cover fairly small areas; in rural areas, a local authority may span several small towns, and large cities are divided into several local authorities. Although bound by national rules and inspected by national entities, each local authority operates its child protective services autonomously.

"The British local authorities provide a useful infrastructure for the development of community-based systems of child protection," Waldfogel observed. "In the United States, in contrast, the local CPS divisions have less autonomy, and their jurisdictions do not always coincide with those of other agencies. For example, it is quite common for a CPS catchment area to be different from a local mental health or public health catchment area, and for all of those to be different from local school districts." The results? More work, more bureaucratic relationships to manage, and dispersed accountability.[16]

"Britain is clearly moving toward what many reformers in the United States think of as the endpoint of CPS reform," Waldfogel said. "This is the point where the two tracks of reform—improving services for children in need of protection and building new preventive services for children in need—converge so that individuals and agencies in the system work together to provide better protection for children. Crucial to this outcome is the need to change frontline practice, the way CPS workers and workers in community agencies approach families, other agencies, and informal sources of support."[17]

So, in most of the United States this type of coordinated, preventive assistance still isn't there. Where are the psychologists and health promotion staff to help new parents see that the safe route for the child is also the best route for them? As long as the state won't provide such guidance—or until it does—hospitals and other organizations must.

Some programs in early preventive intervention do exist in the United States. The child is not removed from the home and the juvenile court doesn't take jurisdiction. Instead, the parent signs an agreement to receive services such as drug or alcohol rehabilitation, anger management, baby care, and living skills.

"The public needs to know that all abusers are not sociopaths and that much abuse and neglect can be prevented," argues Yale's John Leventhal, professor and medical director of child abuse programs, who has worked as a pediatrician in the field of child abuse since 1982. "Often what is needed," Leventhal argues, is "adequate prevention and support for the parents."[18]

"There are models of prevention that work and that should receive funding," Leventhal explained. "As clinicians, we can no longer continue to care for children only after they have been hurt. We need to work much harder before the hurt has occurred."

Given how much there is to learn and the complexity of child abuse and neglect cases, often no single discipline can effectively assess a child's interests and a family's full needs. First Star is therefore developing Multidisciplinary Centers of Excellence (MCEs), intended to offer comprehensive training to professionals responsible for the welfare of abused and neglected children across the United States, such as doctors, judges, lawyers, social workers, nurses, psychologists, and public health workers. Holistic, collaborative approaches to the child's needs and interests are sought by MCE collaborations.

The First Star MCEs will feature multidisciplinary, classroom-based and experiential curriculum modules for students enrolled in schools of law, medicine, social work, education, nursing, public health, and psychology. The MCEs will also offer continuing education courses. A distance-learning component will in the future link partner institutions, and make the curriculum available to individuals nationwide. Conferences will also invite child welfare experts to participate in ongoing discourse about how to better serve abused and neglected children.

Best Interests Across the United States

The National Clearinghouse on Child Abuse and Neglect Information rounded up the best interests of the child statutes for 47 states, three territories, and the District of Columbia.[19] Although all 50 states require that the best interests of the child apply in abuse and neglect cases—the states vary widely in how they actually define the term. As a result, where a child happens to live will determine how the courts respond to his or her case. You can see this in the descriptions of state guidelines for applying the "best interests of the child" to actual procedures. For example, many states don't consider achieving a permanent home for children the highest priority—some don't even include it as a priority. Massachusetts describes the best interests of the child at some length, but with excessive obfuscation. In Michigan love and affection are given priority, as is concern for moral fitness.

Here are the relevant statutes for the state of Alaska:

It is in the best interests of a child who has been removed from the child's own home for the state to apply the following principles in resolving the situation:

- The child should be placed in a safe, secure, and stable environment;
- The child should not be moved unnecessarily;
- A planning process should be followed to lead to permanent placement of the child;
- Every effort should be made to encourage psychological attachment between the adult caregiver and the child;
- Frequent, regular, and reasonable visitation with the parent or guardian and family members should be encouraged; and
- Parents and guardians must actively participate in family support services so as to facilitate the child's being able to remain in the home. When children are removed from the home, the parents and guardians must actively participate in family support services to make return of their children to the home possible.

Numerous studies establish that

- Children undergo a critical attachment process before the time they reach 6 years of age;
- A child who has not attached with an adult caregiver during this critical stage will suffer significant emotional damage that frequently leads to chronic psychological problems and antisocial behavior when the child reaches adolescence and adulthood; and
- It is important to provide for an expedited placement procedure to ensure that all children, especially those under the age of 6 years, who have been removed from their homes are placed in permanent homes expeditiously.[20]

In making its dispositional order, the court shall keep the health and safety of the child as the court's paramount concern and consider

- The best interests of the child;
- The ability of the state to take custody and to care for the child to protect the child's best interests; and
- The potential harm to the child caused by removal of the child from the home and family environment.[21]

On the other hand, Arkansas' description of the child's best interests is—to put it charitably—much less detailed:

> The best interests of the children must be paramount and shall have precedence at every stage of juvenile court proceedings. The best interests of the child shall be the standard for recommendations made by the employees of the Department of Human Services and for juvenile court determinations as to whether a child should be reunited with his or her family or removed from or remain in a home wherein the child has been abused or neglected.[22]

On the other hand, Iowa is no slouch for brevity:

> During the [permanency] hearing, the court shall consider the child's need for a secure and permanent placement in light of any permanency plan or evidence submitted to the court.

Kentucky's language dwells largely on the obstacles the child faces:

> Evidence of the following circumstances if relevant, shall be considered by the court in all proceedings in which the court is required to render decisions in the best interest of the child:
>
> - mental illness or mental retardation of the parent, as attested to by a qualified mental health professional, which renders the parent unable to care for the immediate and ongoing needs of the child;
> - acts of abuse or neglect toward any child;
> - alcohol and other drug abuse that results in an incapacity by the parent or caretaker to provide essential care and protection for the child;
> - a finding of domestic violence and abuse, whether or not committed in the presence of the child;
> - any other crime committed by a parent which results in the death or permanent physical or mental disability of a member of that parent's family or household; and
> - the existence of any guardianship or conservatorship of the parent pursuant to a determination or disability or partial disability.
>
> In determining the best interest of the child, the court may consider the effectiveness of rehabilitative efforts made by the parent or caretaker intended to address circumstances in this section.[23]

Connecticut provides a list of concerns, but specifics are lacking here as well, leaving the determination of best interests to the courts:

> Best interest of the child shall include, but not be limited to, a consideration of the age of the child, the nature of the relationship of the child with the caretaker of the child, the length of time the child has been in the custody of the caretaker, the nature of the relationship of the child with the birth parent, the length of time the child has been in the custody of the birth parent, any relationship that may exist between the child and siblings or other children in the caretaker's household, and the psychological and medical needs of the child. The determination of the best interest of the child shall not be based on a consideration of the socio-economic status of the birth parent or the caretaker. [24]

The District of Columbia, Delaware, Illinois, Massachusetts, Maryland, Maine, North Dakota, Ohio, and Rhode Island all include the child's opinion or preference in their statutes, though some restrict this to children 12 years and older. Here are the relevant Maryland laws:

> In determining whether it is in the best interest of the child to terminate a natural parent's rights as to the child in any case, except the case of an abandoned child, the court shall give primary consideration to the safety and health of the child, and consideration to
>
> - The timeliness, nature, and extent of the services offered by the child placement agency to facilitate reunion of the child with the natural parent;
> - Any social service agreement between the natural parent and the child placement agency, and the extent to which all parties have fulfilled their obligations under the agreement;
> - The child's feelings toward and emotional ties with the child's natural parents, the child's siblings, and any other individuals who may significantly affect the child's best interest;
> - The child's adjustment to home, school, and community;
> - The result of the effort the natural parent has made to adjust the natural parent's circumstances, conduct, or conditions to make it in the best interest of the child to be returned to the natural parent's home, including:
>   - the extent to which the natural parent has maintained regular contact with the child under a plan to reunite the child with the natural parent, but the court may not give significant weight to any incidental visit, communication, or contribution;
>
> *(Continued)*

(Continued)

- o If the natural parent is financially able, the payment of a reasonable part of the child's substitute physical care and maintenance;
- o the maintenance of regular communication by the natural parent with the custodian of the child;
- o whether additional services would be likely to bring about a lasting parental adjustment so the child could be returned to the natural parent within an ascertainable time, not exceeding 18 months from the time of placement. But the court may not consider whether the maintenance of the parent-child relationship may serve as an inducement for the natural parent's rehabilitation; and
- o all services offered to the natural parent before the placement of the child, whether offered by the agency to which the child is committed or by other agencies or professionals.[25]

Florida places first in the suitable placement of a child with a relative:

In a hearing on a petition for termination of parental rights, the court shall consider the manifest best interests of the child. This consideration shall not include a comparison between the attributes of the parents and those of any persons providing a present or potential placement for the child. For the purpose of determining the manifest best interests of the child, the court shall consider and evaluate all relevant factors, including, but not limited to:

- Any suitable permanent custody arrangement with a relative of the child;
- The ability and disposition of the parent or parents to provide the child with food, clothing, medical care, or other remedial care recognized and permitted under State law instead of medical care, and other material needs of the child;
- The capacity of the parent or parents to care for the child to the extent that the child's safety, wellbeing, and physical, mental, and emotional health will not be endangered upon the child's return home;
- The present mental and physical health needs of the child and such future needs of the child to the extent that such future needs can be ascertained based on the present condition of the child;
- The love, affection, and other emotional ties existing between the child and the child's parent or parents, siblings, and other relatives, and the degree of harm to the child that would arise from the termination of parental rights and duties;
- The likelihood of an older child remaining in long-term foster care upon termination of parental rights, due to emotional or behavioral problems or any special needs of the child;

- The child's ability to form a significant relationship with a parental substitute and the likelihood that the child will enter into a more stable and permanent family relationship as a result of permanent termination of parental rights and duties;
- The length of time that the child has lived in a stable, satisfactory environment and the desirability of maintaining continuity;
- The depth of the relationship existing between the child and the present custodian;
- The reasonable preferences and wishes of the child, if the court deems the child to be of sufficient intelligence, understanding, and experience to express a preference;
- The recommendations for the child provided by the child's guardian ad litem or legal representative.[26]

Georgia places considerable trust in the ability of the court to determine a child's best interests once it has also determined by convincing evidence that the parents are incapable of caring for the child:

In considering the termination of parental rights, the court shall first determine whether there is present clear and convincing evidence of parental misconduct or inability. If there is clear and convincing evidence of such parental misconduct or inability, the court shall then consider whether termination of parental rights is in the best interest of the child, after considering the physical, mental, emotional, and moral condition and needs of the child who is the subject of the proceeding, including the need for a secure and stable home.[27]

Oregon leaves definitions to the court and provides only a list of considerations:

In determining the custody of a minor child, the court shall give primary consideration to the best interests and welfare of the child. In determining the best interests and welfare of the child, the court shall consider the following relevant factors:

- The emotional ties between the child and other family members;
- The interest of the parties in and attitude toward the child;
- The desirability of continuing an existing relationship;

(Continued)

(Continued)

- The abuse of one parent by the other;
- The preference of the primary caregiver of the child, if the caregiver is deemed fit by the court; and
- The willingness and ability of each parent to facilitate and encourage a close and continuing relationship between the other parent and the child. However, the court may not consider such willingness and ability if one parent shows that the other parent has sexually assaulted or engaged in a pattern of behavior of abuse against the parent or a child and that a continuing relationship with the other parent will endanger the health or safety of either parent or the child.[28]

Tennessee guides the court with a checklist of circumstances to consider:

In all cases, when the best interests of the child and those of the adults are in conflict, such conflict shall always be resolved to favor the rights and the best interests of the child, which interests are hereby recognized as constitutionally protected, and, to that end, this part shall be liberally construed.[29]

In determining whether termination of parental or guardianship rights is in the best interest of the child pursuant to this part, the court shall consider, but is not limited to, the following:

- Whether the parent or guardian has made such adjustment of circumstance, conduct, or conditions as to make it safe and in the child's best interest to be in the home of the parent or guardian;
- Whether the parent or guardian has failed to effect a lasting adjustment after reasonable efforts by available social services agencies for such duration of time that lasting adjustment does not reasonably appear possible;
- Whether the parent or guardian has maintained regular visitation or other contact with the child;
- Whether a meaningful relationship has otherwise been established between the parent or guardian and the child;
- The effect a change of caretakers and physical environment is likely to have on the child's emotional, psychological and medical condition;
- Whether the parent or guardian, or other person residing with the parent or guardian, has shown brutality, physical, sexual, emotional or psychological abuse, or neglect toward the child, or another child or adult in the family or household;
- Whether the physical environment of the parent's or guardian's home is healthy and safe, whether there is criminal activity in the home, or whether there is such use of alcohol or controlled substances as may render the parent or guardian consistently unable to care for the child in a safe and stable manner;

- Whether the parent's or guardian's mental and/or emotional status would be detrimental to the child or prevent the parent or guardian from effectively providing safe and stable care and supervision for the child; or
- Whether the parent or guardian has paid child support consistent with the child support guidelines.[30]

Like Tennessee, Texas lays out a extensive list of considerations, but once again gives considerable discretion to the court in actual definition and determination.

Wisconsin looks ahead to the likelihood that a child will be adopted. It is not clear whether this means a child will be placed back with unsuitable parents if adoption is unlikely. Certainly this is not the intent, but the wording leaves room for this kind of interpretation by a judge inadequately trained in child protection.

The best interests of the child shall be the prevailing factor considered by the court in determining the disposition of all proceedings under this subchapter. In considering the best interests of the child under this section the court shall consider, but not be limited to, the following:

- The likelihood of the child's adoption after termination;
- The age and health of the child, both at the time of the disposition, and, if applicable, at the time the child was removed from the home;
- Whether the child has substantial relationships with the parent or other family members, and whether it would be harmful to the child to sever these relationships;
- The wishes of the child;
- The duration of the separation of the parent from the child; and
- Whether the child will be able to enter into a more stable and permanent family relationship as a result of the termination, taking into account the conditions of the child's current placement, the likelihood of future placements and the results of prior placements.[31]

Abusing the Term?

Aside from the inconsistencies in the use of the term *best interests of the child*, too often the concept has provided camouflage for what amounts to institutional immorality in the protection of children. Too strong a use of language would you say? Despite decades of emphasis on best interests, by 1990 the U.S. Advisory Board on Child Abuse and Neglect concluded the problem of child abuse and neglect amounts to a national emergency. The board based its conclusion on three findings:

1. Each year hundreds of thousands of children are being starved and abandoned, burned and severely beaten, raped and sodomized, and berated and belittled.

2. The system the nation has devised to respond to child abuse and neglect is failing.

3. The United States spends billions of dollars on programs that deal with the results of the nation's failure to treat child abuse and neglect.[32]

"All Americans should be outraged by child maltreatment," the board concluded. On its heels came a report from the National Commission on Children, chaired by Senator Jay Rockefeller (W.Va.), which stated,

> We could not avoid questioning the moral character of a nation that allows so many children to grow up poor, to live in unsafe dwellings and violent neighborhoods, to lack access to basic health care and a decent education.[33]

Lewis Pitts argued that the concept of best interests itself is not so much to blame as the infrequency with which we apply it effectively. For him, much like Spinak, the issue is how easily we as a nation do indeed allow ourselves to depart from the standard of best interests when responding to the needs of children at risk:

> I think "best interests" is a fully adequate standard. The problem is that it is not followed. We must be careful to not let a focus on the standard lead to failure to boldly point out how frequently and why it is not followed—such as inadequate funding of the entire Child Protective Services process (salaries, foster care rates, training of social workers, attorneys, judges, foster parents, mental health and education services, etc.); the "go along, get along" attitude of guardians ad litem, bureaucratic imperative/protection/turf, egos, etc.[34]

Empty Promises

Do we not understand what children need? "Of course we do," Pitts told us. So, too, do the many experts we interviewed for this book. Research is voluminous on the topic and in general we well understand how children's needs can be met. State constitutions as well as federal and state statutes provide—on paper—for the essential educational and developmental services that children need. The federal Disabilities Education Act promises a free, appropriate, public education to children with disabilities—and that includes the emotional and behavioral disabilities "often present in children involved in the foster care system." The Adoption and Safe Families Act promises speedy and permanent placement of children who enter the foster care system. These promises are important to all children yet the programs charged with providing them are in Pitts' words, "pitifully and disgustingly underfunded."

We've adapted the following scenario, from what Lewis Pitts described, that could be faced by an actual child. We call her Denise. Let's see if her best interests are met.

Returned to her home by Child Protective Services after having been removed due to abuse, Denise finds her situation hasn't improved—in fact, far from it. Her parents repeatedly abuse her, both physically and sexually.

After a lengthy wait, she reenters foster care and is placed with a new family.

But does Denise get the counseling and mental health treatment she needs as a result of being a victim of abuse?

No.

Does she have an attorney to appeal the standard of care she receives?

No.

Denise is Medicaid-eligible; under federal law she's entitled to whatever services are deemed medically necessary by her provider. But does she get those crucial services?

No.

Why not? It happens that appealing to obtain the care she deserves would require filings before a different judge than the foster care judge. Her guardian ad litem—even if an attorney—doesn't get paid to handle such appeals. So there's no appeal, and hence no care.

As a result of her untreated emotional and behavioral disabilities, and all too predictably, Denise gets in trouble at Middle School.

Does she receive a manifestation determination review (aka MDR) as state guidelines would prescribe?

No.

Despite Denise's marked symptoms, and repeated pleas by her foster parents, her school refuses to identify her as requiring special education. Needless to say, without a lawyer Denise can't appeal the school's denial of federally promised services. But the school does take one concrete action: it suspends Denise for her behavior.

(Continued)

(Continued)

Soon thereafter, police arrest Denise on a drug possession charge. The criminal court judge immediately provides her with a public defender to assure that she gets a fair trial. Tragically, he takes no action to sort out the broken, disregarded state and federal laws—laws that guaranteed the mental and health services to keep Denise out of trouble in the first place!

Perhaps Denise's foster parents will complain to the state or local child protection agency about their foster child being denied her lawful mental health and special education services. Perhaps if they do, though, CPS will label them troublemakers. Let's say the foster parents decide to stand up to CPS anyway. Laboring mightily, they manage to find an attorney—one who's willing to dispense with his fee and represent Denise's needs pro bono. Problem solved?

No.

The CPS attorney objects, claiming the foster parents breached confidentiality by talking to the pro bono attorney about Denise's case. Indeed, the CPS attorney threatens to remove Denise to another foster home. [35]

Attempting to serve the best interests of at-risk children is like trying to find your way across a perilous mountain trail strewn with boulders. There are problems with the delivery system that is supposed to protect our nation's children. There are serious problems with abject failure to apply laws that are already on the books. And, yes, there are problems with people who fear that protecting children's rights can go too far.

But we're not talking here about giving children the right to do whatever they please, far from it. We want simply to protect them from the horrors of abuse and neglect—and help them recover from what they've already suffered. To have any hope of accomplishing that, we need to let children be heard in court when their lives become cases of abuse and neglect. They are the victims—let an attorney trained to understand their needs represent them and advocate for them when the help our government promised them fails to materialize. Let them appear before a judge who is, at the very least, knowledgeable on the matters of child abuse and neglect. Can we not improve the child protection system so that children like Denise—in their tens of thousands—don't have to suffer institutional abuse and neglect by local, state, and federal authorities beyond what they've already borne at the hands of adult perpetrators? We address this question at length in Chapter 5.

A Crying Need for Change

Children suffering from abuse and neglect are victims, just as much as adults who are victims of muggings, rapes, and assaults. Why should we stand for laws and systems that are supposed to help these young victims but wind up injuring or distressing them even more? Where legislation isn't being enforced, it needs to be enforced. When lawmakers pass child protection legislation, they need to provide the money to implement it—unlike, for example, Indiana, which passed a child advocate requirement but didn't provide money to pay for the advocates, leaving unrepresented more than 9,000 Indiana children who should have had court-appointed advocates to oversee their abuse and neglect cases.[36] Where such laws are inadequate, they need to be improved. Nowhere in the U.S. Constitution does it say our laws must remain unchanged, or that we have to accept laws that fail to respond to the reality on the ground. Supreme Court Justice Thurgood Marshall explained it this way:

> Moral philosophers may debate whether certain inequalities are absolute wrongs, but history makes clear that constitutional principles of equality, like constitutional principles of liberty, property, and due process, evolve over time; what once was a "natural" and "self-evident" ordering later comes to be seen as an artificial and invidious constraint on human potential and freedom. . . . Shifting cultural, political and social patterns at times come to make past practices appear inconsistent with fundamental principles upon which American society rests, an inconsistency legally cognizable under the Equal Protection Clause.[37]

It's long past time to change the cultural, political, and social patterns that fail to protect our nation's vulnerable children. One way is to generate more complete and consistent definitions and policies across the 50 states regarding the best interests of the child.

"The very smallest favour we should do ourselves if, courtesy of states' rights, we have to live in a country with 2,200 ways of doing the same thing," Peter Samuelson said, "is to compare practices and outcomes by location with each other, draw conclusions on what works best and then apply these best practices nationally. Every national company in America does that every week. When it comes to children, the way we deal with their trauma and grief and victimization depends on where they live."[38]

For our own part, we've scoured the statutes identified by the National Clearinghouse on Child Abuse and Neglect Information. Borrowing liberally, we have made an attempt at a comprehensive list of relevant factors that courts, child protective services, and other agencies ought to consider when determining the best interests of a child who is in jeopardy. We must also take the further step that Lewis Pitts has identified and actually put into action all the guidelines, laws, and promised services that we've supposedly established to protect the children of the United States of America—ones we look at in Chapter 5.

As you read the list that follows, consider: If you had been a child victim of abuse or neglect, and the state were about to determine how your case would be disposed—is there anything below you *wouldn't* want considered? And as an adult, would you tolerate any less?

Factors to Include When Determining the Best Interests of a Child*

Administrative Continuity

- A single judge, whenever possible, hears all successive cases or proceedings involving a child or family.
- The relevant service providers, including the schools, cooperate and coordinate to provide a continuum of services.
- Civil and criminal systems for investigation, intervention, and disposition of the child's case cooperate and coordinate to minimize interagency conflicts and to ensure effective, coordinated response.

Physical Safety and Welfare

The child is able to be safe and healthy and feel secure in an environment that provides adequate food, shelter, medical care, and clothing. The risks attendant to entering and being in substitute care are minimized by thorough screening and monitoring.

The child receives prompt and permanent placement in a safe and stable home. Placement is neither delayed nor denied based on race, color, or national origin of the foster parent or child.

The child is placed with siblings whenever possible, unless determined not in the best interest of a sibling.

---

*From the National Clearinghouse on Child Abuse and Neglect, www.childwelfare.gov.

Moral, Emotional, Intellectual, Social Needs

- The child receives care, nurturance, guidance, supervision, and appropriate discipline consistent with the child's safety and level of development.
- The child is protected from repeated exposure to violence even though the violence may not be directed at the child.
- An adequate social support system consisting of an extended family and friends is available to the child.

Individual Needs

Decisions incorporate consideration of the child's age, fitness, readiness, abilities, and developmental levels, including

- the likelihood of an older child remaining in long-term foster care on termination of parental rights, due to emotional or behavioral problems or any special needs of the child
- the differences in the concept of time of children of different ages
- where the child actually feels love, attachment, and sense of being valued (as opposed to where adults believe the child should feel those things)
- the child's home, school, and community record and the child's adjustment to his or her home, school, and community
- attention paid to the child's background and personal attachments, including family, community, culture, religion, school, and friends
- due consideration given to the child's need for permanence, which includes stability and continuity of relationships with parent figures and with siblings and other relatives

Desires and Wishes

- The wishes of the child as to custodians and living arrangements need to be heard through a client-directed attorney.
- The child's long-term goals and opinion of his or her own best interests in the matter should be taken into consideration.
- The recommendations for the child provided by the child's guardian ad litem or legal representative should also be considered.

Family Bonds

When making decisions regarding placement, consideration is given to

- the love, affection, other emotional ties, and quality of inter-action existing between the child and the parent or parents, siblings and other relatives, or caretakers, including the foster parent and any other residents of the household or persons who may significantly affect the child's best interests and the degree of harm to the child that would arise from permanent removal
- the length of time that the child has lived in a stable, satisfactory environment; the desirability of maintaining continuity, and the potential emotional, developmental, and educational harm to the child if moved from the current placement
- past and present compliance by both parents with their rights and responsibilities to their child. (The results of efforts the parent or parents makes to adjust conduct, home conditions, or circumstances to make it in the best interest of the child to be returned to the parent's home. The extent to which the natural parent has maintained regular contact with the child under a plan to reunite the child with the parent. Whether additional services would be likely to bring about a lasting parental adjustment so the child could be returned within an ascertainable time, not exceeding 18 months from the time of placement.)
- the willingness and ability of the child's family to seek out, accept, and complete counseling services and to cooperate with and facilitate an appropriate agency's close supervision
- the willingness and ability of the child's family to effect positive environmental and personal changes within a reasonable period of time
- whether the child's parents are willing and able to provide the child with a safe environment
- the child's ability to form a significant relationship with a parental substitute and the likelihood that the child will enter into a more stable and permanent family relationship as a result of permanent termination of parental rights and duties
- the depth of the relationship existing between the child and the present custodian

- the child's emotional attachment to the child's current caregiver and the caregiver's family
- the length of time the child has lived with the current caregiver
- the physical, mental, and emotional health of all individuals involved to the degree that such affects the welfare of the child, the decisive consideration being the physical, mental, and emotional needs of the child
- the moral fitness of the parties involved
- the effectiveness, suitability, and adequacy of the services provided and of placement decisions, including the progress of the child or children
- the timeliness, nature, and extent of the services offered by the child placement agency to facilitate reunion of the child with the natural parent; the particulars of the service plan designed to meet the needs of the child within his current placement, whether with the child's family or in a substitute care placement; and whether such service plan is used by the department or presented to the courts with written documentation.

Solutions

People work day and night to assure that children who have been abused or neglected do have their best interests met. These people are genuine heroes to children, but their efforts are constantly blocked by clumsy systems or hampered by government itself. If it seems to you by now that our response to abused children's best interests resembles the too-little too-late response to the victims of Hurricane Katrina—fraught with frustration and unnecessary suffering and death—then you're right. The difference here is that the children don't protest and the press doesn't cover their cries. This broken system is a creeping, long-term curse, lacking the publicity-worthiness of a sudden, unexpected hurricane

In 2001, Minnesota State Supreme Court Justice Kathleen Blatz launched the Children's Justice Initiative, a joint effort by courts and the Minnesota Department of Human Services, which oversees child protection, to improve services for children under state protection.

The same year, the state Supreme Court became one of the first in the nation to open up files and court hearings in child-protection cases.

Traditionally, juvenile delinquency and child-protection cases have been closed to shield children from shame and future harm. Minnesota has apparently asked who is being protected by the closed nature of child proceedings. Significant improvements, then, are obviously possible.

Child advocates and the press need to be able to probe, to ask difficult questions so that other states and the federal government can do right by children at risk. Just like most every other aspect of government, the light of day fosters honesty and encourages those in power to be humane. Children need protection from inept systems. Only openness in procedures of protection and in court can provide that.

The U.S. Constitution Does Not Provide Protective Rights for Children

Judge Charles Gill of Connecticut wrote on this issue:

Members of the general public are astonished when they learn that the Constitution does not really provide any protective rights for our children. However, even the notion that adults have certain protective rights required centuries to evolve from discourses by moral and legal philosophers to codifications in documents such as our Bill of Rights. The same cannot be said for the rights of the child, which for long periods of history were submerged within the rights of the family. The period of transition from the first assertion that children, too, have rights, to the recognition of their individual human rights by binding international law, has taken barely over one hundred years, and has taken place largely without the aid of social scientists and philosophers.

Although numerous other nations have recognized that children have assertible rights in their constitutions, America has made no significant move in that direction. Constitutional rights possessed by other children of the world include protective rights that shield them from parents and family. Those in the front-line trenches of child abuse know full well that the latter are the very people from whom children most often need protection.[39]

Summary

We've asked in this chapter about the best interests of the child by what definition and according to whom. We need to more consistently define this concept that has become so central to child abuse and neglect. We need to question our assumptions, as Hasday argues. We need to avoid falling victim to nice-sounding phrases that really don't mean much but have become widely used to make significant decisions about children's lives.

We need to strike a balance between the concern for child abuse and neglect confidentiality and the need to be able to observe and oversee a system that does not have the excellent track record children at risk deserve. Right now the policy throughout the United Sates is actually "Let someone else decide." This isn't good enough.

Endnotes

1. Mary Ann Mason, *From Father's Property to Children's Rights: The History of Child Custody in the United States* (New York: Columbia University Press, 1994), 59, 82, 121–22.

2. Joseph Goldstein, Albert J. Solnit, Sonja Goldstein, and Anna Freud, *The Best Interests of the Child: The Least Detrimental Alternative* (Free Press: New York, 1996), xix.

3. Ibid., 91–92.

4. Ibid., 227.

5. Ibid., 87–88.

6. Jill Elaine Hasday, "The Canon of Family Law," *Public Law and Legal Theory* Working Paper No. 77, University of Chicago Law School, October 2004.

7. Ibid.

8. petersamuelson.blogspot.com

9. Richard P. Barth and Debra L. Blackwell, "Death rates among California's foster care and former foster care populations," *Children and Youth Services Review,* 20, (1998), 557–604; D. Lindsey, "Family preservation and child protection: Striking a balance," *Children and Youth Services Review,* 16, (1994), 279–294.

10. See Chapter 6, Emerich Thoma, "If you lived here, you'd be home by now: The business of foster care," IPT Journal 10(1998), www.ipt-forensics.com/journal/volume10/j10_10.htm

11. Jane Waldfogel, *The Future of Child Protection: How to Break the Cycle of Abuse and Neglect,* (Cambridge: Harvard University Press, 1998), 162.

12. Ibid., 163.

13. Ibid.

14. British Department of Health, Introduction to the Children Act, secs. 4.1 to 4.4.

15. Waldfogel, *The Future of Child Protection,* 172.

16. Ibid., 164.

17. Ibid., 181.

18. John M. Leventhal, "Editorial: Preventing Child Abuse and Neglect. We (You, Your Colleagues, and I) Have to Do More," *Clinical Child Psychology and Psychiatry* 7(4): 503.

19. The National Clearinghouse on Child Abuse and Neglect Information and the National Adoption Information Clearinghouse, "2003 Child Abuse and Neglect State Statutes Series Ready Reference; Permanency Planning: Best Interests of the Child" (Washington, DC: U.S. Department of Health and Human

Services). Note: "Ready Reference publications contain excerpts of text with citations from specific sections of each State's code that focus on a single issue of special interest. While every attempt has been made to be as complete as possible, additional information on these topics may be in other sections of a State's code as well as in agency regulations, case law, and informal practices and procedures." Note: The above clearinghouses are now the Child Welfare Information Gateway, www.welfare.gov

    20. Alaska Stat. § 47.05.065(4)-(5) (Michie Supp. 1998)

    21. Alaska Stat. § 47.10.082 (Michie Supp. 1998)

    22. Ark. Code Ann. § 9-27-102 (Michie Supp. 1998)

    23. Ky. Rev. Stat. Ann. § 620.023 (Michie Supp. 1998)

    24. Conn. Gen. Stat. Ann. § 45a-719 (West, WESTLAW through 1-1-01)

    25. Md. Code Ann. Fam. Law § 5-313(c) (West, WESTLAW through 2003 Reg. Sess.)

    26. Fla. Stat. Ann. § 39.810 (West Supp. 1999)

    27. Ga. Code Ann. § 15-11-94(a) (WESTLAW through 2000 Gen. Assem.)

    28. Oregon Rev. Stat. Ann. § 107.137(1) (WESTLAW through end of 1999 Reg. Sess.)

    29. Tennessee Code Ann. § 36-1-101(d) (Supp. 1998)

    30. Tenn. Code Ann. § 36-1-113(i) (WESTLAW through 2003 1st Reg. Sess.)

    31. Wisconsin Stat. Ann. § 48.426(2)-(3) (West, WESTLAW through 1999 Act 25)

    32. U.S. Advisory Board on Child Abuse and Neglect, "Child Abuse and Neglect: Critical First Steps in Response to a National Emergency," (Washington, DC: U.S. Government Printing Office, 1990).

    33. National Commission on Children, *Beyond Rhetoric: A New American Agenda for Children and Families* (Washington, DC: U.S. Government Printing Office, 1991), 344.

    34. Lewis Pitts, e-mail interview, February 3, 2006.

    35. Adapted from Lewis Pitts, "Fighting for Children's Rights: Lessons From the Civil Rights Movement," University of Florida Journal of Law and Public Policy 16, no. 2 (2005): 333–34.

    36. Tim Evans, "Protecting Children: 9,000 youths in state lack an advocate; Law to combat abuse, neglect didn't include necessary money," *Indianapolis Star*, August 28, 2005.

    37. City of Cleburne v. Cleburne Living Ctr., 473 U.S. 432, 466 (1985) (concurring in part and dissenting in part).

    38. http://petersamuelson.blogspot.com

    39. Charles Gill, "Essay on the status of the American child, 2000 A.D.: Chattel or Constitutionally protected child-citizen?" *Ohio Northern University Law Review* XVII, no. 3 (1998): 547–48.

3

Lost in the System

Confidentiality and Secrecy

Can we at least agree that the overall state of America's child welfare system is appalling, unnecessarily shoddy, and unworthy of any nation, let alone one of the wealthiest? How can we, 300 million people who almost all love children and wish them the best, have allowed this Hades of awfulness to be perpetrated in our names and on our watch? I hear you say, "Yes, but some places do a great job." Absolutely true, and how crazy is that? Can you imagine a national for-profit company lasting very long if some of its branches did a great job while the others paid no attention to best practices and kept losing, spoiling, and destroying the merchandise? Is it really necessary to let states' rights prevent us from the most elementary top-down types of coordination of knowledge and actions to protect children?

First Star advocates for three key issues to yield tangible long-term benefits for child victims:

- open courts and open records to promote and enforce agency accountability
- university-based, multidisciplinary training and certification for all professionals working to benefit abused and neglected children
- a child's right to professional, client-directed legal counsel

The right to an attorney is one of America's most basic civil and legal privileges. Yet the *First Star National Report Card on Legal*

Representation for Children, issued in April 2007, showed that only 17 states provide client-directed legal representation for child victims in dependency court and foster care proceedings.

> And I hear some say, "There's not enough money to do a better job." Well let me share that I read in the *Los Angeles Daily News* (August 13, 2001) that the annual cost of keeping a child in MacLaren Children's Center, a hell hole so bad it was subsequently closed down as unfixable in 2004, was. . . . wait for it. . . . $336,985. Yes, that is not a typo: It cost almost $1,000 to keep *each child* there *each day* in that awful place! So I phoned the Ritz Carlton and asked how much they would charge for a suite for a year. Prices started at $190,000. Go figure. Of course more money would be helpful. Of course a reordering of priorities in the budget would be great, to give the children who are our only future a better share among the special interest groups with their highly paid and skillful K Street lobbyists. But make no mistake, we could do a heck of a job in improving things if we spent the existing budget better. And for example, an ounce of prevention would save ten times as much in addressing unnecessarily broken lives. Couldn't that be the American Way too?
>
> —Peter Samuelson[1]

At every step in the life of a child at risk, there are people who can help. Many do. But all too often, it seems that blind luck determines whether good care, little care, or no care—or even death—will be the outcome for a child. Is it blind luck? Or is it something else? Is it more about barriers? Barriers to identifying, following, and caring for endangered children.

Barriers have been allowed to arise—and have even been constructed—by well-intentioned legislators, judges, and agencies.

Such barriers cost lives and result in needless agony and death—hinder parents, caseworkers, service agencies, judges, police, oversight committees, child advocates, and even legislators.

They hinder service and they hide incompetence. Sometimes they are even the *reason* for incompetence . . . preventing competent people from giving those children the help they need.

This combination of barriers constructs a maze of child protection services and a maze for the child desperately trying to get help. When the latter maze grows big and complicated enough, getting through it can become a question of blind luck.

Why with so many wonderful people trying to help children who have been abused and neglected have we not constructed a better system, benefiting from ones we already use in some parts of the country? Why does the 2007 UNICEF report place the United States in nearly last place? Why are the children of Portugal so much better off? What is wrong with America?[2]

In the wake of Hurricane Katrina, Louisiana child welfare officials apparently lost track of a four-month-old infant, who died after his father smashed his head into a wall.[3] Indianapolis police arrested 21-year-old Michael D. Sumner, Jr. and 20-year-old Rasheeda D. Williams for child neglect and aggravated battery in the death of their four-month-old son, Michael. They then learned the baby had previously suffered a head injury in Louisiana, and that child welfare officials there had ordered the father to live separately from the infant. Reporters for the *Indianapolis Star* said the tragedy demonstrated the difficulty of monitoring families that move from state to state. Susan Tielking, spokeswoman for the Indiana Department of Child Services told reporters: "Unless a state notifies us of an active case or asks us to be involved with a family, we would have no way of knowing they are here."[4]

What went wrong here? Surely one issue was inadequate reporting when children at risk are moved from state to state, and this definitely was an area where state prerogative wasn't enough. It needed to be addressed nationally. Legislation to improve protection for children who move across state lines—children who might otherwise go missing—was introduced by Representative Tom Delay (R-Texas) and passed by Congress and signed into law in 2006.[5]

We don't usually think about children missing who are supposedly in foster care, but that is exactly what happens in many states. In 2002, when a 15-year-old runaway foster child named Heather Kish was found murdered in Monroe, Michigan, the tragedy riveted the state supreme court's attention on Michigan's 300 other missing foster children.[6]

Consider this. Your state university may have 20,000 full-time students. What would be the public outcry, the newspaper headlines, and the extent of daily police briefings if 300 of those students went missing? It's inconceivable.

To its credit, Michigan's supreme court responded to the problem by ordering the family courts to work with child welfare agencies to find the missing children. Chief judges in the family courts held hearings and called in social workers and everyone else who had information about a given missing child. The judges were required to report their progress in locating the children to the state supreme court. As Chief Justice Maura Corrigan told the Pew Commission, "As a result of this joint effort, last year we located 75 percent of the children who were missing from foster care placements."[7]

Recognizing the need for collaboration and links up the line to the chief justice were key, Judge Corrigan explained,

> The buck stops here with the leadership in the states' highest court, and that's why we are calling on every chief justice in the United States to establish similar positions in their states . . .
>
> This successful effort illustrates the second of our recommendations . . . that courts collaborate with the child welfare agencies . . . we in government are acutely aware of the separation of powers among the three branches. We learn this in school, and we think it's really important. But the distinctions among the three branches do not matter to a child in foster care. It is incumbent on each of us across the branches to collaborate for the sake of these children.
>
> . . . our efforts to reform depend very much on our ability to track the cases in the courts. If you can't track the case, you can't find the missing foster child, and you can't check whether the child is advancing on the road to permanency. And that is our next recommendation, that we need the resources, the training and the performance standards, all the tools that are required to do a good job.[8]

The Confidentiality Barrier

Children in foster care often face abuse and neglect. Getting detailed information about foster children is difficult. So is finding detailed information about the group homes where they live. In an effort to confront this issue, the Children's Advocacy Institute at the University of San Diego and First Star produced a joint report titled "State Secrecy and Child Deaths in the U.S." The Child Abuse Prevention and Treatment Act explicitly requires states to adopt "provisions which allow for public disclosure of the findings or information about the case of child abuse or neglect which has resulted in a child fatality or near fatality." The report compares child death and near death disclosure laws and policies of all 50 U.S. states and the District of Columbia. A grade of "A" is given for the best, most transparent policies, to a grade of "F" for the most secretive or non-existent ones. Only two states earned an "A," 28 states deserved a "C+" or lower, and 10 states actually flunked. This is a must-read report for anyone interested in the care of children who face abuse and/or neglect. Clearly children are being underserved.[9]

Baltimore Sun reporter Jonathan Rockoff found that confidentiality issues make it extremely difficult to hold accountable either those companies entrusted and paid to care for children, or the state regulators who "are supposed to monitor that care."[10] As managing attorney Kathleen Hughes of the Maryland Disability Law Center told Rockoff, "Everything right now is done with this shroud of secrecy, and there's no way to oversee the overseers."[11] Only 16 states had open courts at the time of this writing. In 34 states, the relevant courts are closed.

In a pair of articles by Rockoff, the *Sun* described Maryland's failure to adequately safeguard the 2,700 foster children living in 330 privately run group homes. "Regulators," the newspaper found, "weren't properly overseeing care, spending and staffing at the homes."[12] Many of the children were abuse and neglect victims; some of them needed medical care, even 24-hour nursing. Yet Maryland law, the *Sun* noted, "largely blocks public review of the handling of their cases, even after they have died." It only allows disclosure when prosecutors file child abuse or neglect charges—a rarity.

At least three children's deaths did not receive thorough government reviews, the *Sun* found, and two received no review. The Maryland Department of Health and Mental Hygiene is supposed to report deaths and serious injuries to the Disability Law Center but as the *Sun* report showed, these are difficult to obtain in a thorough and timely manner. Child advocacy experts with whom Rockoff spoke suggested

- giving lawyers for the foster children the authority to decide what information can be released,
- establishing a watchdog agency with the power to review records, and
- requiring county child fatality review teams that examine deaths of foster children to share more information with the public.[13]

A serious problem here is that states like Maryland can have more stringent regulations on confidentiality than federal regulations. So where children live dictates to a large degree whether the state's sluggishness—or even outright failure—to protect them is revealed in time to save their lives.

In the District of Columbia, the *Washington Post* investigated the deaths of 229 children between 1993 and 2000.[14] All had died after coming to the attention of the city's child protective system. In their Pulitzer-winning news articles, *Post* reporters claimed that 40 of the children—mostly infants and toddlers—"lost their lives after government workers failed to take key preventive action or placed children in unsafe homes or institutions." Seventeen were homicides. All were tragic:

- a 15-year-old, wheelchair-bound girl who never received an operation for her painfully curved spine, and died in the hallway of a nursing home
- a 13-year-old boy who "was put on a bus, alone, and ended up dead in a dilapidated house, his body pockmarked with insect bites"
- an 8-year-old boy whose "mentally ill mother . . . stabbed him so many times"

According to the *Post*, "top government officials knew that DC children were dying for avoidable reasons and did little about it. Police officers did not fully investigate abuse reports, leaving children with violent or drug-addicted parents or relatives. Social workers did not adequately monitor neglected children. Frail newborns were permitted to go home to drug-addicted and mentally ill parents without follow-up services. Judges sent children to unlicensed foster homes, or to institutions far from the District where their care went unsupervised."[15]

Post lawyers and reporters obtained thousands of once-secret records of child death reviews. Reporters Sari Horwitz, Scott Higham, and Sarah Cohen charged that although the confidentiality laws had been intended to protect the privacy of children and families, they actually shielded public officials from scrutiny and accountability.[16] The worst details about the tragic deaths of children from abuse and neglect had never seen the light of day.

Without the historic class-action lawsuit that child advocates had filed against the District of Columbia in 1989, the *Post*'s reporters might never have been able to see the damaging confidential reports. Having done so, they found numerous instances of children who died from unsafe facilities, or after "flawed investigations into abuse or neglect complaints," and infants who died after being sent home with known drug-addicted or mentally ill parents. Perhaps worst of all, the reporters found that

In eight years of confidential reports, fatality committee members issued more than 300 warnings about these and other problems in reviews of the 180 deaths, the analysis showed. They proposed specific solutions to the mayor, the D.C. Council, the police chief, the director of the Child and Family Services Agency and the chief judge of D.C. Superior Court. But over the years, even as some officials left and new ones took over, the great majority of the proposed solutions went unheeded.

No one paid any attention to us," said Elizabeth Siegel, a lawyer and fatality committee member.[17]

Using computer analysis of findings by the CFSA and the child fatality review committee, the *Post* identified patterns of mistakes:

- Although the District set up a hotline for health and welfare professionals who are required to report abuse and neglect, people frequently failed to call the number.
- When people did call, investigations were often superficial, and sometimes the result was the death of a child.
- Where social workers opened cases on children, there were "significant gaps" in home visits and on follow-up investigations and activities.
- Children removed from their homes did not necessarily wind up in a safe place or receive needed services.

Eleven drug-exposed or medically frail newborns died between 1993 and 2000 after being released from hospitals to parents with well-documented problems. Because no one assumed direct responsibility, these babies were lost in the system. The reporters blamed vague legal definitions and poor communication among caregivers. They found a startling lack of rules about "whether and when hospitals should release fragile, drug-exposed babies to troubled mothers."[18]

One premature infant, Tyrika, who weighed only 4 pounds 3 ounces at birth had respiratory problems and cried constantly from cocaine withdrawal, a drug dependency she inherited from her mother. CFSA told the hospital's social worker that their quota was full. Sent home when she was only six days old, the baby was later found dead. An electronic monitor provided by the hospital had not been connected. Five years before Tyrika was born, the D.C. fatality committee had asked the city to require follow-up services for families of premature infants. Over the next seven years, the committee recommended 46 more times that hospitals and social workers take steps to protect frail infants, the *Post* reported, "but the warnings, many of which were confidential at the time, largely were not followed."[19]

Why?

So why aren't states doing more follow-up? Why are children still dying when something as simple as a visit from a community health nurse could save their lives? And is the problem the cost, or the people in charge allocating money in ways that don't serve children effectively?

A report by the inspector general for the Department of Health and Human Services, found that foster children in many states don't get regular visits from caseworkers. According to an AP story, although 43 states aim for monthly visits by caseworkers, only a few even come close. In Florida, with 50,000 children in foster care, child and family caseworkers made monthly visits 95% of the time in 2003. In California, monthly visits were only achieved 86% of the time, and in Texas 75% of the time. But in West Virginia, caseworkers only made monthly visits 42% of the time on average. Furthermore, many states couldn't even provide data on monthly visits.[20]

And though certainly admirable, Florida's record was an improvement that the AP story asserted came after highly publicized cases where children "fell through the cracks. The most infamous case was that of foster child Rilya Wilson, whose disappearance when she was five years old forced changes in state childcare. Her body was never found, but investigators think she was killed around December 2000, about 15 months before state DCF officials realized she was missing and reported it to police."[21]

Where such cases fail to make the 11 o'clock news, improvement in follow-up is usually only piecemeal and not—as it should be—wholesale and across the nation. A good share of the blame can also be laid at the feet of the infamous DeShaney decision by the U.S. Supreme Court, which has limited the liability of state agencies for failing to provide effective help and protection to victims of child abuse and neglect.

Admittedly, the issue of confidentiality with regard to children at risk is a delicate one. We want to protect children from invasion of privacy and from making the ordeal they face worse by the addition of public scrutiny. Balancing those concerns, however, is the issue of children not being adequately protected by a system constructed to protect them because of too much secrecy.

The earlier mentioned First Star/Children's Advocacy Institute report "State Secrecy and Child Deaths in the U.S." found that the majority of states fail to release adequate information about fatal and life-threatening child abuse cases, adhering to misguided and secretive policies that place confidentiality above the welfare of children and prevent public scrutiny that would lead to systemic reforms. Only a handful of states fully comply with the legislative intent of federal law mandating public disclosure of the deaths and near deaths of abused or neglected children. The report's authors argue that states withhold critical information that would hold child welfare systems accountable and avert future tragedies.[22]

"When abuse or neglect lead to a child's death or near death, a state's interest in confidentiality becomes secondary to the interests of taxpayers, advocates and other children, who would be better served by maximum transparency," said Amy Harfeld, First Star's Executive Director and a co-author of the report. "Once we know what is broken, we can try to fix it."

"The current emphasis on confidentiality only masks the problems inherent in child protection systems," said Robert Fellmeth, CAI's Executive Director and Price Professor of Public Interest Law at the University of San Diego School of Law. "Public exposure is a critical step toward fixing these problems."

All 50 states and the District of Columbia accept federal funds under the Child Abuse Prevention and Treatment Act (CAPTA). To be eligible for funding, states are supposed to have provisions that "allow for public disclosure of the findings or information about" abuse or neglect cases that result in child death or life-threatening injuries. But few states adequately comply, in part because the public disclosure requirement in CAPTA leaves too much room for interpretation.

If there is incompetence or willful disregard of a child, how are we to know and do something constructive to counteract it if there is no way to understand the situation he or she faces? In the absence of system accountability, much can go wrong and often does with regard to protecting children from abuse and neglect. Lewis Pitts made the following observations about confidentiality:

> I've found over the years that it is the favorite tool of malfeasant county and state officials to conceal their wrong-doing. If you contact them and they perceive you as "looking over their shoulder"—even if your effort is simply to provide representation to insure safety and services for the child—they refuse to give you any information and become hostile.

> In fact, when we do seek involvement it is usually based upon the CPS social workers, local and state mental health officials, the CPS attorney, and the GAL attorney failing to look out for the child's best interest. So they have reason to be ashamed but no right to deny the child access to a lawyer seeking to help.

> A week ago I was in court asking to be appointed pro bono to represent a 3-year-old, severely neglected and most probably sexually abused girl, to insure she got all medically necessary mental health treatment—she had gotten none over the 3-plus months she'd been in foster care. The guardian ad litem (GAL) attorney filed a motion to have me monetarily sanctioned for simply making the request. The judge denied my request and took under advisement the motion for sanctions against me![23]

In court, Pitts recalled, the judge even commented that he did not understand the confidentiality rules. In North Carolina, although abuse and neglect hearings can be open or closed, according to the judge, the files and orders stemming from the hearings are strictly confidential.

If the child requests a hearing be open, so it must be. The catch:

> The GAL attorney speaks for the child and if an 'outsider' is offering to help and implying that the local team has failed in some way, the GAL attorney requests the hearing be closed. As for the girl I tried to help, she's too young to state her own position. Older kids usually are not even consulted on such issues.[24]

Pointing out that the court has a duty to listen to anyone offering information or help regarding a person unable to care for themselves (which includes minors), Pitts said,

> As a general principle all hearings should be open to the public unless compelling reasons justify the judge to order closure. The files, reports, mental health records, etc. deserve more protection—certainly from disclosure to the general public or press. But . . . when an attorney as an officer of the court seeks to represent a child based upon a good faith claim that something is amiss, that attorney should be allowed to see the records.

> We charge adults in open criminal court with heinous crimes and the hearings are open to the public. I have no sympathy for alleged child abusers to be protected from public scrutiny. . . . It would be helpful if the cases involving failures to protect and/or provide necessary services got full public attention. Then we the people would be better able to advocate the changes and appropriations to redress the problems—and save the lives of children.[25]

The First Star Approach

Confidentiality plays a pivotal role in child abuse proceedings. For the system to work, mandated reporters need to feel secure in stating their concerns, children need to be protected from subsequent abuse, and yet families need to be shielded from unwarranted public scrutiny.

However, blanket provisions for confidentiality do not always promote the best interests of child victims and their families. Child protective agencies, medical providers, law enforcement agencies, and even schools routinely report having problems in getting information from one another about the children they are jointly serving.

What Policy Can Do

There is no question but that this is a delicate area. Nevertheless, abused and neglected children can benefit immensely from an environment of openness—sharing of all information potentially relevant to the child or case at issue, including but not limited to records that might otherwise be considered confidential. Amendments adopted in 2003 require state child protective services (CPS) to "disclose confidential information to any Federal, State, or local government entity, or any agent of such entity,"[26] that has a legal responsibility to protect children. However, the types of agencies and agents that need to receive information, as well as the scope of information to be provided, have not been clarified.

Important records should be available to all agencies protecting and representing children with no intrastate or interstate barriers to sharing information. Information should be used to promote public accountability and system reform. Also to that effect, court hearings and records should be open, with judicial discretion to close: As of early 2008, only 17 states permit open courts—California, Colorado, Florida, Indiana, Iowa, Kansas, Maryland, Michigan, Minnesota, Nebraska, New Jersey, New York, North Carolina, Ohio, Oregon, Tennessee, and Texas. (Note: Then Chief Justice of the Minnesota Supreme Court Kathleen Blatz stated that no child has ever been "outed" by Minnesota's open proceedings. Protective protocols apply, as in an adult rape case. The victim is protected.)

First Star recommends the following legislative objectives to benefit children:

- *Promote open courts.* Child dependency courts should conduct open proceedings with judicial discretion to close any hearing or a portion of a hearing if extenuating circumstances exist or for cause shown.
- *Provide information to advocates.* Specifically, provide attorneys and others representing children unrestricted access to court records; give attorneys and others representing a child timely access to the child's records; and encourage child advocates in each state to develop standards for open records.
- *Provide information to parents and providers.* Make records available to parents, foster parents, agencies, and attorneys and

others representing, protecting, and serving the child with no intrastate or interstate barriers to sharing information.

- *Permit agency access to information.* Assure that information affecting the child's safety is provided to the child protection agency with no intrastate or interstate barriers to sharing information.
- *Promote public accountability with information.* Ensure that information is used to analyze the performance of child protection agencies and promote reform through public education.

Eliminate barriers to information posed by HIPAA. Local misconstruing of HHS privacy rules under the health insurance portability and accountability act (HIPAA)—and failure of the rules to have clear exceptions for child protection case situations—hinders information access for advocates, courts, and service providers.[27]

Lost in the System

"There are many telling signs that the performance of officialdom in various jurisdictions leaves much to be desired," said Peter Samuelson. He continued,

Note, for example, that various places have their own awful "specialite de la maison": In a handful of states, including Florida, there are hundreds of children who are wards of the state, but the state cannot find them. They are simply lost. In other places, there are no lost children; all are present and accounted for, but there is no institutional memory: paper files, or a very old computer, high case loads and never the same judge create a regular, never ending cycle where the system cannot remember why, let's say, it took a child into foster care for good reasons. And every so often that system puts such a child back into harm's way and the child is then killed.

When Mayor Williams of the District of Columbia wanted to talk about such a case at a press conference, he had to risk contempt of court in revealing the death of the little girl, Brianna, whom the secrecy was far too late to help. Shine the light of day on the process, put it on the 11 o'clock news, give the children lawyers, train the grown-ups . . . and watch our outcome statistics rise to their rightful place among developed nations. Somewhere better than the lowest 2 percent on the UNICEF chart.[28]

Progress is elusive. Even in 2004, U.S. Representatives Loretta Sanchez and JoAnn Emerson wrote to their colleagues urging them to essentially rededicate themselves to the protection of our nation's most vulnerable children. They asked them to join in two sign-on letters addressed to Secretary Tommy G. Thompson of the U.S. Department of Health and Human Services requesting clarification of the disclosure of confidential information among those needing it to protect children from abuse and neglect. They also requested elaboration on the Safe Act of 2003 section on training appropriate to "the role of any individual appointed by any court to represent a child in a dependency hearing."

Judge Charles Gill followed up on these efforts only to find that nothing came of them. Another effort to save the lives of children at risk for abuse and neglect apparently slipped through the Washington, DC, bureaucratic cracks.

Summary

Indeed the United States is so focused on protecting its entire population from terrorism, that to some the quest for more clarity and greater openness in the pursuit of child protection from terrorism often in their own homes may seem far less pressing. No one would of course say that in so many words. But actions do speak louder than words. We cannot continue to allow the voices of children lost in a system inadequate to their protection to be drowned out simply because they do not yet vote. Confidentiality is an important consideration in the protection of privacy, but when children are dying in obscene numbers in a country that is supposedly advanced in its concern for human rights, something is indeed amiss. And only the cold-hearted, once aware, could turn away and let another child suffer because they were just too busy to care.

Endnotes

1. Peter Samuelson, manuscript comment, May 2006.

2. The United Nations Children's Fund (UNICEF), "The State of the World's Children," 2007, www.unicef.org/sowc07/docs/sowc07.pdf

3. Associated Press, "La. Couple Charged in Infant's Death," *Washington Post*, November 10, 2005, www.washingtonpost.com/wp-dyn/content/article/2005/11/10/AR2005111001012_pf.html.

4. Tim Evans and Vic Ryckgert, "Police Say Abuse Followed Baby to Indy; 4-Month-Old Katrina Evacuee Dies After Brain Injury," IndyStar.com (Website of the Indianapolis Star), November 10, 2005.

5. PL 109-239: Safe and Timely Interstate Placement of Foster Children Act of 2006, GovTrack.us (database of federal legislation, http://www.govtrack.us/congress/bill.xpd?bill=h109-5403

6. Maura Corrigan, remarks, "Fostering the Future: Safety, Permanence and Well-Being for Children in Foster Care" (Washington, DC: Pew Commission

on Children in Foster Care, May 18, 2004), 7-9, www.pewfostercare.org/press/ files/transcript051804.pdf

7. Ibid., 8.

8. Ibid., 8–9.

9. Emily Reinig , Robert Fellmeth, and Amy Harfeld, *State Secrecy and Child Deaths in the U.S.* (San Diego, CA, and Washington, DC: Children's Advocacy Institute and First Star, April 2008). www.caichildlaw.org/misc/State_Secrecy_Final_Report_Apr24.pdf or www.firststar.org/news/report/default.asp

10. Jonathan D. Rockoff, "Critics aim to reduce secrecy in foster care; Children: Advocates strengthen call for public review of records as group home problems come to light," *Baltimore Sun*, April 17, 2005, 1C. See also Jonathan D. Rockoff and John B. O'Donnell, "Reforms proposed, then put on the shelf; Potential remedies for the deep-seated problems have been in the air since 2001, without significant action by the state," *Baltimore Sun*, April 13, 2005, 1A.

11. Rockoff, "Children: Advocates strengthen call," *Baltimore Sun*.

12. Ibid.

13. Ibid.

14. Sari Horwitz, Scott Higham, and Sarah Cohen, "Day 1: Decade of Deadly Mistakes; 'Protected' Children Died as Government Did Little; Critical Errors by City's Network Found in 40 Fatalities; Confidential Files Show Wide Pattern of Official Neglect," *Washington Post*, September 9, 2001, A01.

15. Ibid.

16. Ibid.

17. Ibid. © 2001, *The Washington Post*, reprinted with permission.

18. Sari Horwitz and Scott Higham, "Without Help, Frail Infants Died: Newborns Released to Troubled Mothers with Little D.C. Supervision," *Washington Post*, September 11, 2001, A01.

19. Ibid.

20. David Royse, "Florida ranks high on child visits; A recent government report names Florida among the top states at checking on children in the foster care system," *Miami Herald*, January 5, 2006, 5B.

21. Ibid.

22. "Abused Children Dying Under Shroud of State Secrecy," news release, University of San Diego School of Law, April 9, 2008. http://www.sandiego .edu/usdlaw/about/news/news/index.php?vol=2008&issue=6

23. From First Star interviews, 2004–2006.

24. Ibid.

25. Ibid.

26. Amendment to Section 106(b) of the Child Abuse Prevention and Treatment Act, contained in the Keeping Children and Families Safe Act of 2003. Accessed at http://www.the orator.com/bills108/hr14.html

27. On this last point, the appendix includes Sense of Congress letters that First Star sent to the U.S. Department of Health and Human Services to get the HIPAA legislation correctly interpreted throughout the country so as not to prevent those representing children from accessing their child clients' health care records.

28. http://www.petersamuelson.blogspot.com

4

A Brief History of Child Custody
Issues Related to Abuse and Neglect

Children who came to America as indentured servants without parents were an important part of the story of the colonies' settlement. Although most children who emigrated to New England did so as part of a family, more than half of all persons arriving in the southern colonies were indentured servants and, according to historian Richard B. Morris, most of these were less than 19 years old. The average age was from 14 to 16, and the youngest was six.[1] Many were orphans or poor, thus their indentures were involuntary.

Involuntary apprenticeship was another source of immigrant child labor. In 1617 the Virginia Company asked London's lord mayor to send poor children to settle the colony. He authorized a charitable collection to grant five pounds apiece for equipment and passage; the children would apprentice until age 21 and afterward have 50 acres in the plantation.[2] This arrangement was initiated again in 1619 for "one hundred children out of the multitude that swarm in that place to be sent to Virginia."[3]

Authors' note: This chapter is condensed and adapted with permission from *From Father's Property to Children's Rights: The History of Child Custody* by Mary Ann Mason, copyright ©1994 Columbia University Press. We would recommend Dr. Mason's excellent book most highly to anyone wanting to learn more about the origins and development of contemporary child custody issues in the United States.

Children, like all settlers, did not survive long in deadly Virginia, and in 1622 London sent yet another 100 children, "being sensible of the great loss which [the plantation] lately susteyned [sic] by the barbarous cruelty of the savage people there."[4]

Similarly, in New Netherland (later New York) the West India Company obtained several shiploads of poor and orphaned children from Amsterdam. One official asked for more children in 1658. "Please to continue sending others from time to time: but, if possible, none ought to come less than fifteen years of age and somewhat strong, as little profit is to be expected here without labor."[5]

Other children were tricked into indentured servitude by "spiriters" who won a healthy profit for each child they could deliver to the colonies. By the mid-17th century, victims were being kidnapped and held prisoner until the ship sailed. One father obtained a warrant to search a ship for his 11-year-old son. The search found 11 children taken against their will.[6] The spirit trade provoked public outrage and fear, and in 1664 Charles II's attorney general established a central registry of all servants leaving for the colonies. Those caught spiriting were fiercely prosecuted.

Many children arrived in America with irregular indentures or none at all. Would-be masters had to go to court to set the terms of the indenture. Most common was the term set by the Virginia legislature: "Such persons as shall be imported, having no indenture or covenant, either men or women, if they be above sixteen years old shall serve four years, if under fifteen to serve till he or she shall be one and twenty years of age, and the courts to be judges of their ages."[7] Other colonies set age 18 or marriage as the end-date of indentures for girls. The law did not require masters to teach these children a trade, but rather put the children to whatever service they wished. When the indenture term ended, masters had to give the servant clothes and some provisions.[8]

Although most children were not forcibly imported to the New World without parents, separation from parents and forced labor were common in all the colonies. Many children lost both parents through death or abandonment. Many, if not most, did not stay in either parent's custody until adulthood.[9] Parents very often apprenticed or sent out their children to serve another family at around age 10. Illegitimate children were routinely separated from their mothers when weaned and bound out to a master. Slave children, about one-fifth of the entire child population by 1800, could be sold away from their parents at any time.

Following the first decades of intense immigration, children in New England and some mid-Atlantic colonies were most often involuntarily apprenticed when their parents couldn't or wouldn't care for them properly. Legal adoption did not yet exist and orphanages and child asylums were rare until the late 1700s. The child's settlement town was responsible for his or her welfare, and no town wanted such a burden unnecessarily.

Voluntary apprenticeships occurred when the parent or guardian made a court-approved agreement with a master. Courts treated disobedient and runaway apprentices harshly, extending their indentures from three to five times the number of days they were absent. Rewards were offered for runaway apprentices.

The Father: A Master's Rights

The harsh manner in which colonialists treated children reflected the English law tradition, to which colonial law was firmly tied. Courts frequently were asked to intervene into families on grounds of abuse or neglect, particularly in New England, but they often focused on labor-oriented neglect. Masters and fathers risked losing children if they failed to prepare them for a role in the labor economy. Parents also lost their children if they could not provide economic support. Such children were quickly sent into labor as apprentices in other households.

Children were crucial to the colonial labor force and were often employed like adult workers. Children were seen as economic producers; in the labor-hungry colonies, small hands could not be idle. A child's labor was a commodity that could be sold or hired out by fathers and assigned by masters. The mutual obligations of a master-servant relationship best describes the legal bonds between the man who held custody and the child, who held rights similar to those of an employee. The household head, whether father or master of indentured servants, had complete rights to the children's labor and strict obligations for their training and education. The right to a child's labor was seen as recompense for the father's support. This mutuality was a relatively recent development. Ancient English tradition required only that the father control the child's education and religious training. The Elizabethan poor laws added the duty of maintenance and support.[10] Mutuality was contrary to Roman law, where the father enjoyed absolute power, and in the early Roman republic, according to the historian Dionysius, "the atrocious power of putting his children to death, and of selling them three times in an open market, was vested in the father."[11]

Colonial America expanded these mutual obligations beyond the English tradition. The duty to educate and provide religious training was enlarged to include vocational training. In New England, local governments insisted that parents train their children to be literate, religious, and economically productive citizens.

Colonial fathers had paramount rights to the association and labor of their children. Association included the right to send the child to live with another relative or family or to apprentice the child; the father did not need the mother's consent for either action. By today's standards, this marked legal emphasis on the father's role to the mother's exclusion may seem out of touch. However, the colonial father performed many tasks that today are shared or handled by the mother. Most 17th- and 18th-century fathers were farmers, the rest mostly artisans or tradesmen who worked at or near home. According to historian John Demos, fathers were not only a daily visible presence but took charge of their children's education and moral supervision. Children turned to their fathers for guidance, not to their mothers.

The Mother: Legal Impotence

The mother was an assistant with few enforceable rights or responsibilities toward her children. Although mothers played a larger role with infants, and necessarily worked closer with their daughters, they were not the central figure in their children's lives. Blackstone stated the English common law simply: the father had a natural right to his children and the mother "was entitled to no power [over her children], but only to reverence and respect."[12] A free white mother could lose her children on account of poverty, divorce, widowhood, or illegitimacy. A slave mother's child could be sold away at any moment.

The colonial mother also had few obligations toward her children. A New England mother only needed help the father teach the children to read, but Virginia women also helped with religious education.

Under English common law, a married woman could not own real or personal property. All that she brought to her marriage became her husband's. She could not make a contract, execute a deed of gift or write a will unless her husband consented.[13]

Early in the new republic, judges in custody disputes relied more on English precedents than their own newly emerging case law. Fortunately those precedents offered choices, letting judges be flexible. No known English court gave custody to a mother over an unfit father until 1774. In Blisset's Case, chancellor Lord Mansfield let a mother keep her six-year-old when the bankrupt father mistreated them both.[14] Lord Mansfield put forth the innovative notion that "the public right to superintend the education of its citizens necessitated doing what appeared *best for the child* (our italics), notwithstanding the father's natural right." This case planted the germ of what became the best interest standard in America, though it established no lasting change at the time. On the other hand, Rex v. DeManneville (1804)[15] exemplified the doctrine of a father's paramount right to his children. When a mother ran away from an allegedly brutal father, Lord Ellenborough of the King's Bench returned the child to her father, even though "she was an infant at the breast of the mother."

Although individual children may have been loved and protected— even spoiled—the law principally enforced the labor relationship and paid little heed to their need for nurturing. The best interests of the child slowly developed as a legal concern in the new republic when, for a growing class of parents, child labor needs became less urgent, and children were assigned an emotional value, enhanced by the romanticization of mothers.

Child Custody Law in the New Republic, 1790–1890

The legal and social status of the child was slowly and relentlessly transformed during the first century of the republic. The colonial view of children as helping hands gave way to a view that children had interests of their own. Increasingly, these interests became identified with the nurturing mother. This significant shift in perspective changed the legal forms of custody in the 1800s. As a transitional period in child custody law, the century was filled with contradictions and inconsistencies. Women's rights were suspect, yet motherly love was idealized. In the same state, one court might uphold the primacy of fathers' rights and another would defend mothers as the natural guardians of young children. Although seen to need protection and nurturing, children were regularly apprenticed or sent to factories at age 10 or 11.

The modern legal arrangement of adoption was developed to meet the needs of children for family nurturing. Most changes favorable to children, though, were confined to private disputes over child custody. Children who became dependents of the state due to their parents' death, abandonment, or poverty did not fare as well, nor did slave children freed during the Civil War. Until the late 1800s most communities' guiding principle was to relieve the public of economic burdens rather than cater to a child's best interests. Poor law officials wielded almost unlimited custodial control with little legislative or court supervision. By 1900, many judges still recited the common law maxim that "the natural right is with the father, unless the father is somehow unfit."[16]

Early U.S. Cases

In the earliest cases, the child's best interest was associated with the mother's special capacity to guide and nurture. In 1809 in Prather v. Prather, the first published decision to defy the paramount rights of fathers, the court awarded the youngest child, a five-year-old girl, to the mother.[17] The husband had turned out his wife and brought another woman into the house in open adultery. Incensed by the injustice to the mother, the South Carolina court described her as "a prudent, discreet and virtuous woman." The court, in fear of defying the weight of common law, passed the responsibility of strictly enforcing it to higher courts. "The Court is apprised that it is treading on new and dangerous grounds, but feels a consolation in the reflection that if it errs, there is a tribunal wherein the error can be redressed."[18]

In 1842 New York's highest court, in Mercein v. People, replaced the common law tradition of paternal authority with a natural law argument in favor of mothers, stating: "By the law of nature, the father has no paramount right to the custody of his child."[19] The court gave custody of a sickly three-year-old daughter to her mother, explaining that the law of nature gave her "an attachment for her infant offspring which no other relative will be likely to possess in an equal degree, and where no sufficient reasons exist for depriving her of the care and nurture of her child, it would not be a proper exercise of discretion in any court to violate the law of nature in this respect."[20]

In a vivid illustration of the seesaw-like ambivalence of 19th-century courts, the state's supreme court two years later delivered custody of the little girl to her father. This court rebuked the natural rights reasoning, claiming that father's right should prevail because "it has not been denied that he is the legal head of the whole family, wife and children inclusive; and I have heard it urged from no quarter that he should be brought under subjection to a household democracy. All will agree, I apprehend, that such a measure would extend the right of suffrage too far."[21] Joining in the opinion, a second judge invoked divine law. "It is possible," he wrote, "that our laws relating to the rights and duties of husband and wife have not kept pace with the progress of civilization . . . But I will not enquire what the law ought to be . . . I will, however, venture the remark . . . that human laws cannot be very far out of the way when they are in accordance with the law of God."[22]

In 1850, 80% of the population lived rurally, and most remained so by century's end.[23] Child labor was an economic necessity in those areas. Nevertheless, courts across the country, from the deep rural south to pioneering California, increasingly showed concern for the child's welfare and endorsed the mother's nurturing nature.

My own explanation of why even rural judges shared this growing solicitude is the development of a uniform culture based on mass circulation magazines and books. Between 1784 and 1860, at least 100 new magazines appeared, most devoted to women's interests.[24] Communication among the colonies had been limited, so cultural differences and social values developed independently. But the newly united republic began to develop a mass middle-class culture extending from fashion to child raising, aimed at the literate urban housewife with the leisure time to read. Literate women in small towns and farms read the magazines as well. Judges were certainly part of this new middle-class elite, even in small rural towns.

Maria Barbour, age nine, was indentured to Benjamin Gates in 1865 by her mother, a widow. The indenture was set to last until Maria turned 18, but after three years her mother, in a better position, asked to have the child returned. She claimed the indenture contract was technically defective, citing defects in its execution. Dismissing the defects, the judge found that the mother had indeed severed her right to legal custody, but nonetheless found her the better custodian, "because of all the affection she must feel for her offspring."[25] The court returned the child to her mother, claiming, "The laws of nature have given her an attachment for her infant offspring which no relative will be likely to possess in equal degree." In this decision the court rejected well-established indenture law, under which the child had no rights and the contracting parent could sue only on the terms of the contract.[26] The judge looked to the child's interests rather than the imperfections of the contract, and determined on the basis of natural law that the child's nurturing was best performed by her mother.

In those times, women fought for property rights that had been held exclusively by their husbands. These included the rights to control their own wages and inheritance, to equal control of their children's custody—and complete control when their husbands died—as well as an equal right to make indenture contracts that bound their children.

Thus, a fundamental ideological conflict developed between a strategy seeking legal and civil rights for women directly, and a judicial deference to the cult of motherhood that gave women limited benefits only in relation to their children's interests. By 1887, 30 states had granted women rights to wages, property, litigation, and contracts, but few states expanded women's rights to their children.

By century's end, only nine states and the District of Colombia gave mothers the statutory right to equal guardianship.[27] Most men and even some women's rights advocates feared too many rights would tempt women to take their children and leave the family. The California legislature used just this argument to defeat an equal guardianship bill.[28] Many judges still recited the common law maxim that "the natural right is with the father, unless the father is somehow unfit."[29] However, the laws regarding bastardy, custody following divorce, testamentary guardianship, and voluntary and involuntary apprenticeship were fundamentally altered by the new attitude toward children.

In addition, the modern legal arrangement of adoption was developed to meet children's newly recognized needs for family nurturing. The common law emphasis on bloodlines connection had been the major barrier to legal adoption in England, but had long been permitted in countries with civil codes and different attitudes toward inheritance. Led by Massachusetts's landmark adoption law of 1851, by the end of the 19th century, virtually every state gave adopted children the same rights as birth children in a family. The spirit of equal opportunity enabled a new definition of family, based not on blood but on nurture.[30]

The new adoption statutes usually included two elements: judges must deem the adoptive parents fit, and the natural parents, if alive, had to consent.[31] Exceptions to the latter were made where, as in the New York statute, a father or mother "adjudged guilty of adultery or cruelty and who is, for either cause, divorced, or is adjudged to be an insane person or an habitual drunkard, or is judicially deprived of the custody of the child on account of cruelty or neglect."[32]

The Courts

The courts increasingly awarded children to their mothers in custody disputes—not under the dangerous doctrine of women's rights but rather under the newly developing rule of the best interests of the child. But such disputes were usually related to divorce or separation.

Since the beginning of the republic, judges had wielded individual discretion in all matters of family law. They established what historian Michael Grossberg terms a judicial patriarchy, where they used their own judgment to interpret English common law and their state's legislative mandates. They were supported in this by the English courts' increasing use of chancery courts to determine the welfare and property of minors under the doctrine of parens partriae. The English chancery courts had sometimes overridden common law provisions, which gave fathers paramount control, in order to protect children whose fathers were grossly immoral or heretical.[33]

In America, judges gradually extended this equitable tradition to consider the interests of the children against those of their parents, even when there was not gross abuse. With slight regional differences, judges all over the growing nation shared the same emerging middle-class values about the family's role, the need for child nurturing, and the special moral and religious capacities of women as mothers.

Evolution of Best Interests Standard and Tender Years Doctrine

Torn between common law rights of the father and the child's best interests, judges eventually favored the best interests standard. For very young or female children, this became associated with the mother. Courts' tendency to award infants to their mothers became known as the Tender Years Doctrine. The almost universal exception occurred when the mother was considered unfit, usually on moral grounds.[34]

Perhaps the greatest legal advance for children and their mothers (or at least for mothers with means of support) occurred with the transformation of bastardy laws. The common law definition of an illegitimate child as filius nullius gave way to legal recognition of the mother–child bond. Mothers frequently raised their illegitimate children, but had not been supported by the law. By 1900 most states declared the child a member of his or her mother's family, with a right to inherit from the mother.[35] The mother, in turn, gained what had been the father's prerogatives when parents were married.

Indenturing of minors was fast disappearing as the 19th century ended. Taking children from their families to live in a stranger's home was no longer approved. In apprenticeship disputes, judges began releasing minors to their families if they considered it in the child's best interests. The concept of nurture also forced some courts to reject apprenticeship arrangements in favor of child welfare.

The changing demand for child labor also helped break the back of voluntary apprenticeship. Artisans and small tradesmen were being replaced by factories and mass production, and child labor was particularly suited to routine and repetitive tasks. The southern textile industry was based largely on child labor. From 1880 to 1910, manufacturers reported one-fourth of their workforce was under 16 years old, and many cases of child labor went unreported. Children of seven or eight commonly doffed spun cotton and performed casual labor.[36] By 1880 the Census Bureau estimated that 17% of children aged 10 to 15 worked outside the home. This ignored the children under 10 and those working in home production or on consignment from manufacturers.[37] Children still worked, perhaps in greater numbers and under worse conditions than before, but now they remained in the custody of their own parents; their employer had only limited control over them at the workplace and no obligation for their welfare.

"Placing Out"

Although voluntary apprenticeships waned, most involuntary apprenticeships changed legal form to "placing out" and became the primary custody arrangement for tens of thousands of abandoned and indigent children in the late 1800s. Most were placed in rural homes where their labor was exchanged for room, board, and education. Although custody and control remained with the association, and it could terminate the arrangement at any time,[38] the hope was that some children would be adopted by their placement family. In this sense, placing out attempted to straddle the line between the economic arrangement of involuntary apprenticeship and the child-nurturing focus of adoption.

Charles Loring Brace, founder of the New York Children's Aid Society in 1853, introduced the placing out system in America as a good, cheaper alternative to the asylum, almshouse, or house of correction. In its first 25 years, the society placed 40,000 homeless or destitute children from New York City into farm homes.[39] Other associations placed untold thousands as well. After an initial screening to weed out "the mentally defective, diseased and incorrigibles," children ages five to 17 were sent to rural communities in East Coast, western, and southern states. Farm families quickly took the children, but the experience was not always positive and many critics denounced the system. Lyman P. Alden, school superintendent in Coldwater, Michigan, observed that

> It is well known by all who have had charge of the binding out of children that the great majority of those who are applying for children over nine years old are looking for cheap help; and while many, even of this class, treat their apprentices with fairness, and furnish them a comfortable home, a much larger number of applicants do not intend to pay a quid pro quo, but expect to make a handsome profit on the child's service.[40]

The State as Superparent: The Progressive Era, 1890–1920

> The rich cannot say to the lowly, "You are poor and have many children. I am rich and have none. You are unlearned and live in a cabin. I am learned and live in a mansion. Let the State take one of your children and give it a better home with me. I will rear it better than you can." The deepest, the tenderest, the most unswerving and unfaltering thing on earth is the love of a mother for her child. The love of a good mother is the holiest thing this side of heaven. The natural ties of motherhood are not to be destroyed or disregarded save for some sound reason. Even a sinning and erring woman still clings to the child of her shame, and though bartering her own honor, will rarely fail to fight for that of her daughter.[41]

Thus Georgia's appellate court reversed a trial court that had awarded custody of Mrs. Moore's three illegitimate children to an orphanage. The trial court had relied on a Georgia statute that any child under 12 could be removed to an orphan asylum or other charitable institution if it "is being reared up under immoral obscene or indecent influences likely to degrade its moral character and devote it to a vicious life." Without questioning the statute, the appeals court said the trial court had failed to prove Mrs. Moore was "of an immoral character, unsuitable and unable to rear the children."[42]

In this case, the court struggled with two powerful, sometimes contradictory principles. One was a belief in the importance of preserving the family, no matter how poor. The other was the conviction that the state must intervene to protect children from abusive, neglectful, or immoral parents. These two principles had a profound effect on child custody decisions in the first two decades of the 20th century. They prompted state courts like Georgia's to abandon the common law doctrine allowing the exploitation of children. Instead, both courts and legislatures formulated new rules aimed at protecting children.

For example, the concept of the child's best interest was extended to poor children. In a radical departure from traditional poor law principles, the state tentatively committed to allow poor but worthy mothers to keep custody of their children. Poor children who would have been bound out to a master in return for labor in the colonial years, and placed out to labor on a midwestern farm or sent to an almshouse or orphan asylum in the 19th century, were now more frequently supported in their mothers' homes. (Rarely was support provided if the father were present.) If that failed, or if they had no suitable parent, children were increasingly placed in a foster home, which was considered a substitute family rather than an orphanage, or put up for adoption by a new family.

State legislatures also acted to protect children in other important ways during this era, adopting a huge amount of child welfare legislation. The hours and the workplaces where children could labor were closely regulated; other laws dictated the establishment of public schools and required attendance of all children. A juvenile court system was put in place in many states. State legislatures diluted judicial discretion in dealing with the welfare of children, confining it within an elaborate statutory scheme.

At the same time, the divorce rate was exploding, and both courts and legislatures were concerned about the impact this social change might have on the future of the family. Legislatures passed strict laws, often buttressed with severe criminal penalties, to compel child support from all fathers, including those who lost their children by judicial decree following divorce. Overall, both courts and legislators paid far less deference to fathers, virtually ignoring their common law rights to the custody and control of their children.

In effect, the state became the superparent, generous and nurturing, but judgmental. It made the final decisions on how children should be raised and with whom they should live. In assuming this role, the state finally shattered the common law relationship between parents and children. Child labor legislation now severely restricted the right to the child's services. The right to custody, once absolute, could now be severed if the father or mother misused their authority in an abusive or neglectful manner. Finally, the obligation to educate passed from the parent to the state. The public school teacher, not the father or mother, would control the child's education and a good deal of the child's socialization.

Child Saving and Childsavers

The new concern for the welfare of the children was part of the larger, broader reformist movement placed historically in the Progressive era. During this era, states intruded into the privacy of families in a manner not seen since the selectmen of Massachusetts visited homes to determine whether children were behaving well and receiving religious and civic training. Childsavers, as they were called, were originally a large and very active coalition of volunteer philanthropists, Women's Club members, and assorted urban-based professionals who rallied against the mistreatment of poor and abused children toward the end of the 19th century. In the Progressive era, the child-saving movement was increasingly dominated by the developing profession of social work. In contrast to the volunteer childsavers, social workers were trained, paid, and career minded. They focused more on providing services to support a child within his or her family, rather than simply removing a child from a cruel environment.

Julia Lathrop, the first chief of the Children's Bureau, created by President Howard Taft in 1912, had been the first woman member of the Illinois Board of Public Charities in 1892, the organization responsible for orphaned, abandoned, and neglected children, and in 1899 helped found the Chicago Juvenile Court, the first in the country and the model for the nation. Thereafter, her career soared with the rapidly evolving child welfare movement. Her commitment to children was deeply felt. "Sooner or later," she declared, "as we choose, by our interest, or its lack, the child will win."[43]

She was a member of a dedicated group referred to as social feminists, who turned away from the 19th-century feminists' focus on individual property and civil rights for middle-class women, and instead focused their attention on poor children and their families.

By supporting rather than challenging the family and the role of women within it, social feminists achieved important political gains, including suffrage and equal custodial rights for mothers—goals that had eluded their more individualistic 19th-century predecessors. Most of the leading social feminists of the early 20th century supported women's suffrage, but based their argument on family welfare rather than individual rights. The nonthreatening argument that the vote was a means for mothers to promote the family, not their own political interests, proved to be the winning strategy in persuading all-male legislatures to grant female suffrage.

This same argument in favor of mothers promoting their children's interests permitted the passage of legislation giving mothers equal custody rights to fathers—a victory not attainable by the first wave of feminists, who fought for equal rights for married women. Social feminists, allied with philanthropists, juvenile court advocates, and other reform-minded groups, pushed for a broad program of child protection and support legislation that often benefited their mothers as well. Legislative emphasis on children's rights rather than those of their parents was a winning approach. As Florence Kelley remarked in regard to the common law as interpreted by Blackstone, "nowhere in the Commentaries is there a hint that the common law regarded the child as an individual with a distinctive legal status." However, she believed that the Progressive era began by recognizing "the child's welfare as a direct object of legislation."[44]

Social feminists promoted family interests while redefining the relationship between children, parents, and the state. They abandoned the 19th-century policy of family privacy, which effectively gave parents or, most often, fathers, the right to complete control of their children, as long as they supported them. Instead, the social work profession recognized the role of the state as parent as well. In fact, the state, as represented by its agents, child welfare workers, became the superparent, determining the conditions under which natural parents could raise their children. Critics of the newly developing "helping profession" of social work claim that social workers set out to undermine the family culture of poor immigrants and replace it with their own middle-class values. Historian Christopher Lasch maintains that social workers, through children's aid societies, juvenile courts, and family visits, "sought to counteract the widespread 'lack of wisdom and understanding on the part of parents, teachers, and others,' while reassuring the mother who feared, with good reason, that the social worker meant to take her place in the home."[45]

Still, the new social work philosophy emphasized maintaining poor children in their families, if fit. This was probably the most significant shift in American poor law philosophy on child custody since the Elizabethan Poor Laws of 1601 mandated the apprenticing of poor, idle, or vagrant children.[46] Propelling this was the emerging belief that poverty did not necessarily reflect moral weakness; social conditions could force otherwise worthy people into poverty. Much of the debate in the Progressive era focused on how to support parents so they would not be forced to give up their children. The first White House Conference on the Care of Dependent Children, called by President Theodore Roosevelt in 1909, offered this agenda:

> Should children of parents of worthy character, but suffering from temporary misfortune, and the children of widows of worthy character and reasonable efficiency, be kept with their parents—aid being given to parents to enable them to maintain suitable homes for the rearing of the children? Should the breaking of a home be permitted for reasons of poverty, or only for reasons of inefficiency or immorality?[47]

Reformers quickly took the position that poverty alone did not justify removing a child from his or her parents; only severe physical abuse or neglect or lack of moral fitness provided sufficient grounds.

During the Progressive era, for the first time the state took seriously its role as child protector. All states wrote legislation defining abuse and neglect and sanctioning child removal. Theoretically the state had been permitted to intervene to protect children under the English common law doctrine of parens partriae as defined in the 17th-century Blisset's Case; in reality family privacy and parental autonomy had held sway. The state was represented by local poor law officials who were ill-equipped to handle even abandoned and orphaned children. They had little energy left for children in families.

The stirrings of child protection grew out of work for the protection of animals. Starting in 1874 with the New York Society for the Prevention of Cruelty to Children, such societies sprang up about the country. Popularly called the Cruelty, at first they were staffed by volunteers whose mission was to look after poor children in the streets and bring those who were ill-used or hired to beg before the courts.[48] Later, most Cruelties, staffed with paid social workers, supervised troubled families and provided them a variety of services.

After the initiation of the first juvenile court in 1899, cases of dependent, neglected, and delinquent children under 16 soon moved to the new courts. Loosely written laws gave much discretion to juvenile court judges as protectors of children, including the power to remove children and make them wards of the state. In 1915 the Cook County Juvenile Court handled 1,886 cases of dependency—which included parental neglect, abuse, and abandonment—compared with 3,202 charges of delinquency.[49] Criminal abuse complaints against parents were handled in the criminal courts.

Ironically, although Cruelties began in reaction to cruel treatment of children by parents, children were rarely removed because of physical cruelty. Nor were their parents punished. Acceptance of corporal punishment in the name, at least, of discipline was such that laws were more likely to protect parents than punish them.

Furthermore, according to historian Elizabeth Pleck, the anticruelty societies worked more on investigating complaints against drunken and neglectful parents than on rescuing physically abused children. Of the Pennsylvania Society to Protect Children from Cruelty, Fleck found that from 1878 to 1935 only 12% of its cases concerned child cruelty. The society intervened, she claims, mostly in immigrant poor and working-class homes. The occasional investigation into a middle-class home was handled gently, with slight risk of removal.[50]

By the end of the era, only five western states (California, Montana, North Dakota, Oklahoma, and South Dakota) included excessive use of parental authority as a reason for removing a child. Eighteen states defended parents' rights to use physical discipline, and nine excused them from murder if death occurred while lawfully correcting the child. (If excess force was used, manslaughter could be charged.) South Carolina apparently even defended the use of knives in discipline. "Provisions on killing by stabbing do not apply to a person, who in chastising or correcting a child chances to commit manslaughter without intending to do so."[51] South Dakota presented a curious hybrid:

> Abuse of parental authority subject to judicial cognizance in civil action brought by child, relative, or office of poor. Child may be freed from dominion of parent. Homicide excusable when committed by accident or misfortune in lawfully correcting child, with usual and ordinary caution, and without unlawful intent.[52]

More often, neglect rather than abuse prompted intervention and sometimes removal of children during the Progressive era. Neglect included parental incompetence, not properly caring for the needs of a child, and parental unfitness, usually immoral behavior or drunkenness.

Neglect based on parental incompetence, the most common ground for removal, was most problematic for Progressive reformers and the courts. Parents who could not properly clothe and feed their children were most often victims of poverty, yet the new view of child nurture was that poverty alone should not be the basis for the removal of a child. At the same time, public and private support of poor parents was often inadequate for the basic obligations of parenting. Courts struggled to reconcile this new doctrine rejecting poverty as the ground for removal with the fact that children were indeed neglected when their parents were extremely poor.

Child Placement

What happened to children when they were removed from their families because of abuse or neglect or abandoned by their parents through illness or inability to support? They were often removed temporarily and then returned home. For many children, this became a familiar pattern. The Cruelty often sponsored temporary shelters and churches and other charities sponsored orphan asylums. There was, however, a steady move toward placing children in homes. With the Progressive focus on family as the best institution for raising children, placing out was widely adopted and modified by the proliferating children's home societies.

Adoption was the hoped-for goal of a child placed out. By the Progressive era, it was clear that few orphaned and neglected children would be adopted. Most adoptive parents preferred healthy children under four years of age. Strict adoption laws in most states meant birth parents kept their rights unless convicted of abuse or neglect (a rare event), and both parents had to consent for the child to be adopted. Courts exercised wide discretionary powers in considering the adopting parents' race, sex, age, wealth, and religion.[53]

For most dependent or neglected children, a family situation could only be achieved by placing out. As reformers passed laws restricting the use of children in factories and as street peddlers, children's aid societies were sending them to hard labor on faraway farms in western states. Such children were seldom well supervised, and agencies frequently lost contact with placement parents. Newly organized children's home societies sought to end child labor exploitation, using placing out to meet families' emotional rather than economic needs. These homes came to be known as foster homes. A popular women's magazine, the *Delineator*, campaigned for home placement in the early 1900s.

Despite such campaigns, free placements could not be found for many children, compelling children's home societies to consider paid placements. Homer Folks, a major figure in child protection, advocated paying for children's board in families when necessary, the model for the contemporary foster care system. To the claim that there were more free home placements available than children to fill them, Folks replied,

It is true as regards healthy infants, and in some seasons of the year, for children evidently able to work. It is not true with regard to ordinary boys from four to eight or ten years or age, it is not true as regards delicate or unattractive children, or children who may be reclaimed by parents.[54]

Initially paid placements or boarding out were opposed on grounds of cost and that they countered the spirit of charity. The children's home societies claimed that paying families was soulless and commercial. But the only alternative for children of the wrong age or sex, unattractive or beset with physical or emotional disabilities was orphan asylums. The above included most children, and orphanages continued to provide for the majority. In the 1923 census, the first accurate account of child placing, 64% of dependent and neglected children were still in orphan asylums, 23% were in free home placements, and 10% were in paid placements.[55] The number of adopted children was not reported.

In the Best Interests of the Child? 1960–1990

By the late 20th century, child custody law had permeated the casual discourse of everyday life; indeed, few households were untouched by a custody matter. A child born in 1990 had about a 50% chance of falling under court jurisdiction involving where and with whom the child would live. Unlike previous eras, in which custody involved orphans or neglected children, most custody matters resulted from the exploding divorce rate. The state increasingly intervened, sometimes removing children from their families, as the number of single-parent families below the poverty line swelled.[56]

Divorce, increasing poverty, and a startling upsurge in illegitimacy once again rearranged the tentative symmetry between mother, father, and the state. State legislatures and courts weakened divorcing mothers' claims to child custody, systematically wiping out the maternal preference or tender years doctrine and leaving only the vague best interests of the child standard. Procedures changed as well; mothers, fathers, and the court called expert witnesses, usually mental health professionals, to help the court choose between legally equal adults, and mediation was increasingly an alternative. Children remained the silent party in custody disputes, rarely given voice until adolescence. Some states did provide for the appointment of a child advocate in custody disputes. The duty of the advocate was to speak for what he or she determined to be the child's best interests.

The state took an ever more active role as superparent, providing more economic support while dictating stricter standards of behavior to mostly poor families. As single-parent poor families grew rapidly, the state no longer distinguished between worthy and unworthy mothers as a criteria for support; however, its social service arm vigilantly supervised the behavior of those it supported, with the threat of removal and ultimately termination of parental rights.

New custodial issues forced a redefinition of parenthood. Many nonbiological parents with no legal rights to custody and control played central nurturing roles for the children who lived in their homes. Foster homes became the state's preferred choice for its dependent children, but foster parents, who sometimes raised the children until adulthood, held the legal status of a vendor under contract. Finally, new reproductive technology tested the legal definitions of *mother* and *father*.

Removal of Children and Termination of Parental Rights

By the second half of the 20th century, child protection organizations initiated by the Progressive era's volunteer childsavers had become large publicly funded bureaucracies staffed by social workers. The third wave of feminists showed little interest in child welfare, instead focusing on equal opportunity for women outside the family. In all fairness, little room existed for volunteers in the well-organized world of child protection. The state as parens partriae had almost completely assumed the role of child protector, intervening in families to supervise conduct toward their children and, often, to remove them temporarily or permanently. Following an adjudication of abuse, neglect, or dependency (parents unable or unwilling to care for the child), the court appointed a temporary or permanent guardian who could be an individual, a state agency, or a private institution. The guardian was responsible for the child's well-being, but this did not involve terminating all parental rights nor necessarily a transfer of custody. Sometimes the state would claim custody and place the child in a foster home. More often, the child would be returned home under the guardian's supervision. In both circumstances, the natural parents still claimed residual rights and obligations, including visitation, the right to refuse adoption, and the duty to support. Ultimately, if the child was removed from the family for a lengthy time, the state determined whether to terminate parental rights.

The balance between the state as child protector and parents' rights to custody and control tilted toward the state. The state intervened at an unprecedented rate, providing support and sometimes removing children when the support could not, in the state's opinion, cure the families' problems. Publicly supported child protection agencies still enjoyed some autonomy, but federal control grew, exacted by Supreme Court decisions governing removal and termination of parental rights, and by laws mandating uniform requirements in return for federal funds.

Perhaps the greatest federal contribution to child protection, mandatory reporting began in 1974 with passage of the Child Abuse Prevention and Treatment Act.[57] This act offered funds to states that required their medical professionals, educators, social and childcare workers, and police to report suspected physical and sexual abuse, physical neglect, and emotional maltreatment. Failure to report triggered civil or criminal penalties. The general public was also encouraged, but not required, to report suspicion of child abuse. Many states already had such laws; most others followed suit.

The effects were immediate and dramatic. In 1963, about 150,000 children had come to the attention of public authorities; by 1982, it soared to 1,300,000. Social service organizations increasingly intervened in custodial matters; removing children and terminating parental rights also became more common. After thorough screening of child protective agency reports, more than 400,000 families came under home supervision.[58]

Responding to this rapid rise of intervention into private homes, parents' rights advocates and critics of child protection philosophy questioned the state's procedures. How were agencies defining abuse and neglect? Were definitions based on an ethnocentric vision of middle-class family life? Was foster care in the best interests of the children?[59] Were mothers on Aid to Families with Dependent Children (AFDC) getting unfair scrutiny while richer families escaped the attention of child protection agencies? And was the basic right of parenthood being terminated without due process?

At the core was the fundamental question of what constituted neglect and abuse. Severe physical abuse certainly existed in broken bones and serious bruises, but other manifestations of abuse and neglect were more difficult to measure.

Meanwhile, a new category of abuse made a powerful entrance in the 1980s. Child sexual abuse, unknown in previous abuse and neglect statutes, became prominent in child removal allegations. The states rewrote the laws to include this category. Reports increased dramatically, but whether the reporting requirements had uncovered abuse that had always existed, or a new and real upsurge, was unknown. Child sexual abuse allegations differed from neglect, or even many physical abuse complaints, in that criminal convictions were sought even when the offender was a parent. Even if a jury could not convict beyond a reasonable doubt, a civil action could mandate removal for the child's safety. Criminal and civil trials of sexual abuse were notoriously difficult to pursue because the child was often the only witness, and frequently under age five with limited language skills. Physical evidence was often ambiguous or nonexistent, so courts commonly relied on sexual abuse experts who interviewed the child. Courts viewed such testimony skeptically, but a sexual abuse allegation almost always triggered a child's removal, at least temporarily, from custody of the suspected adult. Sometimes this meant placing the child in the custody of social services.

Children of poor parents were more likely to be removed for reasons of abuse and neglect. The law no longer recognized poverty alone as a ground for removal, but several factors made poor parents more vulnerable to state intervention and removal. First, immigrant and minority parents were more likely to be poor, and some of their cultural styles were unacceptable to the white middle class. Second, parents on public assistance were scrutinized by social workers in a way other parents were not. Third, poverty was sometimes linked with patterns such as drug or alcohol abuse that could provoke child neglect or abuse.

To complaints about cultural bias, courts usually held up the state's action on the basis of the best interests of the child. A New York court, for example, rejected the argument that "impossible barriers" were created for poor black parents by making them comply with "bourgeois urban" customs in maintaining a visitation schedule, "To accept [this argument] would constitute regression to the period when the rights of parents were treated as absolute, and would negate the rights of children."[60]

The Supreme Court addressed social service intrusiveness into the privacy of families receiving public assistance in 1971. The plaintiff, Barbara James, refused to allow a scheduled home visit by a caseworker as a condition of continuing AFDC payments for her son Maurice, age two. The mother refused the visit on Fourth Amendment grounds of unreasonable search and seizure.[61] She introduced affidavits from 15 other AFDC recipients who complained of intrusive and unannounced visits by social workers. Writing for the majority, Justice Blackmun noted as an aside that Maurice showed evidence of a skull fracture, a dent in his head, and a possible rat bite. The Fourth Amendment did not cover the home visit because it was made by a caseworker, during working hours, with no forced entry or snooping, Blackmun stated, "The caseworker is not a sleuth but rather, we trust, is a friend to one in need."

The final and most dramatic step the state took as *parens partriae* was termination of parental rights. With this step, the state, as the social service agency, could retain guardianship and place the child in long-term foster care or, when possible, assign full custody and control to adoptive parents. Natural parents became legal nonentities, foregoing even visitation rights. Government agencies had to make reasonable efforts to restore children to families after removal. But for many families, in the judgment of social workers, reunification was not possible.

What right did parents have to protect against such agency decisions? What kind of due process? Ultimately, the Supreme Court in Santosky v. Kramer considered the procedures affecting termination of parental rights.[62] The Santosky family had pursued the case through several appeals. Petitioners John Santosky II and Annie Santosky were the natural parents of Tina and John III. In 1973, after incidents reflecting parental neglect, Kramer, commissioner of Ulster County's Department of Social Services, initiated a neglect proceeding and removed Tina from her home. Ten months later he placed John III with foster parents. Simultaneously, Annie Santosky bore a third child, Jed, who was immediately transferred to a foster home on grounds of imminent danger. Two more children were born later and remained in their parents' custody.

In October 1978 Kramer petitioned the Ulster County Family Court to terminate the Santoskys' parental rights of the three children. Acknowledging that the Santoskys had maintained contact with their children, the judge found those visits "at best superficial and devoid of any real emotional content." After deciding that the agency had made "'diligent efforts' to encourage and strengthen the parental relationship," he concluded that the Santoskys were incapable, even with public assistance, of planning for the future of their children. Termination of parental rights was granted, and this decision was affirmed on two procedural appeals, but the U.S. Supreme Court disagreed:

> Even when blood relationships are strained, parents retain a vital interest in preventing the irretrievable destruction of their family life. If anything, persons faced with forced dissolution of their parental rights have a more critical need for procedural protections than do those resisting state intervention into ongoing family affairs. When the State moves to destroy weakened familial bonds, it must provide the parents with fundamentally fair procedures.[63]

The court insisted on a standard of clear and convincing evidence, demanding more than a preponderance of evidence but less than the beyond reasonable doubt required in criminal matters. In another case involving termination of parental rights, however, a divided court decided that parents do not have right to counsel in termination hearings because their physical liberty is not at stake.[64]

Foster Care and Adoption

A child relinquished by parents, or removed through state intervention, was placed in one of three custodial situations: guardianship (usually with a relative), short- or long-term foster care, or adoption. Through the 19th century, guardianship was the only alternative to orphan asylums or binding out for children whose parents could not care for them. Guardianship probably would have been informal, with no court involvement. Adoption and foster care evolved in the second half of the 1800s in an effort to replace apprenticeships and orphanages with a family model.

Adoption was not an option for all children. As mentioned previously, child advocate Homer Folks argued that "delicate" and "unattractive" children or children that might be reclaimed by parents were harder to place. Older children were particularly difficult to place in the late 20th century because there was no longer a demand for their labor. Minority and mixed race children were also more difficult to place, as were children with emotional or physical disabilities.

Early in the 20th century, most unplaceable children would have gone to an institution run by a voluntary agency. By the second half of the century, the state had nearly usurped the role of private voluntary (usually religious) agencies, and the familial model of foster homes replaced the institutional model of orphanages. In addition to sheltering orphans or abandoned children, foster homes provided short-term care for children under the state's protective jurisdiction who were returned to their parents when the home situation improved. Many parents also voluntarily placed their children in foster homes without court intervention. It was not always clear how voluntary these placements were, in the face of social worker persuasion.[66] In theory, foster homes were a temporary respite until return to family or adoption. In fact, many children spent nearly all of their childhood in the twilight zone of temporary foster care.

Foster families usually were licensed by the state, which regulated home size, number of children, and age of parents. The social service agency paid a monthly fee for each child, but kept legal responsibility for the child and could terminate the foster relationship. Like stepparents, foster parents had physical custody but no legal claim to the children. For many, this was extremely frustrating; they had developed familial ties—sometimes over many years—yet their foster children could be removed at will.

A class action suit filed to correct this inequity claimed that foster parents had a constitutionally protected interest in the children they cared for, which demanded a full hearing before children were removed from their care. The suit eventually reached the U.S. Supreme Court, but only words of solace were the result:

> The importance of the familial relationship, to the individuals involved and the society, stems from the emotional attachments that derive from the intimacy of daily association, and from the role it plays in "promoting a way of life" through the instruction of children, as well from the fact of blood relationship. . . . For this reason we cannot dismiss the foster family as a mere collection of unrelated individuals.[67]

Despite these words of solace, the court deemed New York's procedures adequate and did not provide the sought relief. Nor did it say that foster parents had a constitutional right to continued custody of their foster children.

Summary

The history written by Mary Ann Mason reveals how views of what matters in determining the "best interests" of children at risk have changed over time—sometimes because of legal decisions and sometimes because of cultural shifts in priorities or ways of seeing what can be called our moral duty to children.

We learn from this work, too, that how we see what matters is influenced by the times in which we live and that we should always be aware of the sources of our attitudes so that we do not inadvertently harm children. We should be aware, too, as we'll discuss in Chapter 8, of how political views influence our care of children, that is, whether we prioritize their care or allow, by distraction or dismissal, their issues and concerns to vanish from our consciousness.

Endnotes

1. Richard B. Morris, *Government and Labor in Early America* (New York: Columbia University Press, 1946), 391.

2. Abbott E. Smith, *Colonists in Bondage* (Chapel Hill: University of North Carolina Press, 1947), 148.

3. Great Britain, Privy Council, *Acts of the Privy Council of England*, 1619–1621 (London, 1930), 118, in Robert Bremner, *Children and Youth in America*, 4 vols. (Cambridge, MA: Harvard University Press, 1970) 1:8.

4. Quoted in Smith, *Colonists in Bondage*, 149.

5. *Documents Relative to the Colonial History of New York* (Albany, 1856–1887), 2:52, in Bremner, *Children and Youth in America*, 1–23.

6. Smith, *Colonists in Bondage*, 73.

7. *Virginia Statutes at Large*, 1:441–42, quoted in Bremner, *Children and Youth in America*, 1:23.

8. Walter Clark, ed., *No. Car. Records* (Goldsboro, N.C., 1904), 23: 62–66, in Bremner, *Children and Youth in America*, 1:116.

9. R. W. Beales, "The Child in Seventeenth-Century America," in *American Childhood: A Research Guide and Historical Handbook* (Westport, CT: Greenwood Press, 1985), 15–57.

10. Doris Foster and Henry Freed, "Life with Father: 1978," *Family Law Quarterly* 11(4)(1978): 322.

11. As quoted in William Forsyth, *Custody of Infants* (London: Rayner and Hodges, 1850), 8.

12. William Blackstone, *Commentaries on the Law of England*, 3rd ed. (New York, 1900/1758), 1:453.

13. Tapping Reeve, *The Law of Baron and Femme, of Parent and Child, of Guardian and Ward, of Master and Servant, and of the Powers of Courts of Chancery* (New Haven, 1816), 70–72.

14. Lofft 748, 98 Eng. Rep. 899 (K.B. 1774).

15. *Connecticut Records*, 2:328, as discussed in Edmund S. Morgan, *The Puritan Family* (New York: Harper & Row, 1966), 37.

16. Foulke v. People, 4 Colo. App. At 528(1894), quoting the leading doctrine of Lord Mansfield in Blisset's Case, 1 Lofft 748, 98, Eng. Rep. 899 (K.B., 1774).

17. 4 Desau. 33 (S.C. 1809).

18. Ibid., 44.

19. Mercein v. People ex rel. Barry 25 Wend. 64,101 (N.Y.) 1840.

20. Ibid., 104.

21. People v. Mercein, 3 Hill 399, 418 (N.Y.) 1842.

22. Ibid., 422.

23. Ansley J. Coale and Melvin Zelnick, *New Estimate of Fertility and Population in the United States* (Princeton, NJ: Princeton University Press, 1963), 34–35.

24. Carl N. Degler, *At Odds: Women and the Family in America from the Revolution to the Present* (New York: Oxford University Press, 1980), 277.

25. People v. Gates, 57 Bard. 291, 296 (N.Y. 1869).

26. Many states had laws that allowed the child to reject a voluntary indenture, but only after the age of 14.

27. Michael Grossberg, *Governing the Hearth: Law and Family in Nineteenth-Century America* (Chapel Hill: University of North Carolina Press, 1985), 247.

28. Reta Dorr, *What Eight Million Women Want* (Boston: Small, Maynard & Company, 1910), 94.

29. Foulke v. People, 4 Colo. App. At 528 (1894), quoting the leading doctrine of Lord Mansfield in Blisset's Case.

30. "Rev. John Eliot's Records of the First Church in Roxbury, Massachusetts," in Sixth Report of Boston Record Commissioner (Boston, 1881), 187.

31. Bremner, *Children and Youth in America*, 1:105.

32. Cotton Mather, *A Christian at His Calling: Two Brief Discourses, One Directing a Christian in His General Calling: Another Directing Him in His Personal* (Boston, 1701), 36–45.

33. Grossberg, *Governing the Hearth*, 236.

34. Joseph R. Long, *A Treatise on the Law of Domestic Relations* (St. Paul: Keefe-Davidson, 1905), 321.

35. Grossberg, *Governing the Hearth*, 219.

36. Jaquelyn Hall, James Leloudis, Robert Korstad, Mary Murphy, Lu Ann Jones, and Christopher B. Daly, *Like a Family: The Making of a Southern Cotton Mill World* (Chapel Hill: University of North Carolina Press, 1987), 56.

37. David Smith, Sandra Smight, Fred Doolittle, "How Children Used to Work," *Law and Contemporary Problems* 39(3)(1975): 99.

38. Susan Tiffin, *In Whose Best Interests? Child Welfare Reform in the Progressive Era* (Westport, CT: Greenwood Press, 1982), 90.

39. Bremner, *Children and Youth in America*, 2:291.

40. Lyman P. Alden, "The Shady Side of the Placing-Out System," in Bremmer, *Children and Youth in America*, 2:298

41. Moore v. Dozier, 128 Ga. 90, 57 S.E. 110, 96–97 (1907).

42. Ibid., 92–94.

43. As quoted in Jane Addams, *My Friend Julia Lathrop* (New York: Macmillan, 1935), 213.

44. As quoted in Susan Tiffin, *In Whose Best Interests?*, 46.

45. Christopher Lasch, *Haven in a Heartless World: The Family Besieged* (New York: Basic Books, 1977), 14.

46. For the New England colonial version of the Elizabethan Poor Laws, see *Laws and Ordinances of New England, An Abridgement of the Laws in Force and Use in Her Majesty's Plantations* (London: Parker and Smith, 1704), 23.

47. *Proceedings of the Conference on the Care of Dependent Children*, 1909, 41, in Bremner, *Children and Youth in America*, 2:358–59.

48. Extract from *Ninth Annual Report of the State Board of Charities of the State of New York, Relating to Orphan Asylums and Other Institutions for the Care of Children* (Albany, 1876), 306–08, in Bremner, *Children and Youth in America*, 2:192.

49. Tiffin, *In Whose Best Interests?* 219.

50. Elizabeth Pleck, *Domestic Tyranny* (New York: Oxford University Press, 1987), 84–85.

51. South Carolina Code of Law, 1922, in Chester Vernier, *American Family Laws* (Stanford, CA: Stanford University Press, 1931), 4:46.

52. South Dakota, comp. 1. 1929, in Vernier, *American Family Laws*, 4:46.

53. Vernier, *American Family Laws*, 4:282.

54. Homer Folks, "Family Life for Dependent Children," in *Care of Dependent, Neglected, and Wayward Children*, edited by Charles Bartwell and Anna Spencer, 75–80, in Bremner, *Children and Youth in America*, 2:321.

55. In Tiffin, *In Whose Best Interests?*, 105.

56. In two decades, families maintained by women alone increased from 36 percent to 50 percent of all poor families. Of the net increase of 129,000 poor families in 1983, 95% were headed by women See U.S. Bureau of the Census, *Money Income and Poverty: Status of Families and Persons in the United States: 1983* (Washington, DC: U.S. Government Printing Office, 1984).

57. 42 U.S.C.A. Sec. 5101–106. The act was renamed the Child Abuse Prevention Adoption and Family Services Act of 1988.

58. Douglas Besharov, "Doing Something About Child Abuse: The Need to Narrow the Grounds for State Intervention," *Harvard Journal of Law and Public Policy* 8(1985):545.

59. Legal scholar Michael Wald, analyzing the research on children in foster care placement, concluded that social, emotional, and academic development were negatively affected by removal of children and placement in foster care. See Michael Walk, *Protecting Abused and Neglected Children: A Comparison of Home and Foster Placement* (Stanford, CA: Stanford University Press, 1985), 9–13.

60. In re 71 Misc. 2d 965, 337 N.Y.S. 2d 203 (1972).

61. Wyman v. James, 400 U.S. 309.

62. Santosky v. Kramer, 455 U.S. 745 (1982).

63. Santosky v. Kramer, 455 U.S. 745 (1982), at 754.

64. Lassiter v. Dept. of Social Services of Durham County, 452 U.S. 18 (1981).

65. Folks, "Family Life for Dependent Children," in Bremner, *Children and Youth in America*, 2:321.

66. Robert Mnookin, "Foster Care—In Whose Best Interest?" *Harvard Educational Review*, 43(1973):599.

67. Smith v. Organization of Foster Families for Equality and Reform, 431 U.S. 816 (1977).

68. Muller v. Oregon, 208 U.S. 412, 421 (1908).

69. "Letter to the President of the United States Embodying the Conclusions of the Conference on the Care of Dependent Children," Proceedings of the Conference on the Care of Dependent Children, 1909, 192–97, in Bremner, *Children and Youth in America*, 2:368–79.

5

Silenced by the Law

An Even More Modest Proposal

Two hundred and seventy-six years ago, the British satirist Jonathan Swift shocked everyone with a modest proposal: in the midst of a famine, Ireland could escape the burden of poor children by. . . . well, eating them. The author of *Gulliver's Travels* pointed out that his society was unwilling to actually feed these hungry, dependent children, so what would be so shocking about eating them? He reminded everyone that the moral decision to let the children die had already been made by default by the government and by the people who elected it. So what, he wanted to know, was so wrong with his proposal? If nothing else, it would be less wasteful.

Swift's *Modest Proposal* would be altogether too shocking, excessive, and ridiculous for our times. So allow me to propose something infinitely more humane and generous for our nation's million plus abused and neglected children: Let's treat them legally like animals.

We've long demonstrated that we are prepared to protect and nurture our pets much better than we'll ever agree to watch over other people's children. We have extensive laws that protect animals from abuse and neglect, and in many situations these legal protections are much better than those we apply to children in harm's way. In these United States, a man who beats his dog is uniformly prosecuted, but a man's right to beat his child is inherently protected. A century ago, laws protecting animals were already in place. Let us recall that the very first organization to stand up for children was an animal rights charity. Go figure.

Punishment to Fit the Crime?

In September 2005, the national media pounced on the story of 11 Ohio children confined to cages by their adoptive parents. "Although most of the 'boxes' were not locked," authorities said in a statement, "the children were afraid to leave their 'boxes' at night even to use the bathroom because an alarm would sound and the parents would react in anger."[1] The children's crates were fashioned from wood and chicken wire and clearly did not include the designer mattresses that cushion America's most pampered pets (Asprey and Garrard, for example, offer a handcrafted chocolate brown alligator-skin pet carrier with cashmere throw for $19,000).[2] The children, all of whom have special needs, were removed from the home and are now in different foster care. Although the parents are under investigation, criminal charges have not yet been filed.

In a 2004 issue of the *Stanford Law Review*, Jill Elaine Hasday noted that

> By the end of the nineteenth century, a majority of common law courts held that a parent could inflict reasonable or moderate correction on his child, and rarely convicted a parent for exceeding the bounds of reasonableness or moderation. [As of 2004], every state still recognizes a parent's authority to impose corporal punishment on his child. At least thirty states and the District of Columbia, for instance, have codified a parent's right to inflict 'reasonable' corporal punishment. At least thirteen states have codified a parent's right to impose corporal punishment in slightly different terms. These statutes preserve a substantial portion of the common law regime.[3]

No Political Will on Children

Let's be honest here. There is no decisive will in government or among the majority of voters to put children first. We don't agree with giving children national primacy as the future of our society. So why don't we 'fess up and use the existing framework of laws that protect animals? Just define children before age 18 as animals and, bingo, we'll go a long way toward providing the protections kids have in other countries. OK, so we've decided the United States should be the only nation of 179 to not ratify the UN Convention on the Rights of the Child. But at least by giving children the rights we give animals in this country, we might reduce the thousand-plus who die each year of abuse or neglect, and the couple of million who suffer with no right to a lawyer, no right to sue for redress when the government harms them, no right to be heard when their fate is being determined, no right to be safe. And who knows, we might even find a few of those many children who are wards of a state that the state has yet to list.

Why We Don't Put Children First?

We give an elevated national standing to so many worthy issues: national security, the fight against terrorism, rebuilding the Gulf States, Social Security, tax cuts, and so on, not to mention pork-barrel projects for politicians of every stripe. These issues for good or bad are given a kind of golden ticket among national priorities. Without debating any of them here, we do ask why the position of children as our gating factor, the glass ceiling of future prosperity, stability and arguably as our only future, has not been given at least a couple of those golden tickets. OK, so two might be too many. But what about the same little brass ticket we give to pets?

Impact of Ignoring Children's Needs

How did we develop this blind spot? Is it that children don't vote? Is it that they don't lobby? Is it that we still viscerally feel that children are the chattel property of their parents? Is it that we still have the Victorian sense children are imperfectly developed grown-ups, not fully human until they come of age? Are we always to be the nation that believes in fixing things after they break, rather than avoiding the breakage through prevention? Can't we find enough political will to rise above policies that are invariably reactive and rarely preemptive? Do we really believe grown-ups have bigger rights to abuse and neglect than children have to be protected from the abusers and neglecters? Yet isn't that totally short-sighted when the children mostly outlive the parents and when we know abuse and neglect often roll from generation to generation?

My Modest Proposal

We know that more than half of all adult male prisoners were abused or neglected as children. We know that a lack of prenatal care greatly increases the cost of remedial medical and other services after birth. We know that education can break cycles of poverty and low adult achievement. We know these things and yet our nation consistently relegates the fate of children to the bottom of the totem pole of priorities. We appropriately spend billions of dollars to defend our nation but only a relative handful of pennies to ensure that it will be a safe home to valuable citizens for generations to come.

Let's be honest with one another. There is no political will to put children first. So let's just agree to put them tenth by defining them as animals. It will be a huge step-up among national priorities for the abused and neglected children who are currently not even standing on the ladder.

Oh, and by the way, if you think this idea is daft, there is an alternative. We could treat the kids as human and actually protect them better. That's why we have First Star. No point cursing the gathering darkness. Candles, anyone?

—Peter Samuelson[4]

Note: Peter Samuelson is a film producer, founder chairman of the Starlight Starbright Foundation (www.starlight.org), and founder president of the First Star Public Policy Initiative (www.firststar.org).

The blind spot we want to illuminate in this chapter is the way abused and neglected children are silenced by the legal system—as Peter Samuelson described, treated worse than animals. In the courtrooms of many states they are to be seen, but not heard. One of First Star's primary goals is to overcome such antiquated notions and to ensure that children are actually heard by our courts. How? By having the right to an attorney.

Some people might argue that children are already guaranteed protection under the Constitution. After all, in 1967, the United States Supreme Court ruled that "neither the 14th Amendment nor the Bill of Rights is for adults alone" and that "under our Constitution, the condition of being a boy does not justify a kangaroo court."[5]

Two years later, in *In re Gault,* the Supreme Court made yet another reference to children that any rational person would expect to have ensured their rights as Americans: "Constitutional rights do not mature and come into being magically only when one attains the state-defined age of majority. Minors, as well as adults, are protected by the constitution and possess constitutional rights."[6]

The "YES" States		Notes
Alabama	New Jersey*	*In abuse & neglect proceedings
Arkansas*	New Mexico**	**When children are over 14 years
Colorado	New York*	
Connecticut	North Carolina	
District of	North Dakota	
Columbia	Oklahoma	
Kansas	Pennsylvania	
Kentucky	South Carolina*	
Louisiana*	South Dakota*	
Maryland	Utah	
Massachusetts	Virginia	
Michigan	West Virginia	
Nebraska	Wisconsin	
Mississippi	Wyoming	

The "NO" States		Notes
Alaska**	Minnesota	GAL not required to be an
Arizona*	Missouri	Attorney
California*	Montana	*An Attorney or CASA may serve
Delaware*	Nevada	as GAL
Florida	New Hampshire***	**Appointment of Attorney or
Georgia*	Ohio	GAL at Court's Discretion
Hawaii	Oregon	***Court may appoint Attorney
Idaho	Rhode Island	when child's expressed interests
Illinois	Tennessee	conflict with GAL
Indiana*	Texas	****Court may appoint GAL or
Iowa*	Vermont****	counsel for child
Maine	Washington*****	*****Court may appoint an
		Attorney if Child is 12 years or
		older

These are statements of crystalline clarity by the highest court in the land. Yet American children have been treated as property and as objects of court proceeding for so long that it's become the fossilized way many public officials think about children and their relationship to the law. Nearly four decades after that important Supreme Court decision, *In re Gault,* four states fail to require that children be provided with attorneys in court proceedings.

No national standard is in place to ensure children meaningful access to the courts. Children have not been granted the right to traditional legal representation in hearings at which their interests are at stake.

Where children have been removed from their family, or there is an effort to remove them or to bring them back, most people believe they have a lawyer. In most cases, they do not, or the lawyer they have acts as a guardian ad litem. The guardian's duty is not to the child but to the court.

Every child in every proceeding that affects that child's interests is entitled to traditional, competent legal representation. Without it, children are disadvantaged by the system that claims to protect them.[7]

I Hear You Knocking—But You Can't Come In*

You might call Gregory K. the Rosa Parks of the children's rights movement. In 1992, 10-year-old Gregory had been left double-parked in Florida's foster care system well beyond the statutory time limit. A family was ready to adopt him, but the child protective services (CPS), which had custody of Gregory, refused to initiate termination of parental rights proceedings. Gregory found a lawyer who knocked on the courthouse door on his behalf, petitioning for termination of parental rights and to be adopted. The entire time Gregory languished as a ward of the state in foster care, his appointed guardian ad litem never met nor spoke with him about his needs and desires. Predictably, the CPS lawyer moved to dismiss Gregory's petition, claiming he lacked the standing and capacity to bring any legal action.

By claiming his right to be heard on the matters of his own safety, liberty from state custody, and desire to live in a permanent loving family, Gregory aroused national attention. The Legal Action Project of the National Committee for the Rights of the Child filed an amicus brief and appeared in court opposing the CPS's motion to dismiss. Others supported Gregory's position, thus strengthening a nascent movement for children's right to be heard.

---

*From Lowry, Bross, Dicker, and Pitts, *Perspectives on Child Advocacy Law in the Early 21st Century,* 2000 Foundation for Child Development and the American Bar Association Fund for Justice and Education.

The trial judge denied the CPS motion and ordered a hearing on the petition for termination of parental rights. The subsequent trial was televised nationally on Court TV. Based on strong evidence, the judge ordered parental rights terminated. The adoption was approved and Gregory became part of a wonderful family. The CPS then appealed the decision. The Florida court of appeals reversed the trial judge's decision, holding that as a minor Gregory did not have the capacity to bring the action—even though he had a meritorious claim. However, because CPS had filed its own petition to terminate parental rights (out of embarrassment at the unlawful amount of time Gregory had spent in foster care) the appeals court was able to let the adoption stand.[8]

Even when children have attorneys, a blind spot regarding their rights seems to operate even in the most sensitive circumstances. We proceed now to the West Coast for the case of Marco Barrera's eight-year-old son and 14-year-old daughter.

When Barrera was convicted of murder in San Fernando, California, two of his children were called to the witness stand during the death-penalty phase of the trial. But the attorney representing the children only learned about it in the newspaper—weeks after they had already testified in the penalty phase.[9]

Lawyer Lisa E. Mandel had been present when the children testified during the evidentiary part of the trial for first-degree murder, where Barrera was convicted of killing two small children and burying their bodies in a forest. But Mandel wasn't even notified that Barrera's children were to be put on the stand once again—in the phase where the jury would decide whether their father should be executed—to testify about their feelings toward him and whether they wanted to have contact with him again.

Mandel pointed out that just as prosecutors wouldn't contact adult witnesses without going through their lawyers—so they should not call child witnesses without their attorney's consent: "In no other circumstances, if a person is represented, do you circumvent their attorney."[10] She asked for a protocol to ensure that minors' attorneys be notified when the children are called to testify in court.

Both stories show how children—for a long time—have not had rights like those of adults and their voices are often not heard over the din of ignorance sounding around them.

A Little History

Until the 1960s, children in dependency court proceedings rarely got a chance to make their voices heard. Judges relied on social workers to investigate abuse cases and make recommendations on each child's behalf, based on the best interest standard.

The Supreme Court case in *In re Gault* held that every child accused of a crime has a constitutional right to an attorney. But for a child subject to an abuse, neglect, or termination of parental rights proceeding, the right to a lawyer still depends on where he or she happens to live—because the law varies from state to state.

Abused children's needs for legal representation wasn't addressed until the Child Abuse Prevention and Treatment Act (CAPTA) passed in 1974. The act made states provide a guardian ad litem to every abused or neglected child whose case requires a court proceeding. Depending on the state, however, a guardian ad litem might be a trained attorney, a lay professional from the fields of social work or psychology, or a non-professional citizen volunteer. A 1996 amendment requires states that receive funding under the law to give appropriate training to people who represent children in abuse cases. Today, nearly every state requires that a lawyer, a guardian ad litem, or both be appointed to a child in dependency court proceedings.

Children in dependency court proceedings tend to have one of the two following types of legal representation.

Advocate-Driven Representation

A court appoints a guardian ad litem (GAL) and in some cases a court-appointed special advocate (CASA) volunteer to establish the child's best interest by gathering information and monitoring the surrounding circumstances.

A guardian ad litem isn't necessarily an attorney. Indeed, many states have no minimum education requirements for the guardian ad litem, nor are caseload restrictions in place to ensure that every child receives a basic standard of care. Although guardians ad litem take the child's point of view into consideration when preparing a recommendation, they aren't legally obligated to represent the child's expressed preference, nor are they bound by the same confidentiality laws as traditional attorneys. Thus, a guardian ad litem's role is significantly different from that of an attorney.

A court-appointed special advocate is a volunteer who accompanies a child to dependency court proceedings. Begun in Washington State in 1977, the CASA program was devised as a fact-finding method where a community volunteer meets with a dependent child to gather information and then acts as liaison between the child and such interested parties as parents, foster parents, guardians, social workers, counselors, and any guardian ad litem or attorney assigned to the case. The Victims of Child Abuse Act of 1990 authorized a court-appointed special advocate "to every victim of child abuse or neglect in the United States that needs such an advocate."[11] The special advocate acts in concert with those promoting the child's best interests but also conveys to the judge the child's expressed wishes—even when those wishes conflict with the child's best interests.

Client-Directed Representation

The American Bar Association (ABA) puts it succinctly: "The term 'child's attorney' means a lawyer who provides legal services for a child and who owes the same duties of undivided loyalty, confidentiality, and competent representation to the child as is due to an adult client."[12]

Traditional, client-directed, or expressed interest attorneys are governed by the Model Code of Professional Responsibility, the same code that governs attorneys who represent adults. Such attorneys must abide by the child client's expressed wishes for the objectives of the representation while counseling them on those objectives. Traditional representation further requires a presumption that a child client is competent to participate in the course of his or her representation, absent a showing to the contrary.

The National Association of Counsel for Children has amended the ABA and Model Code standards to provide an alternate representation scheme in certain circumstances, particularly where very young children are concerned. If the attorney believes that the child's expressed preference conflicts with his or her best interests, a guardian ad litem should be appointed to advocate the best-interests position. The attorney may counsel the child about what may be in his or her best interests; however, the child may decide which position to advocate in court. Where direct danger is likely to result from advocating the child's preference, the attorney–client privilege may be abrogated. The ABA also states that a "nonlawyer [GAL] cannot and should not be expected to perform any legal functions on behalf of a child." Once established as the child's attorney, the lawyer should remain in this role for the rest of the court process.[13]

Should a Child Have a Say in Court?

In the 1960s and 1970s, children's rights as a concept really began to enter the legal dialogue. According to law professor Martha Minow, during the

1970s many lawyers, scholars, and activists became involved in a "children's liberation" movement proposing that questions of children's competence should be argued on a case-by-case basis and that children deserve the right to participate fully in society.[14] Another group of activists argued that instead of simply liberating children from the constraints of childhood status, the emphasis should be on providing protections, services, and adequate care.[15] This was a dramatic departure from the common view of children as property and gave great hope at the time to some child activists.

However, as Gary Debele wrote, "a legal ambivalence came into the children's rights movement over the last several decades." The courts were concerned about providing children with rights that would "inject conflict and individualism into the sphere of family life and disturb the usual arrangements of caring for children."[16] By the 1980s, the movement for children's rights had secured neither a "coherent political and intellectual foundation" nor a "viable constituency with political clout."[17] The 1990s brought efforts to redistribute resources to meet children's varied needs, but this would have required legislation, something children have difficulty influencing as they do not vote.

Children have been denied basic rights and so remain the most vulnerable group in our society. The system has no direct responsibility for children. When children's needs are in direct conflict with those of adults, children very often lose out. An important option still on the table is support for international human rights for children. This would recognize for each child the right to express views freely in all matters affecting the child, and the opportunity to be heard in any judicial or administrative proceedings in accordance with procedural rules of national law. The United States still refuses to sign the UN Convention on the Rights of Children.

What madness is this? Why would we keep children from having a say in their futures? We all know that children can be easily led and often don't know what is best for them—but should this potentiality preclude all input? How can we insist that we're guided by the child's best interests when we don't even know from the child what he or she has experienced and what he or she wants? This contradicts constitutional due process.

> We in the U.S. do not believe that we should railroad a person for expedience. We still put murderers—murderers caught in the act, when we have eyewitnesses saying, "yes, this is the guy"—we still put them through the process. We do any number of things to ensure that this process is fair, even though we know the defendant is guilty and it's a

waste of time from the "common sense" point of view. We have a fair system that makes sure that every adult has due process. We are always trying to take shortcuts with kids. Would we ever allow a CASA to represent an adult? Of course not.

—Shari Shink
Executive director
Rocky Mountain Children's Law Center[18]

If we fear that a child and attorney could convince a judge to approve something harmful to the child, then we're placing very little faith in judges' and lawyers' ability to sort out which desires are reasonable and preferable.

This may be the most important decision that may be made in the life of this child . . . and the state is making it. If the state fines you $25.00 and you're facing a possible 24 hours in jail, you have the right to a jury trial and legal counsel, but the same state affords no such right to a child it is involuntarily placing somewhere for ten or fifteen years. Why is that? Meanwhile, constitutional doctrine gives every parent in danger of being declared unfit the right to counsel if an attorney might make a difference in the outcome—effectively granting all parents counsel (Lassiter v. DSS 452 U.S. 18 (1981)). But an often less articulate child— also a person under the Constitution—being deprived by the state of one or both parents and forced to accept a stranger and placement as dictated by a court, has no such assured right. Why is that?

—Robert Fellmeth
Director, Children's Advocacy Institute
Price Professor of Public Interest Law
University of San Diego[19]

Validating the Decision in the Child's Mind

If the child's wishes are not voiced to the court, the judge's decision will not be legitimate in the child's eyes. Numerous studies have shown how important it is for the child to feel like they have a stake in the venture.

Even when no physical abuse is alleged, such as the case of the alcoholic parent whose child is regularly absent from school, it's crucial to have the judge hear the child's point of view. Then the court can get together with the advocates and service providers involved to coordinate prevention, because the best interests of the child are to address the alcoholism as the underlying cause of the neglect.

I'm not supportive of sending any child back to abusive parents, but it is very important to hear from the child in a way that's expressed through a professional legal advocate. Ultimately, we want to know the particulars of why the child wants to be with his parent despite the parent's perceived unfitness, and whether it is an unfitness that can be addressed.

—Lewis Pitts
Senior managing attorney
Advocates for Children's Services
Legal Aid of North Carolina[20]

Only Lawyers Can Provide Due Process

Although guardians ad litem can be very helpful, they can't provide the due process that is the constitutional right of adults. Colene Robinson, formerly of the National Association of Counsel for Children, explained it this way:

Someone in that role has an inherent conflict because they're charged with presenting the child's best interests. A child understands when the person is conflicted, and he isn't going to open up to someone he sees playing both sides like that. The client-directed attorney is different. When you build the trusting relationship, the child confides more readily and you get a situation that the child wants and can live with—it doesn't do any good, for example, for a CASA to come in and say the child should go to a group home if the child is just going to run away. Having that tenuous a relationship between supposed representative and child can't yield a good result, and a lot of times, the result might be unrealistic. It seems hard to believe—if the whole child protective services system is set up to help children—that you wouldn't listen to what they have to say. That's just so patronizing . . . I like to think that most places recognize that, and have client-directed representation, especially for the older kids.[21]

A layperson looking after your interests just isn't the same as a member of the bar arguing for you in the language and manner that a judge expects and understands.

Why an attorney? Because these are legal proceedings. There is testimony, a legal standard, evidence. Only an attorney can bring a writ to stop the county from violating the law or failing to perform for the child as the law requires. Only an attorney can appeal an improper decision. Only an attorney can make the kinds of arguments judges understand and accept.

Why an attorney? Because they deserve a voice in the decision about where they will live and with whom; because the decision is likely to be better if they have an attorney raising issues and presenting evidence from their perspective; because only an attorney can challenge the county and the court by way of appeal; and because every other party has one—although each of them is generally better able to present their own cases without counsel than are young children.

—Robert Fellmeth[22]

Why Can't the Judge Do It?

Most skeptics of legal representation argue that the judge will look out for the child's interests—or that we don't need the complication and expense. Yet parents are entitled to legal representation (often at taxpayer expense) even if they have prior convictions or pose an abusive threat. So what are these states saying? That they can't afford to protect children? The situation reminds me of Oliver Twist, porridge bowl in hand, begging: "Please, sir, I want some more." Heck, it's the least we can do. Children at risk often have experienced terrible and even unspeakable treatment. To deny them the defense of one who truly speaks the language of the court is to jeopardize them yet again—only this time knowingly.

Shink argues convincingly: "Judges cannot make decisions without information, and the lawyer can provide the court with information—factual, unadulterated information. We simply cannot assume that inundated, overburdened caseworkers are going to do that—they don't. The court needs a total picture to make a decision, and instead most hearings last three minutes."[23]

Lewis Pitts expressed it another way:

Client-directed representation in no way supplants the trial judge as the ultimate decision-maker. It just empowers that judge to make the most prudent and wise decision as to what's in the best interests of the child. If I could ask people just one thing when they disagree with the notion that kids need attorneys, it would be this: would you be satisfied if you were that party, with all those interests at stake, to be told "Hey, you don't need an advocate—we'll figure it all out and tell you the answer."

Would you consider that you'd been treated with the value and sacredness that all humans have?[24]

Although judges may fervently wish to protect the children who appear before them, they are supposed to be impartial. For a judge to fully appreciate the child's position and needs, he or she should hear the argument of a qualified attorney. Lay representatives of children aren't trained to do this. Sure, they may care immensely for the child, but do they have the legal expertise to persuade a judge who's accustomed to legal rather than social or personal arguments? Not likely.

Why Can't Social Workers Do It?

Most social workers are diligent, hard-working, caring individuals with specialist training. So why can't the social worker or the court-appointed special advocate represent the child adequately in court?

"A caseworker has divided loyalty," Jane Spinak explained. "The caseworker is responsible to the agency, as well as the family, and not just to the child. There is always the potential for a conflict among (those) positions. In addition, the caseworker's obligations range, from state to state, depending on state law. The caseworker simply doesn't have undivided loyalty to the child."[25] And, as described in Chapter 7, they simply don't have the time to represent children given their caseloads.

Moreover, neither a caseworker nor a CASA can offer the child confidentiality, Spinak pointed out, so the child may not be willing to speak freely about her concerns or wishes. A lawyer assigned to represent a child "has undivided loyalty and can be an independent advocate for the child . . . can ensure confidentiality in most cases and encourage the child to say 'this is what is happening in my life; this is what I want to happen.' The lawyer then has the opportunity to counsel the child, to develop a strategy for securing the child's interests, and to explain what the child wants to the court. No one else can have that role."

As Pitts put it, "Whether the GAL is a trained caseworker, with specific knowledge and expertise at parsing issues and convening the appropriate resources and services, or whether it's a limitedly trained lay person who got one heart string tug and decided to become a volunteer—how do we know about the independence of that person? This is tough work. You can't wing it."[26]

How Old Should a Child Be to Have a Voice?

If indeed children were given a voice in court, a question would arise. When is a child old enough to have that voice bear substantial weight? In other words, is there an age at which children are typically mature enough to think and speak rationally for themselves? This is a difficult question to answer, especially given that children are not all alike and many abused children lag behind developmentally. Many experts favor the age range of 14 to 15 as a time when children have in fact matured enough to provide input regarding their care and protection.[27] Given how difficult it is to determine the ability of adults to know what is in their best interests, we can expect that knowing whether a child is competent in this regard is likely to be difficult as well. This doesn't mean, however, that we should exclude children from participation. They are the ones who have had the experiences relevant to their care and should at least be heard.

What if the Child and Lawyer Disagree?

Let's accept that a client-directed attorney can uniquely represent a child's stated interests. Okay—then what is the attorney supposed to do when a child client wants to return to an abusive or neglectful home? An attorney doesn't necessarily have to represent the desires of a client who's engaged in self-destructive behavior. Robert Fellmeth explained: "An attorney is allowed—and sometimes obliged—to recuse himself (and) withdraw from any client, adult or child, who is uncooperative, unreasonably refuses to follow his advice, with whom he cannot work or deal, or who is engaged or wants to engage in unlawful acts."[28]

On the other hand, Fellmeth continued,

What is the harm in having the child's preferences a part of the process, assuming all of the dangers and facts are presented to the court by a party to the proceeding—which is likely? It is true that the child may have his or her preferences because of bonding, lack of maturity, lack of information about choices . . . but the court is able to weigh that. Indeed, children generally will telegraph their lack of basis without the kind of artifice that more often characterizes adult testimony.

The point is, there is some value in having the child's preferences a part of the process for many reasons:

First, sometimes the child is right.

Second, although parents may be abusive, foster care is sometimes abusive as well. This is the state serving as parent, and the track record in most states is inconsistent at best. The statistics on what happens to foster children emancipating from the system hardly warrants categorical confidence.

Third, the child deserves to be part of a process where his or her views are at least considered seriously. Should not a parent, in any context, hear out a child and solicit his or her feelings and perspective? Isn't there value to that?

But beyond all of the above is the reality of dependency proceedings. Explore the hypothetical further. The proceeding does not merely determine whether the child should be detained, or whether a parent is fit, but where the child should go and what should happen to the child— whatever the future relationship with the parent. If the child is to go back to the home, will "family preservation" services be provided? Which ones? Will they protect the child? If the child is removed, what "reunification" services will be provided to the parent? The law requires "reasonable services." Are they effectively protective? If parental rights are to be terminated, where is the child to go? We are deciding the future of a child, possibly for the rest of his or her childhood.

Ann Haralambie, author of *The Child's Attorney,* described how some jurisdictions have handled the difficult question of what can be done when a child's expressed interests are not what his or her attorney zealously advocates:

> In some jurisdictions, an attorney who disagrees with the child's wishes is expected to fully present the client's expressed wishes and is permitted to explain why the attorney disagrees. This role would initially appear to offer a sensible blending of the traditional roles of attorney and guardian ad litem. . . . However, there is an inherent conflict of interest in such a situation, and no other client would tolerate an attorney presenting the client's case and then arguing why the client is incorrect. The better approach is for the attorney, advocating the child's wishes, while requesting appointment of a guardian ad litem who would be free to advocate the child's best interests irrespective of the child's position.[29]

Haralambie provided some factors to be considered by lawyers when representing the expressed wishes of a child. One aspect, she suggested, in determining the reasonableness of a child's position is whether his or her safety can be assured. Children who have been abused may not know any other way of living. They may feel that they do not deserve love or that they are to blame for the abuse. They may have been threatened or may even feel that they need to take care of a parent. Foster care may be a frightening unknown to them. Only by understanding what motivates children to prefer danger to safety can an attorney with or without a guardian ad litem influence them to choose safety.

As noted above, the maturity of a child is relevant. As children mature, attorneys should pay greater attention to their wishes. Often the age of seven has been used as the point at which the child can participate in decision making about his or her future. Of course, children vary developmentally, so seven is merely a beginning point. There are times when an even younger child can add input to his or her future in meaningful ways. Haralambie observed that as children get older, though this can also be true of young children, what they want may be the only thing they will go along with. "Indeed," she wrote, "children can be very effective in sabotaging almost any court orders involving them with which they strongly disagree."[30]

Attorneys should get to know the children they represent and consult development specialists for guidance. They should communicate with children to explain what is happening at each step along the course of representing their interests and help them to understand their rights and those of anyone contesting their expressed interests. If an attorney is not proficient in this area or if a particular child is resistant to help, then he or she should seek assistance. Any attorney representing children in abuse and neglect cases should be trained in this area and in child development. But even when they have been trained, mental health experts, child development experts, and guardians ad litem can be and should be brought in to assist if the attorney believes that some or all of what a child is advocating may put him or her in harm's way.

Sometimes an attorney must identify when state agencies are not making reasonable efforts to provide quality services to a child client. If the child has been in foster care and moving from home to home, he or she may have been labeled a troublemaker but in fact need medical attention or counseling. The child may be clinging to the hope of being reunited with parents, even when this is not feasible. It's part of an attorney's responsibility to understand a child client, not merely to represent his or her interests in terms of placement. Haralambie tells of her experience representing six children whose mother, an alcoholic, could not rehabilitate enough to take custody of her children. The children had a strong affiliation with the mother, however, and did not want to be adopted. Each time they went to court they and the mother would go away disappointed. Eventually, Haralambie helped the children realize that reunification was not possible but, because she knew of their bond with their mother, arranged foster homes rather than seeking adoptive placement. A case like this can be very difficult. For example, one or two of the children might well have wanted to be adopted. Haralambie got to know the children well enough to understand their desires and by doing so identified a solution that worked for all.

Children are not able, as a rule, to articulate their needs with the same understanding and conviction as adults. This is why they need to be represented by attorneys who can argue for them and understand, appreciate, and work with the complexities inherent in such representation.

Shari Shink

One of the critical roles of an attorney is to counsel the child about viable options to present to the court. As the attorney, you can move the child to believing there are better options than the one he or she initially proposes. And by taking the time to explore the child's suggestion with the child, by giving that option weight, even if you come to a different result, the child will perceive the process as fair.

I can tell you that in my 27 years of representing children, I only have one case in which I had to decide between either doing what my client wanted or doing what I thought was best. I went into court and said exactly the opposite of what my child client wanted. In the end, it worked out—the judge ended up placing the child back with the child's family, which the child wanted, no further abuse occurred, and eventually the child was moved to a better situation. I felt so bad about what I had done, though, that I promised myself that I would never do it again. I have worked hard to establish relationships with my child clients that allow them to trust me and to be willing to take my advice. In another case, the child wanted to live with an ailing grandmother; I simply told the child this wasn't a good option, that his grandmother wasn't well or strong enough to be able to take good care of him. But I did a number of things to show him that I cared about what he thought. He eventually came around to seeing that that was probably true.[31]

Colene Robinson

It's an adversarial system. And that adversarial system is in place so that every position can be heard and considered. In the end, even if what a child wants can't work, there might be elements that the court may want to listen to. Let's say the child wants to go back to living with an alcoholic mother for reasons x, y, and z. The court won't return the child, but recognizes that the x, y, and z have value. The court can gain from that, and in its order at least address those points, which are certainly going to be relevant, and relevant to that child. If you didn't have anyone representing the child, no one would hear the x, y, and z. We as outsiders might say, "of course the child can't live with two alcoholic parents." But if we look at the facts, maybe the child is 17 years old and doing well in school and is so self-sufficient at this point that even though the parents drink and it's not the ideal family life, it's at least a loving, stable bond that might be best for the child—especially when the alternative is going to a group home, when you know the child is just going to run away, or being sent from placement to placement.

Children should have expressed-interests representation. As I said, it's an adversarial system. The judge should be hearing all of the evidence and deciding. Remember, there is a judge presiding. As an attorney, if I do my job well and I win, that's because the decision represents a good result for the system.[32]

Jane Spinak

Part of it is looking at what the role of the lawyer is generally. If the attorney for the child serves as an independent voice, that voice can provide the judge with a sense of how the child is feeling and what the child wants to have happen, even if the judge ultimately decides that the particular course of action is not in the child's best interest. The lawyer's argument may be in conflict with the caseworker or the CASA or the court's view of the child's best interests. The role of the lawyer for the child is to advocate what I call the child's counseled wishes. It's not the first thing out of the child's mouth. The lawyer has had the opportunity to hear the child, talk to the child, gather information, and then be the voice to say to the judge, "This is what my client wants." But the judge is the decision maker. The judge has the opportunity to hear the independent voice of the lawyer and then ask, "What does this mean to me?"

"When the lawyer explains what the child wants, the judge then has information that might qualify his or her decision. For example, if the lawyer indicates that the child wants to return home, part of the obligation of the lawyer is to say, "these are the reasons my client wants to return home, these are the ways to keep my client safe, and these are things that my client understands are necessary and is willing to do to stay safe," especially an older client. Even for a younger client, though, the process may reveal more complexity about the child's life to the judge. The lawyer has an obligation to talk to the child about what could happen: "if the judge says that it's unsafe for you to live at home, how would you respond?" And maybe that would be when the child would say, "if my brother is there, I'll be safe" or "my grandmother lives next door." If there's not a lawyer present to have that conversation in confidence with the child, the judge might never get the information. The child may be unwilling to say anything without the promise of confidentiality. Once the child has shared the information, the lawyer can discuss with the child whether the child wants that information disclosed to the court. The information may allow the judge to then say, "well, maybe I can't simply send the child home, but I can, under certain circumstances or conditions." Alternatively, the judge might think, "given the interest that this child has in returning home, even if I don't think the child ought to, I have to think seriously as a judge about what would allow this child to have an ongoing relationship with this parent," because the child and the parent have that right until parental rights are terminated.

The opposite might also occur. The lawyer may provide information that the client wants the judge to know that confirms for the judge that the child should not go home. The ultimate decision might be influenced strongly in one way or the other. It's very hard for the court to make the right decision both for the short term and over time without an independent voice saying to the court, "this is what this child wants."[33]

Lawyers Will Need to Spend Time With Kids

Shari Shink

But today in America, children don't have lawyers that spend enough time with them. At the Kempe Center, I did a study of children's relationships with their lawyers. I interviewed 47 kids. And 45 of them said, "If I trusted my lawyer, I would do what my lawyer said was best." We're still not where we need to be, because most kids don't have lawyers, but the truth of it is that kids really want guidance and direction. They want someone to take control of a situation that for whatever reason has gotten out of control. In my experience, if there's a disagreement between what I think should happen and what my child client wants, either I come to move closer to what the child wants because I'm impressed with their sincerity, or I bring them to my side. So you tend to eliminate the controversy—but you have to take the time. You have to listen and talk.[34]

Attorneys Must Be Trained to Interview Children

This issue deserves more than a cursory overview. We explore it further in Chapter 7, which focuses on training those involved in child protection. Two areas of child development of significant interest to an attorney should be the children's memory and susceptibility to influence. The 1995 publication of *Jeopardy in the Courtroom: A Scientific Analysis of Children's Testimony* by Stephen Ceci and Maggie Bruck raised the level of attention given to false reports of abuse and to failures to substantiate actual abuse. Children's memory issues and suggestibility are especially important in abuse cases where medical evidence is not available and young children have difficulty explaining details. Without an understanding of how memory and suggestibility affect a child's view of abuse, reports of it, and expressed interests, attorneys may believe that a child is lying or does not understand what is going on and is therefore incapable of offering reliable input into his or her future.

Research indicates that a child's ability to tell about an event is determined by cognitive ability as well as language ability. In *Investigation and Prosecution of Child Abuse,* for example, one team reports that

> Narration of life events by children is also a skill with clear developmental trends in both the amount and type of information reported. Preschool children are still learning the "rules" involved in telling about an event. Young children generally report the usual aspects of an event. As the child matures, she reports the more unique and distinctive aspects of an event. . . . Young children's narratives, consistent with their egocentric perspectives, are sketchy, lack detail, and are loosely organized. They have not mastered the convention of telling a story from beginning to middle to end. Thus, they can appear confused, disorganized, and inconsistent in their recounting of events. Their expectation is that the adult already knows what they are going to report.[35]

Young children may answer questions they don't fully understand, sometimes merely to please adults or because they don't comprehend the significance of understanding a question before answering. While it is easy to find a child's inconsistencies as reason to distrust her comprehension of the world around her, it can just as easily be the inability of the interviewer to present questions effectively that leads to this observation.

Suggestibility pertains to the extent to which children can be influenced by a host of external factors. Below is a list of factors associated with child susceptibility:[36]

The Interviewer's Mindset

Interviewers who begin with assumptions about what the child knows may elicit that information from a child even if it is erroneous. Children may be swayed by adults' interpretations of events that children do not understand well.

Stereotypes

When children are repeatedly presented with negative stereotypes, such as the bad man, they are more likely to report negative information that conforms to the stereotype.

Delay

Children's memory for details fades more quickly than that of adults, especially for peripheral details. This leaves the child more vulnerable to suggestions about those details.

Intimidating Environment or Interviewer

Children are more likely to agree with the suggestions of an intimidating interviewer. There are conflicting research results as to whether children actually adopt the suggestions of an intimidating interviewer or simply conform to the demand of the situation by agreeing.

Form of the Question

Children provide more erroneous information in response to yes or no questions than to open-ended questions.

Inducements to Keep a Secret or a Lie

By age five, children frequently lie or omit information to protect the adults who have asked them to do so.

Source Monitoring

Young children have more difficulty than do older children or adults with remembering the source of their knowledge, and in determining whether it happened to them or whether someone told them it happened.

Leading or Misleading Questions

Not all leading questions have an equal impact on the child's account. Children will have a hard time correcting the interviewer when coercive questions are asked. Misleading questions can be a source of postevent contamination that can affect the recall of preschoolers.

This information on memory and suggestibility alone indicates the complexity involved in understanding a child. The need for training of attorneys and all those involved in representing and supporting children who have experienced abuse or neglect is obvious. Although we argue here that children should be represented by attorneys, we also argue that the quality of that representation depends to a large extent on the training provided prior to such representation and the attorney's ability to recognize when he or she needs to bring in additional experts to assist.

It's important to note that the ability of an attorney to provide this kind of necessary attention to a child depends also on his or her caseload. When we propose such attention to children's needs we need to be sure that attorneys have the help they need to provide it and are given a level of pay that is an incentive to provide quality representation.

A Bright Spot

We could approach the issues in this chapter by failing to provide legal representation altogether, or we could give children the right to be heard and the right to independent, trained counsel, and work out either state-by-state or nationwide guidelines for when and how attorneys might deviate from their client's expressed wishes and add their own observations. Even with guidelines, however, there will be room for interpretation. Best practices training for attorneys regarding how to handle a variety of difficult situations likely to arise when representing children should be required and at a very high standard as children are our most vulnerable citizens.

A bright spot in this effort took place in Atlanta in 2005. Federal district courts are the highest trial courts in the country. Judge Marvin Shoob has been with the U.S. District Court of Georgia's Northern District since President Jimmy Carter appointed him in 1979. Shoob "has made a career of speaking his mind—and following the dictates of his conscience," according to alma mater Georgia Tech's alumni magazine,

> It's been 51 years since Marvin Shoob was a foot soldier in World War II. But one searing experience still haunts him. . . .
>
> I was in a shell crater at an outpost when five or six Germans came up through the fog—all kids, 16, 17 or 18—with their hands up to surrender. I told them to come on into the crater. I was holding a rifle on them when, a few minutes later, a lieutenant walked by and said, "What are you going to do with them, soldier?" I said, "I don't know what to do; I don't have any place to take them, lieutenant." He made them lie down, and he sprayed them with an automatic rifle—they were crying and screaming—and he killed them all. I was there with the bodies all night. I was 20 years old at the time."
>
> That was the night that Shoob, now a senior U.S. district judge, quit waiting for others to decide the right thing to do. "Since then I have always

tried to do what I think is right, regardless of the consequences," he said. "My position has been and continues to be that I am going to call them as I see them. I didn't take this position to waffle on major decisions."[37]

On February 8, 2004—for the first time in U.S. history—Shoob ruled that abused and neglected children in Georgia's child welfare system have a right to an attorney at every major stage of their experience in state custody.[38] The decision came in the ongoing civil rights class action lawsuit, Kenny A. v. Perdue. "This is a landmark decision nationally and a huge victory for the rights of abused and neglected children," said Ira Lustbader, associate director of Children's Rights, the national advocacy organization that filed the lawsuit in 2002.[39] In his ruling, Judge Shoob denied efforts to prevent children from having their day in court, and ruled that enough evidence existed to proceed to trial on the claim of 3,000 abused and neglected children in the Atlanta metropolitan area that they were denied effective assistance of counsel while in the state's custody.

The metro Atlanta area includes Fulton and DeKalb counties. Children's Rights claimed that each child advocate attorney assigned to represent abused children in Fulton County had an average caseload of more than 400 children, more than four times the recommended number, and that attorneys in DeKalb County had more than 182 children. The national standard for such caseloads is no more than 100 children per attorney. Children's Rights argued that such high caseloads prevent children from getting effective legal assistance in a system plagued with dangerous deficiencies.

Judge Shoob concluded that plaintiff foster children have both a statutory and a constitutional right to counsel in all major child welfare proceedings. In the Atlanta area, these proceedings include

- an initial 72-hour detention hearing in which the juvenile court determines if the child should be placed in out-of-home foster care or returned to his or her parents,
- the adjudicatory hearing where the juvenile court determines whether in fact the abuse occurred,
- the dispositional hearing where the juvenile court determines where and with whom the child will be placed,
- periodic reviews of a child's status while in foster care, and
- proceedings in which the juvenile court determines whether to terminate the parental rights of a particular child's parents.

Rejecting the argument that lawyers from the state's attorney general's office representing children during foster care were adequate (such attorneys also represent Georgia's foster system and therefore such problems as children placed in overcrowded and inappropriate homes, shuffled from one home to another, and the overuse of institutional facilities for children), Judge Shoob found that children are entitled to representation by separate counsel at all times.

Previously, children in Georgia's welfare system received lawyers only when the state sought to terminate their parents' rights. Marvin Ventrell, who heads the National Association of Counsel for Children, appeared as an expert witness for the plaintiffs. Ventrell said that although there was a right to counsel in delinquency cases, ironically, abused and neglected children don't have that right. But if an appeals court agrees with Judge Shoob and thus creates case law, "It would be one of the biggest steps toward justice for children that we could make."[40]

The late Senator Hubert H. Humphrey once said, "The moral task of government is how it treats those in the dawn of life—the children; those in the twilight of life—the aged; and those in the shadows of life—the sick, the needy and the disadvantaged." Giving to children their most fundamental legal rights is a human and moral obligation, a task not yet fulfilled. The time to right this wrong is now.[41]

Endnotes

1. "Children allegedly caged during daytime," Thomas J. Sheeran, Associated Press, September 20, 2005.

2. "Absolutely barking," Meg Carter, *The (London) Independent*, June 2, 2004, 1.

3. Jill Elaine Hasday, "The Canon of Family Law," *Stanford Law Review*, Vol. 57, December 2004.

4. Peter Samuelson, "An Even More Modest Proposal." The Huffington Post, August 18, 2008. http://www.huffingtonpost.com/peter-samuelson/an-evan-more-modest-propo_b_118741.html

5. See Marcia Robinson Lowry, Donald C. Bross, Sheryl Dicker, and Lewis Pitts, *Perspectives on Child Advocacy Law in the Early 21st Century* (Washington, DC: American Bar Association Center on Children and the Law, 2000).

6. Planned Parenthood of Central Missouri v. Danforth, 428 US 52 74 (1976).

7. "Right to Counsel Principals," First Star working documents, http://www.firststar.org/policy/rtc.asp

8. Lowry, Bross, Dicker, and Pitts, *Perspectives on Child Advocacy Law,* 34.

9. Jean Guccione, "Case Sparks Debate Over Testimony by Children; Courts: Lawyer Says New Rules Are Needed To Protect Minors' Interests," *Los Angeles Times*, August 3, 2001.

10. Ibid.

11. *Victims of Child Abuse Act of 1999*, Public Law 101-647.

12. American Bar Association "Standards of Practice for Lawyers Who Represent Children in Abuse and Neglect Cases," approved by the American Bar Association House of Delegates, February 5, 1996, www.abanet.org/child/repstandwhole.pdf.

13. Ibid.; "American Bar Association Standards of Practice for Lawyers Representing a Child in Abuse and Neglect Cases," www.abanet.org/child/rep define.html.

14. Martha Minow, "What Ever Happened to Children's Rights?" *Minnesota Review* 80(267)(1995): 269–70.

15. Ibid. See also Gary A. Debele, "A Children's Rights Approach to Relocation: A Meaningful Best Interests Standard," *Journal of the American Academy of Matrimonial Lawyers* 15(1998): 75–118.

16. Ibid., 93.

17. Minow, "What Ever Happened to Children's Rights?" 287.

18. Telephone interview by Jenny L. Miller with Shari Shink, Executive Director, Rocky Mountain Children's Law Center, 2004.

19. Telephone interview by Jenny L. Miller with Robert Fellmeth, Director, Children's Advocacy Institute, Price Professor of Public Interest Law, University of San Diego, 2004–2006. Interview conducted in connection with First Star research.

20. Telephone interview by Jenny L. Miller with Lewis Pitts, Senior Managing Attorney, Advocates for Children's Services, Legal Aid of North Carolina, 2004–2006.

21. Telephone interview by Jenny L. Miller with Colene Robinson, formerly of the National Association of Counsel for Children, 2004–2006.

22. Miller interview with Fellmeth.

23. Miller interview with Shink.

24. Miller interview with Pitts.

25. Telephone interview by Jenny L. Miller with Jane Spinak, Clinical Law Professor, Columbia University, 2004–2006.

26. Miller interview with Pitts.

27. See John E. B. Myers, *Child Protection in America: Past, Present, and Future* (New York: Oxford University Press, 2006).

28. Miller interview with Fellmeth.

29. Ann M. Haralambie, *The Child's Attorney: A Guide to Representing Children in Custody, Adoption, and Protection Cases* (Washington, DC: American Bar Association, 1993), 13.

30. Ibid., 32.

31. Miller interview with Shink.

32. Miller interview with Robinson.

33. Miller interview with Spinak.

34. Miller interview with Shink.

35. American Prosecutors Research Institute, *Investigation and Prosecution of Child Abuse*, 3rd ed. (Thousand Oaks, CA: Sage Publications, 2004), 32.

36. Ibid., 33.

37. Lisa Crowe, "The Uncommon Candor of Judge Shoob," *Tech Topics* 31(3)(Spring 1995). http://beta.gtalumni.org/Publications/techtopics/spr95/shoob.html

38. Children's Rights news release, February 8, 2005.

39. Ibid.

40. Shaila Dewan, "Abused Children Are Found Entitled to Legal Aid," *The New York Times*, February 9, 2005.

41. Claudia J. Kennedy and Sherry Quirk, "Legal restrictions harming kids in child welfare system," *Chicago Sun-Times*, May 22, 2004.

6

Foster Care Today

"When I moved into Group Home C, I was 12. They promised me that this would be my home until I turned 18. I had been in so many other places before. 'C' was the first place that I really settled down. After I lived there three years, they decided to change it into a program where you only stayed for one year. I couldn't believe that they could do that!"[1]

—A foster child

On a cloudy Friday in spring 2006, the melting snowpack from northern California's massive mountains had caused flood warnings on rivers near the state capital Sacramento.

But California lawmakers that day heard a different kind of flood alert as William Bell, president of Casey Family Programs, spoke to the state assembly's select committee on foster care.

> Action is essential, Because if nothing changes, the outcomes for our most vulnerable children only worsen. Consider the next 15 years—to the year 2020.
>
> If nothing changes in the U.S. child welfare system, nearly 14 million confirmed cases of abuse and neglect will be reported. . . . 22,500 children will die of abuse and neglect, 9 million children will be placed in foster care, and more than 300,000 children will age out of foster care without adequate supports to successfully transition to adulthood. Of those 300,000 transitioning youth, 75,000 will experience homelessness, and 54,000 will become involved in the criminal justice system.

And for every young adult incarcerated, they do so at a cost of approximately $22,650 a year. That means for every former foster youth who is incarcerated—with an average prison sentence of about four and a half years—our state governments will spend about $102,000 in an effort to rehabilitate a life we could have positively influenced for so much less.

The bottom line is this: advocating for and supporting change for our most vulnerable children is the right thing to do and ultimately costs us so much less. Think of the value and contribution of those lives—as opposed to their cost—when they are given a path to success.[2]

Bell spoke eloquently of the one million children abused and neglected each year, of the overrepresentation of minority children in juvenile welfare and justice systems in California and across the country, of the struggle faced as children aging out of foster care try to build productive lives.

Every year in our country, more than 20,000 youth in foster care turn 18 and leave the system, often with little or no financial and family support. In California, that number is 4,000. The starting point they need is permanence—or, in simpler terms, lifelong connections with caring adults, who can help them transition to the workforce or higher education. Who among us was prepared for adulthood at 18 without the support of family and community?[3]

Twenty-five years earlier another Bell, the spouse of U.S. attorney general Griffin Bell, had led a commission that denounced the nation's foster care system as "an unconscionable failure," which harmed large numbers of the children it purported to serve. The commission cited constant movement of children from one foster home to another, inadequate payments to foster families—in some states less than the cost to kennel a dog—federal welfare money being used for foster care but not adoption; judges' reluctance to sever family ties no matter how unfit the family, and a hodgepodge of practices and rulings. "A surer system for harming children could hardly be invented than that which has grown up, like a pernicious weed, in the operation of foster care," the report had charged.[4]

How much has really changed in the last quarter century? For one thing, more has been learned about the system—a lot more.

Foster Families Challenged on Every Side

"Foster families are critically important; they can offer immediate comfort and stability to children in crisis," a 2005 *Baltimore Sun* editorial noted.

"But that is only if they do not fall into crisis themselves because of a lack of adequate support. That means money and services, as well as ensuring that caseworkers aren't so overworked that they have to overlook the small problems of a couple of families so they can put out another family's conflagration. Those small problems could well become next week's big disaster."[5]

The editors' words were directed at the state of Maryland, which had—for each of three succeeding years—cut state funding for local agencies to help foster parents with important things like child care, doctor and relative visits, transportation, and unexpected expenses like new beds or winter coats. A low monthly stipend that hadn't changed in a decade was also contributing to the state's hemorrhaging of foster parents at a time of unprecedented growth in the need for them.

People who have been in foster care generally consider it a positive experience in their lives. A national survey of child and adolescent well-being conducted by the Children's Bureau in the Department of Health and Human Services found that 90% of children age six or older who have spent a year or more in foster care "have positive views" of the people they live with, and more than half of the children report they were placed in better schools and neighborhoods. The same researchers, however, found that organizational problems such as large caseloads, high staff turnover, and data limitations compromise efforts to serve and monitor foster families.[6] Foster parents "often complain about receiving inadequate training; less than one-third report being well prepared, and often there is no reinforcement of what is learned in the training once the child comes home."[7] Many foster families cease foster parenting within their first year after finding the experience "overwhelming and frustrating."[8]

A glut of negative portrayals of foster parents on television and in movies and popular fiction doesn't help either. Positive media coverage is "heavily outweighed" by those negatives, according to researchers Bill Grimm and Julian Darwall. Moreover, such portrayals are made for an audience "largely ignorant of who foster parents are, what they do, and why they choose to open their homes to foster children. Most members of the general public do not have relatives or friends who are foster parents. Most do not know a foster parent. Few have ever been in juvenile or dependency court." Without such direct knowledge, people use popular media to form their opinions and, given the powerful images conveyed, "it is no wonder that a substantial number of people view foster parents as self-interested and uncaring."[9]

How have youths in the care of foster families fared? Almost simultaneously with *The Sun* editors' plea for more state support, Seattle-based Casey Family Programs had published its ground-breaking Northwest Alumni Study, which examined how 659 former foster youths in care between 1988 to 1998 had fared.[10]

Conducted by researchers from the University of Washington, Harvard, and the University of Michigan working with the Oregon Department of Human Services and the Washington State Department of Social and Health Services, the study looked at the long-term effects of foster care on adults now aged 20 to 33. The subjects were from Oregon and Washington but, the researchers asserted, the findings indicate national trends. The 659 respondents had spent an average of six years in foster care, suffering a mean placement charge rate of 1.4 placements per year.

Despite such challenges as unstable living conditions and abuse, more than 20% of adults who had been in foster care were doing well. On the other hand, posttraumatic stress disorder appeared twice as often as it does among U.S. war veterans. And most foster care alumni still faced major challenges in mental health, education, and employment. A third were living at or below poverty level, a third had no health insurance, and nearly a quarter had been homeless some time after leaving foster care.[11] Some of the key mental health and education findings are revealing.

Diagnoses in the year before the interviews showed that 54.4% had one or more mental health disorders.

- 25% suffered from posttraumatic stress disorder.
- 20% suffered major depression.
- 17% suffered social phobia.

Although alumni were as likely as members of the general population to complete high school, they were six times more likely to use GED credential programs to do so.

- 65% underwent seven or more school changes from elementary through high school.
- 56.5% earned a high school diploma.
- 28.5% obtained a GED credential.
- 42.7% had some education beyond high school.
- 20.6% earned a degree or certificate after high school.

- 16.1% earned a vocational degree (21.9% of those 25 and older).
- 1.8% earned a bachelor's degree (2.7% of those 25 and older).

William Bell summarized the study to California lawmakers:

While the study documented many success stories, other results we saw were disturbing. Particularly when examining issues regarding how foster youth transition to adulthood. The study showed that foster care alumni—in far greater proportion than the general population—suffered serious mental health issues, were far less likely to pursue and attain a college degree, and experienced difficult employment and financial situations that often led to unemployment, homelessness, and a lack of health insurance and medical benefits.

Taken individually, any one of these areas—mental health, education or employment—could knock a young adult off a path toward building a successful life. But when taken together, they present a nearly impossible set of obstacles for many foster youth.

In truth, when we fail to put in place comprehensive policies rooted in permanency and reinforced by adequate funding, training and essential relational and physical supports for children and youth in care, we are, to a very practical degree, failing them, and failing the communities in which they begin their independent adult lives.[12]

According to a 2004 report by the Packard Foundation, over the past two decades, the foster care system has dealt with an "unprecedented rise" in the number of children in foster care, as well as policy changes and "organizational impediments" (bureaucratic roadblocks) that complicate efforts to serve the children in foster care.[13]

To place the 799,000 children currently in foster care in perspective, consider them a city. Such a city would be one of the 30 largest in the United States. It would rank with Boston, Denver, Las Vegas, Oklahoma City, and Seattle, and be much larger than Minneapolis, Oakland, Atlanta, and Kansas City.

According to federal researchers, 60% of the children in protective care are there as a result of parental neglect, the rest because of emotional, physical, or sexual abuse. Of children who have been in foster homes for at least a year, 58% believe they will live with their parents again.[14]

Figure 6.1 shows the number of children in foster care in the United States. The 2005 estimate reflects a dip in numbers. But Robert Fellmeth of the University of San Diego warns against taking this to mean things are getting better. For some children they are. There are more children going into kin guardianship, especially in those states where there is reasonable financial support provided to the guardians. Fellmeth adds that there are more states trying some form of family preservation. Some are using probate court to establish relative guardianship, which saves money, and avoids foster care inclusion.

Fellmeth suggested a hard look, though, at the pendulum swing here in the effort to not remove children from families where abuse is suspected or even evident. "The safeguards where you remove too easily are many—hearings, an attorney for the parent, mandate to reunify, clear and convincing evidence standard and so on but in the other direction—not removing when you should have steps taken to protect him or her. . . nothing."[15]

The Children's Advocacy Institute, of which Fellmeth is the director, shared with us some as yet unpublished research findings that should raise a caution flag for those considering quick fixes in protecting children: "We got more information disclosed in California post 2005 (a real battle) and . . . surveyed about 5 months of 'deaths of children (not in foster care) from abuse or neglect'—75% of them had prior reports to CPS, and in over half of all these deaths, we traced the cause of death to the very subject matter of the CPS report."[16]

The Foster Care System Today

"There was this lady and her husband, and the old lady worked with deaf kids. The people were real nice. And one of the kids staying there was deaf in one ear. So he and I had fun and stuff. Everything was fine. I was there for about six months. I had to leave because it was a temporary placement. It was uncomfortable. Places that are temporary are usually the places that you want to stay anyway. That's how the thing is."[17]

—A foster child

Over the last 10 years, concerns about the child welfare system have led to reform efforts through targeted legislation, improved oversight, and increased data collection. Nonetheless, the system is still troubled by high rates of placement moves of children who stay in care, barriers to adopting children who are not likely to go home, high reentry rates for children who

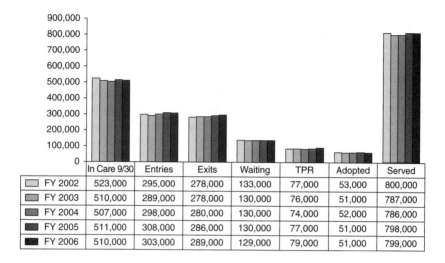

Figure 6.1   Trends in Foster Care and Adoption Fiscal Years 2002–2006

Source: AFCARS data, U.S. Children's Bureau, Administration for Children, Youth and Families.[18]

do return home, and particularly long stays of African American children. (For a summary of types of foster care placement, see Table 6.1.[19])

In a 1997 study, Richard Barth found that age and race tend to be a major factor in finding placements for foster children.[20] According to Barth, for children four to six years of age, the odds of being adopted are

Table 6.1   Type of Placements for Children in Foster Care, 2003

Type	Percent	Number
Foster family home (nonrelative)	46	239,810
Foster family home (relative)	23	121,030
Institution	10	51,370
Group home	9	45,700
Pre-adoptive home	5	24,650
Trial home visit	4	19,700
Runaway	2	10,560
Supervised independent living	1	5,570

Source: Grimm and Darwall 2005.[21]

five times lower than infants. Barth also attributed the long stays in foster care for African American children partially to the inadequate services provided to both these children and their families and to the short supply of African American adoptive homes.

As of 2001, about 38% of children in foster care were black, 37% were white, 17% Hispanic, and 8% of other racial-ethnic origin. Nearly 75% of foster care children were older than five. The average age was 10½ years.

"What should be a temporary safe haven has become a long ordeal for many children in foster care,"[22] said William H. Gray III, former House representative from Pennsylvania, president of the United Negro College Fund, and vice chair of the 2004 Pew Commission on Children in Foster Care. The chair was Bill Frenzel, Republican representative from Minnesota. "Almost half of the kids in foster care are there at least two years. Almost 1 in 5 children are there five or more years, and it's not unusual for them to move from one foster home to another to another without notice, without any expectation that their next home will be anything other than another temporary way station, without knowing if or when they will ever go home or join a permanent family."

Gray described several of the young people:

> The first thing that he did every day when he got home from school was to check whether his belongings had been packed.
>
> We met a young woman who learned from an early age to carry her school records with her so that every time she moved to a new foster home in a new school district she could show the principal what grades she should be in.
>
> We met twin sisters who spent their whole childhood apart from each other because they were put in different foster homes. They used to run away just to see each other and spend time together.
>
> No child should have to do that. No child should have to live this way. All children need safe, permanent families that love, nurture, protect and guide them.[23]

Federal Inflexibility Hurts Foster Kids

Federal laws passed in the 1990s have created a straitjacket that actually creates disincentives to successful foster care, according to Fostering Results, a Chicago-based research and education group based at the University of Illinois. "Promoting better outcomes for children in foster care means tackling the single greatest stranglehold on child welfare innovation—a federal financing system that favors interminable foster care stays over other services and options that can provide children with safe, permanent families."[24]

Federal funding for foster care—specifically, Title IV-E of the Social Security Act—was intended to help states remove children from dangerous homes and provide short-term foster care. As the largest source of federal money for child-welfare services, Title IV-E amounts to 53% of total spending on child welfare in the nation, but only kicks in once the child becomes a foster child.[25] In some ways, the effort actually backfired because intervention services still lacked federal funding. The problem was documented by the states' nationwide failures in the recently completed Child and Family Service Reviews, failures that jeopardized some of the $4.6 billion Title IV-E money that states received to help care for poor children.[26]

The *San Francisco Chronicle* described it this way:

> Perverse federal-financing rules have forced counties to needlessly remove thousands of children from their homes in order to provide them with any services. Even then, the funds are used mainly for board, care and administration . . . Financially-strapped counties are often left to find additional funding for other services, such as counseling and preventive programs. This rule has created a system that rewards failure.[27]

The "fundamental gap between outcomes and the strategies required to produce them reflects just one way in which the rules governing federal financial participation have not kept pace with what is needed to serve children and families," the Fostering Results report stated, somewhat more diplomatically.[28]

The federal straightjacket meant that states couldn't spend federal foster care dollars "on the services and strategies that could actually help give children safer, more stable, permanent homes. The report also shows that when states have been granted more flexible use of federal funding through 'waivers'—and then required to measure the results— several of those states have achieved success in reducing the number of children in foster care and the length of time that children spend in the foster care system."[29] The federal money could be used to pay foster parents and institutions, but it could not be spent on services to help families stay together, like mental health or substance abuse counseling.

Since 1995, states have been able to seek waivers to IV-E restrictions for demonstration projects to help find new approaches to child welfare service delivery. Such waiver projects are time-and-place limited, but even so more than half of the states have now at least attempted them— despite the fact that they involve no new money, but only more flexibility with existing dollars. Several of the more successful efforts are worth noting:

> Illinois used its waivers to subsidize private guardianship and give 6,800 children stable, permanent homes. The state reinvested the $28 million in federal "savings" it gained into other services, which helped reduce children in foster care from 51,000 to 19,000 in five years.

> Connecticut's waiver used federal funds to offer intensive residential mental health services to children in need, which cut the time they had to spend in foster care and improved their behavior once they returned home.

> Delaware cut by nearly one-third the time that children of drug and alcohol abusers spent in foster care, through a waiver program to identify families that needed immediate substance abuse treatment and services.

It took California two years to get congressional authorization for its Title IV-E waiver program. Indeed, the waiver was signed on March 31, 2006—the day the waiver authority was set to expire. The waiver was restricted to 20 counties in the huge state, however, and will expire after five years.[30] According to the Packard report, 25% of all children in foster care live in 12 cities and three of those cities—Los Angeles, San Jose, and San Diego—are in California. Researchers say such cities are perfect places to experiment with reforms.[31]

According to Lucy Hadi, head of the state's department of children and families, Florida's waiver, also obtained under the wire in 2006, "provides unprecedented flexibility for the state to use federal foster care funds for a wide variety of child welfare services such as early intervention and intensive in-home services." "It puts use of funds in line with program goals and good practice." That includes in-home services that help children remain at home "when this can be accomplished safely," "earlier and safer reunifications" and expedited permanency when reunification is impossible. "More importantly, the waiver can now support an array of services that address child well-being that cannot currently be funded through federal funds," Hadi added.[32]

The Straightjacket Tightens

In March 2006—10 years after Washington granted states a little flexibility to use their share of federal funds to improve foster care—the straightjacket was tightened once more. Programs that helped to stabilize families rather than remove children were about to go begging again. The federal budget reconciliation bill of 2006, which passed in Congress, allowed the Title IV-E waiver program to expire as of March 31. Once again, federal funding would cover only board, care, and administrative costs once a child is in foster care.

The *San Francisco Chronicle* put it this way:

> While the federal government requires that "reasonable efforts" be made by states to avoid removing a child from his or her home, such antiquated federal-financing rules practically promote it. . . . Federal financing for foster care demands a major overhaul. States should not have to apply for and await approval of waivers that only serve as temporary Band-Aids to a system-wide crisis.
>
> Programs that prevent children from going into the system should be a mandate, fully funded by the federal government, not something that has to be requested by a state in order to implement. If the government truly wants fewer children in the system, it must back its stated intentions with real dollars.[33]

Foster Care "Drift"

> *"When I was in the D's (foster home), I joined a police department. I was in a junior police academy. And I had graduated from the academy and everything. I made corporal so I was doing real well there. And a promotion was coming up. And then I left. I just started my first year in high school, and then I just disappeared and couldn't go."*[34]
>
> —A foster child

The system does not help to facilitate adoption or even permanency in many states. Often, it actually makes any kind of settled life nearly impossible for children in foster care.

The phrase *foster care drift* refers to situations when children are removed from their home on a temporary basis and then remain in out-of-home care for long periods of time.[35] Researchers often cite drift as a major issue that affects children in the foster care system. According to experts children with a higher number of placement changes are known to experience a decreased likelihood of reunification,[36] greater severity of behavior problems,[37] and more time in residential care.[38]

One in four boys in Cook County, Illinois, who enter the state's foster care system end up accused of crimes in juvenile court, new research indicates. Also, the more often boys move between homes within foster care, the more likely they are to have run-ins with police. For girls, at 8%, the correlation is much weaker. So found a massive study, undertaken by the University of Illinois Children and Family Research Center, of abused and neglected children in Cook County. The study also found that abused children removed from their parents were twice as likely to enter the juvenile-court system as those who returned to their parents' home.[39] On the other hand, although foster home changes are often attributed to children's behavior problems, only 20 percent are actually behavior related.[40]

Exploring the causes of placement change for a sample of 1,084 foster care children over one year, child placement expert Sigrid James found seven of every 10 changes occurred as a result of system or policy changes. The study defined such changes as "moves made to implement procedural, policy or system mandates." This included a variety of possible changes including routine moves from short-term facilities and moves to reunite siblings. Reviewing the research literature, James found other nonbehavioral reasons for placement changes include mismatching of child and family characteristics, unrealistic expectations by the foster family, and unforeseen life events.[41]

That would be cold comfort to Christine, who spent two months waiting for acceptance into the Apple Valley, California, school district. Christine was one of several foster children who have faced long delays in being enrolled in school there, according to the *Victorville Daily Press*. State law requires immediate enrollment of foster children, yet nearly every child at Christine's foster facility endured long delays—sometimes up to six months.[42]

When the children finally enter a classroom, they have to struggle to catch up on work where they've missed months of instruction. The school superintendent claims a lot of work needs to be done to glean the children's individual needs—but somehow non-foster children manage to enter the school district with no such delays.

A Hopeful Sign

One of the most difficult problems facing those trying to improve foster care and adoption from foster care is the loss of hope that grows with the child. With each additional year of age, a child becomes less adoptable. Can you imagine feeling completely unwanted? Is there much that is worse? Yet, foster children know that as they get older, families fear taking them into their homes. Perhaps some of these fears are legitimate. At the same time, so many children out there need homes and so many adults could love them. We need desperately to find ways to bring them together, to dispel the myth that an older child will only bring heartache. One article provides hope even as it recognizes the difficulties inherent in adopting foster children. But as we tell our own children, whom we adopted, "anything worth doing is difficult."

Monday, May 29, 2006

When Foster Teens Find a Home

More families are adopting older kids. But taking in an adolescent can create a new set of challenges for the parents and the child

By Anita Hamilton, *Time* Magazine

When Sabreena Boyd was 11, she stood before the congregation at the New Jerusalem Full Gospel Church in Muscatine, Iowa, and asked for a new family. A member of the church's Sunday school, she had recently been placed in a foster home after her mother could no longer care for her. "I gave a speech saying that I wanted to be adopted by a Christian family, a loving family," recalls Sabreena, now 20. Stuart and Tina Juarez, a recently married couple who heard her speak that day, were impressed by Sabreena's maturity and after much soul searching decided to give the girl a home. "We just knew we had to do it," says Stuart. "We saw a child in need, we prayed about it, and everything just fell into place."

Hamilton explained that Sabreena's experience of being adopted is on the increase.

"Over the past few years, the number of 12- to 18-year-olds adopted out of foster care has risen sharply, from 6,000 in 2000 to 10,000 in 2004. That's thanks, in part, to financial incentives and intensive campaigns to persuade people to take in some of society's most unwanted children. Monthly foster-care subsidies, which used to stop after a child was adopted, now continue typically until age 18 and average about $500 a month. In addition, the federal tax credit for adopting has more than doubled, from $5,000 in 2001 to $10,630 in 2005. And both national and state websites like adoptuskids.org and cominghomekansas.org have launched online photo galleries of older kids available for adoption.

(Continued)

(Continued)

Child-welfare advocates applaud the trend. Young people who "age out" of foster care because they fail to get adopted by the time they turn 18 are especially at risk for homelessness, unemployment, and incarceration. "When you grow up in foster care, you just don't get the skills it takes to develop a successful adulthood," says Brenda McCreight, author of *Parenting Your Older Adopted Child*.

It's important to mention that Sabreena did not make the Juarezes' lives easy. She ran away and got pregnant. She was a teenager being asked to change her life and it wasn't easy. It takes determined people who will love a child despite the letdowns to help a child rebelling.

This is Sabreena's story and that of three other children all indicating that adopting teen foster children is not an easy road, but as any parent can vouch, teens are rarely easy and it's important to know that going in.

Overcoming a Lost Childhood

Sabreena Boyd learned to cook, clean and take care of herself when she was just 7 because, she says, her birth mother was often too drunk or strung out on drugs to watch over her. After she moved in with the Juarezes, "I was told that I needed to try to live the rest of my childhood," says Sabreena. "But what does being a kid mean? I don't think I've ever gotten that explained to me."

The girl clicked right away with her adoptive dad Stuart, now 39 and a Baptist minister. Soon after she moved in, they painted her bedroom her favorite color—sky blue. And after school, Stuart would talk with her about her day. "It was me and Dad all day, every day," says Sabreena, who never met her biological father. Getting along with her new mom Tina, a state clerical worker, also 39, was harder. Says Sabreena: "We didn't have anything to say to each other. The only time we would talk was about chores." Says Tina: "Dad was the friend. Mom was the parent."

Like most teens, Sabreena didn't enjoy being told to put the dishes away or leave her bedroom door unlocked. But instead of sulking when she got really mad, she would run away—sometimes for a few hours, sometimes for a few days. At first when Sabreena disappeared, the Juarezes would call the police and go looking for her. But "that became very old because we could never find her," says Stuart. Eventually, they began leaving a sleeping bag outside the back door as a reminder that even if she didn't want to come inside, she never had to sleep on the streets. When she did come home, the Juarezes would talk to her about what happened and either ground her or give her extra chores. One technique, suggested by counselors, was called "time in," which meant that Sabreena had to stay close to her parents and do whatever they did.

But then Sabreena got pregnant. "It was very shocking," says Tina. "All the values we tried to instill, for a brief moment in time went out the window." Their disappointment was so intense that they wouldn't even drive her to doctor's appointments. "We stepped back as parents," admits Stuart. When the baby girl died just a few days after she was born, Sabreena felt even more alienated from her adoptive parents and ran away again.

It was only when Sabreena left home a few months later to attend Iowa State University, where she is now a senior, that she was able to restore her relationship with Stuart and, for the first time, establish a true bond with Tina. "I missed her more. I used to call her all the time and say, 'Mom, I love you,'" Sabreena recalls. She drew even closer to her parents after she married and became a mother. "I get another shot at Sabreena through her daughter," says Tina. "I can establish a relationship with her on another tone."

Respecting the Outsider

Unlike Sabreena, Dan Knapp never ran away or openly clashed with his adoptive mother. "He never gave me a problem. He just made me proud," says Jackie Knapp, 53, a single mom who is the education director at a Christian center in Elmira, N.Y. Placed in foster care at age 9 after his father died and his mother was unable to care for him on her own, Dan moved in with Jackie and her parents the next year. Now 24, he still remembers the meeting he attended in which his birth mother told the social worker that she was relinquishing her parental rights: "I was devastated," he says. "I was hearing my mother say she doesn't want me."

Such feelings of abandonment by the birth family are common among older adopted kids and can make it hard for them to trust any adult. "That your mom, the person who is supposed to be there for you no matter what in life, is the first person who actually wasn't there for you—that can be very painful," says Barry Chaffkin, a co-founder of the New York City–based adoption-services agency Changing the World One Child at a Time.

Now a college graduate and program coordinator at a teen center in Watkins Glen, N.Y., Dan says that in some ways he has always felt like an outsider. When his last name was changed to Knapp, after Jackie legally adopted him when he was 14, "I expected everything to magically change, and it never did," he says. "I still felt like I was a foster kid." He recalls how upset he felt when Jackie's mother occasionally introduced him as her adopted grandson and how his cousins always seemed to get more presents than he did when the extended family exchanged gifts at Christmastime. Moreover, he says, he and Jackie "never really connected on an emotional level."

After Dan got his driver's license in high school, he started spending less time at home. He also stopped talking at meals or skipped them altogether. "I kind of just closed off," he says. Jackie noticed the change in him but opted for a tolerant approach. "I just took it that he's a teenager," she says. "I just kind of gave him his space."

(Continued)

(Continued)

Then Dan went to college, and they started instant-messaging each other to stay in touch. Although he and Jackie IM several times a week and Dan says he would like to work on their relationship, one of the few times he remembers calling Jackie "Mom" to her face was four years ago at church. "She was at the altar praying, and I put my arm around her, and I called her Mom. I think she cried," he says. Jackie says she knew all along that it would be hard for Dan to call her Mom. "I realized that it was because of the loss of his own mom," she says, adding, "I don't know if he'll ever really get over that, but I'm hoping."

Balancing Family Loyalties

Many adopted teens are torn by split allegiances to their birth and adoptive families. A tall, bubbly 16-year-old who plays drums and dreams of being a pilot or neurophysicist, Lamar Stapleton says being in foster care "taught me a lot about life. When push comes to shove, you've only got yourself and your family." And by family, he means his birth family. In November, Lamar and his younger sister Nasia, 14, were adopted by Shirley Williams, 61, a single parent in New York City's Harlem who had already raised five of her own children.

Lamar, who had been in foster care since he was 4, is grateful to have a permanent home. He always calls Williams Mom, and he makes a point of hugging her every day and telling her that he loves her, but he says, "Seeing her as my mother—I don't think I can ever really do that because that would be blocking my [biological] mother out of my life." He continues to hope that he can find his missing birth mom and has even searched for her "once or twice" on the Internet. Having his sister with him helps, but sometimes the stress of dueling loyalties makes him moody. "He holds a lot in. I keep telling him it's not good holding in," says Williams. Admits Lamar: "I think I have less feelings than everybody else. Being in the [foster care] system kind of dilutes your emotions. I basically have two feelings. I am either happy or angry."

Experts acknowledge the conflict that many adopted teens experience and say letting them maintain a relationship with their birth parents (when safe) can help provide more continuity in their tumultuous lives. "We try to help kids realize that you're not replacing one family with another. You're building on," says Chaffkin, who counsels foster kids who are considering being adopted. Tina Juarez says one of the most important lessons she learned while raising Sabreena and the two younger children whom she and Stuart have also adopted is "Don't try and take their prior life away because they'll resent you for it."

Accepting the Wild Child

Yevonda Graham's childhood memories are mostly the stuff of nightmares. In and out of 36 foster homes, Vonda, now 22, says she was sexually abused by relatives, molested by a foster parent and raped as a teenager. By the time she got to the home of Dale Graham and Karla Groschelle in Whitley City, Ky., at 17, she had been in eight hospitals and three group homes and had just run away from her last foster home. Arriving at the couple's house for what she expected to be yet another short-term placement, she remembers, "I was so nervous, and I was just thinking to myself, Is this going to be another bad foster home?"

Instead she found that for the first time in her peripatetic life, she felt at home. Karla and Dale "didn't seem fake," she says. "Usually when I'd act up, my [other] foster parents would just send me away, but they didn't. They stuck in there with me." Even when Vonda's date wrecked Karla's brand-new Durango on prom night, Vonda remembers fondly that Karla was worried more about whether Vonda was hurt than about the car. In fact, for the first several months, things went so well that one evening Vonda sat Karla and Dale down in the living room and asked whether they would adopt her even though she was about to turn 18. "I wanted a place to always come home to," she says. "In a foster home, once you're 18, you're out." Recalls Dale, a sculptor: "She said she wanted a family that would always be there for her and for somebody to walk her down the aisle when she got married. Her approach was very sincere."

Vonda's adoption was finalized three weeks before her 18th birthday, but she's still waiting for her happy ending. At 13 she received a diagnosis of bipolar disorder. She never stayed on the prescribed medications but did get hooked on the painkiller OxyContin. ("I forget my problems. I forget everything," she says of her addiction.) When Karla, now 47, and Dale, 53, tried to intervene, Vonda resisted. Karla, a therapist, says Vonda once agreed to enroll in a rehab program and then checked herself out just three hours after she arrived. She was arrested in 2002 for breaking into a house to steal money for drugs and has been in and out of jail since then on charges including theft, identity theft and intoxication in a public place.

A 2005 study by Casey Family Programs, a foster-care foundation, and Harvard Medical School found that 54% of young adults formerly in foster care as adolescents (including those who later got adopted, aged out or were reunited with their birth family) have mental-health problems, including post-traumatic stress disorder and depression. "A big part of our counseling is telling parents how to ride this roller coaster," says Kathy Boyd, supervisor of post-adoption services in Chester County, Pa. No matter how rocky things get, Boyd advises parents never to cut off communication. "Even if the child is rejecting you 100%, call, write, keep that door open so a big chasm doesn't occur and that kid is never willing to open that door again." But she also tells parents to "take care of themselves and to accept that they cannot do everything. We're careful not to lay more guilt on the parents." Karla and Dale say their home is open to Vonda as long as she stays clean. But they have also come to accept that their daughter will make the ultimate choice about how to lead her life. "All we can do is be there for her and be supportive when she's going down the right direction and try to redirect her when she's going the wrong way," says Dale. That kind of commitment is what being a parent—to any child—is all about.

Training for Foster Families

"As for my foster parents, they made me the person I am today. They took in a heap of hideous mass and transformed a terrified child into a functional, responsible human being. . . . The Turnboughs were a godsend, with something so simple as teaching me how to walk, talk, and act like a normal child, while assuring me that I was worthy and could overcome any challenge that life had to offer. . . . The general public rarely, if ever, hears of the love and compassion for what some folks dub F-parents—as if the words foster parent belonged to a deadly epidemic."

—Dave Pelzer, author of *The Lost Boy*, of his
foster parents, Harold and Alice Turnbough

According to Brenda Jones Hardin, "making better training available to foster parents is essential." The Packard-affiliated researcher cited the complaints foster parents make about inadequate training:

Less than one-third report being well prepared.

Often there is no reinforcement of what is learned in the training once the child comes home.

Effective foster parent training models exist, but they are not used consistently across local child welfare organizations.

For many foster parents, the fragmentation and irregularity of support can be traumatic.[43]

As a result, Hardin reported, many certified foster families grow dissatisfied and quit within their first year of service. "Although better training is not the sole solution," Hardin explained, "It is one way to enhance the experience of foster parents and to motivate them to continue to serve. When foster parents receive quality training, they are more likely to retain their licenses, have greater placement lengths, and provide more favorable ratings of their experiences as foster parents."[44]

Aging Out of the System: Where Do I Go From Here?

"They're suddenly let loose in the world in a way that a family would never do it. They don't have jobs when they get out; they don't have places to live; they don't have money for food. They're really up against it."[45]

—Irving Piliavin, Professor Emeritus,
University of Wisconsin–Madison

Most 18-year-olds are contradiction personified. They're more street-wise than some grown-ups about many things in the world, yet remarkably naïve about economic reality: idealistic in some ways, yet jaded in others; struggling against constraints on their individuality, yet driven to ape their peers; compelled to strike out on their own, yet (increasingly, these days) dependent on their families. In a society such as ours, where most sons and daughters depend on their families until they are well into their 20s, if not longer, an 18-year-old is, relatively, a babe in the woods. Few 18-year-olds in our experience would be able to tackle the modern world in all its complexity, opacity, ruthlessness, and competitive indifference without the personal, moral, and financial support of a devoted family. It's hard enough to get by even with such support.

Yet each year, as many as 25,000 young people are released from foster care into the world on their own, many of them with little or no money, belongings, preparation, or guidance. For some, resilience and luck enable them to achieve productive lives. Others face a day-to-day struggle to survive and get by. All too many end up in desperate circumstances.

"As others before us have observed, Americans regard teenagers as the least lovable of our children," Martha Shirk and Gary Stangler wrote in their inspiring and compelling book *On Their Own: What Happens to Kids When They Age Out of the Foster Care System.* "Can we really hope to generate public support for enhancing the prospects of a subset of America's least lovable children? We think so."[46] Why? Their research showed that when people learned of the outcomes for children who age out of foster care, they expressed "surprise and dismay."

In Milwaukee County, 150 teens age out of the foster care system every year. The Lad Lake agency has had some success using a hands-on approach with former foster children, according to the *Milwaukee Journal Sentinel.*[47] The program operates with three caseworkers, two of them part-time. From the mid-1980s, the Bureau of Milwaukee Child Welfare attempted to prepare foster children for independence with 16 weeks of classes on such topics as personal finance, job interviewing, and dealing with landlords. In 1999, after passage of the federal Foster Care Independence Act, the state of Wisconsin formed an Independent Living Advisory Committee and adopted the Lad Lake approach, which included using foster parents and social workers to help the adolescents learn independent living skills. Some foster children "can participate in a supervised independent living program while remaining wards of the state. Then, when they age out of care, youths can sign up for Lad Lake's Connections program" where caseworkers help them find apartments and jobs.[48] Participants also receive some assistance with security deposits and rent for the first year. Some of the youths also are eligible for W-2, food stamps, and other assistance.

Teens must request the program. Asking for such help can be hard, especially at an age when youth feel that they've had enough of the child welfare system. Some just move back in with their parents. Worse is when youth run away from their foster homes and disappear. In 2004, of 454 eligible youths in Milwaukee County only 260 signed up. "A lot of 18-year-olds don't believe they need us, then they come back when they're 19," Karie Brophy, independent living coordinator for Lad Lake, told the *Journal Sentinel*.[49] Those who participate can stay with the program until they are 21, or 23 if in college, and caseworkers are available to help out with emergencies.

"It's kind of like we're their parents," Brophy said. "We teach and support them without carrying them." According to the *Journal Sentinel*, the Connections program received $218,000 in 2004 and Wisconsin received $1.9 million in yearly federal money "for independent living services and $600,000 for education and job training for former foster children."[50] A follow-up study of youth in Wisconsin, Illinois, and Iowa showed similar trends.

Irving Piliavin, a retired University of Wisconsin-Madison professor who co-authored the 1998 study, said teens leaving the system remain vulnerable.[51]

> "Programs such as Connections are a good start but don't go far enough," he said. He would like to see a system in which teens who age out of foster care receive a bank of emergency days. When rough times hit, they should have a place to go where they would be housed, fed, and protected, he said, adding that this idea has not received much support because many consider it too expensive.[52]

A Proposal for University-Based Foster Care

"We can't solve problems by using the same kind of thinking as when we created them."

—Albert Einstein

The proposal described here was developed by Kathleen Reardon as a way to bring the resources of universities to the problem of foster care.

The idea of campus-based foster care programs emerged from a discussion we were having while interviewing and researching for this book. We spoke about the limitations of foster care and the feelings of children who are fostered. Such children often feel trapped in a system that cares for their basic needs but doesn't seem to pay attention to them as people. One child described foster care as "a storage place. You were alive but not living." Others see it as "a system of punishment," one "that messes you up" and one you'd better not get used to because "they will move you, they will toss you around like a ball." These children often don't feel that anyone listens or believes them and often do feel that the people who decide their fate don't know them as anything other than a number.[53]

Add to this the hazards faced and created by many young people who exit the foster system—family dissolution, substance abuse, homelessness, domestic violence, and losing their own children to foster care. The abrupt end of support or supervision at age 18 contributes to many deficits for these young adults. Clearly, the present overloaded and overstressed system isn't working for many children or the adults they will become.

Over time, certain notions of how to cure a long-term problem have taken hold and become dominant. Many children have suffered and are suffering as a result. By accepting the status quo, we pass our troubles along to future generations, perpetuating them at colossal societal and human cost.

The answer is not to blame an overloaded system, but to relieve it with something that works. That something needs to be multilayered, capable of meeting the needs of abused and neglected children at many levels. Certainly, we need to encourage more individual families to take in foster children. We also must do more to train, assist, regulate, and support them. In reality, though, a tremendous shift in that direction— necessary though it may be—is unlikely to be achieved any time soon. That is why the issue of how to improve institutional foster care is a subject worthy of urgent attention.

This is where universities and colleges come in. Consider the environment that university and college campuses provide for their own students. Many students arrive feeling lonely, confused, or apprehensive, sometimes even isolated. Yet, within days or weeks, most are becoming or have become part of the campus culture. The support systems are there: counselors, peers, older students, support staff, and professors, all of whom can be turned to with issues. There is no foster mother or father, but rather a spectrum of resources for dealing constructively with academic and personal concerns. The whole student is the concern of any university or college worthy of a sound reputation. Doesn't this begin to sound like a reasonable model for how we could help foster children as well?

Family fostering works for many children—and for some of them it works well indeed. It would be a mistake to uproot children from supportive, familiar families if there are means to keep them there. But when such measures fail or are unavailable despite diligent efforts, we need other programs that respond thoroughly and appropriately to the foster child.

Good professors—and indeed all good teachers—know that when new students come to our office doors looking bewildered, often enough they're not there just to learn more about the subject. Very often they need to connect with someone. Each professor or lecturer is one lifeline among the many available to them.

Foster children need multiple lifelines too. They need them sooner and for longer. One possible advantage of campus-based residential care for foster children is competition for funding. Conducting federally or privately supported projects in professional, ethical ways is required by the rules of academic research. Stringent requirements minimize the likelihood of haphazard research, especially where human subjects are concerned. Fierce competition helps ensure adherence. Funding agencies therefore take university-based grant proposals seriously. No system is perfect, of course, but research universities and colleges are set up to ensure that funded projects are undertaken in the manner proposed. University and college grant awards require thorough applications and experts committed to carrying out the projects. Even if universities and colleges benefit financially, as they will, our concern is that the child benefit as a whole person. Because Kathleen has been a principal investigator on grants and has served as a reviewer for the National Institute of Health, she knows the level of competition out there. This competition can serve the needs of at-risk children who have been removed from their homes, by providing acknowledged experts planning residential programs for children who've waited too long and for those who are about to enter the foster system for the first time.

Substantial governmental funds are already being deployed to support children in far-from-ideal institutional foster care. This support averages $4,000 per child per month nationally. The cost per child per year was $220,000 at McLaren Hall, the Dickensian warehousing facility for foster children recently closed by Los Angeles County. The new university-based model proposed would ultimately save money and, more important, it would both allow children to be children, and serve society by better preparing them to successfully join family foster homes when possible, and in any case to live more fulfilling and productive lives. Of course, depending on the school, there is the benefit of access to specialists in medicine, psychology, sociology, communication, and education.

There is one other great plus to this proposal. College and university campuses have hundreds—sometimes even thousands—of young people interested in giving their time to worthwhile causes. They are at college for four or more years. Whether they major or do graduate work in social work, psychology and other social sciences, education (including special education), child development, family relations, communications, business, bioengineering, theatre, or chemistry, they can help foster children feel that people and society truly care about them. For starters, a campus-based program modeled on Big Brothers and Big Sisters would be quite feasible. People to help with homework, to play ball, and to talk are readily available on campuses. After graduation, or in graduate school, kids helped in this way are good sources for young, enthusiastic employees in the area.

We would want to be very concerned with who receives grant awards. Children should be housed properly, served excellently, and not used as guinea pigs. But these and other concerns are highly addressable.

In this context, the model of Hope Village, a program in Mississippi that is admired by First Star, warrants further examination. Hope Village has created individual cottages, staffed by married couples who live in the cottages full time, enabling long-term bonding and a familial atmosphere for the two to six children fostered in each cottage. Economies of scale and supervision stem from grouping the cottages on a single campus where activities and services can be coordinated centrally as appropriate.

The proximity of many colleges and universities to urban areas will be helpful as foster children are encouraged to maintain positive linkages to friends, relatives, and places as appropriate. At the University of Southern California, for example, we are surrounded by a huge, low-income, inner-city area where a large number of children who cannot be locally accommodated in individual family foster care are regularly exported over large distances to institutional care in different parts of sprawling Los Angeles County.

Many colleges and universities have excellent on-campus or campus-affiliated elementary and secondary schools. Given the right kind of support, it is likely that many foster children could be successfully tracked from these schools into higher-level education and good jobs. Children at such programs would be far less likely to fall off the cliff of supervision and support that is unfortunately too frequent across the United States. The key is support every step of the way and affection, familiarity, and consistency for these children. The responsibility of taking children onto (or nearby) campus may seem daunting to some, especially when some of them have special needs, but we are convinced of the potential.

Much needs to be considered, but we're on the right track if we think of how many options are likely to emerge.

Summary

Clearly, there are no easy answers to the question of how children removed from homes or parents should be cared for. Yet this is the very reason why we need to become more imaginative in doing so. Too many children are lost in the system and then abandoned by it when they turn 18. Again, surely we can do better. Our government representatives need to become very well aware of the suffering of children in their districts. They and we are responsible for those whose lives are turned upside down by the tragedy of abuse and neglect. This chapter is a start in providing a picture of the urgency of the situation. Each child's situation requires special consideration by people expertly trained to serve his or her best interests.

Endnotes

1. Susan Kools, "Self-Protection in Adolescents in Foster Care," *Journal of Child and Adolescent Psychiatric Nursing* 12(4)(October 1999): 139.

2. Testimony of William C. Bell, president and CEO of Casey Family Programs, before the California Assembly Select Committee on Foster Care, San Francisco (May 12, 2006).

3. Ibid.

4. Spencer Rich, "U.S. Foster Care Is Termed Harmful to Many Children," *Washington Post,* April 24, 1979, A2.

5. "Fostering families," *Baltimore Sun,* editorial, May 13, 2005, 18A.

6. Cheryl Wetzstein, "Child-Welfare System Flooded; Group Reports Judges Are Frustrated by Numbers," *Washington Times,* July 5, 2004, final edition, A04. The HHS study cited in the story involved 700 children, ages one to 15, and their representatives. More than 400 of those children were age six or older.

7. Sandra Stukes Chipungu and Tricia B. Bent-Goodley, "Meeting the Challenges of Contemporary Foster Care," *The Future of Children: Children, Families, and Foster Care* 14(1)(Winter 2004): 85.

8. Ibid., 75.

9. Bill Grimm and Julian Darwall, "Foster Parents: Who Are They? Reality v. Perception, Part II," *Youth Law News* 26(4)(2005).

10. Peter J. Pecora, Ronald C. Kessler, Jason Williams, Kirk O'Brien, A. Chris Downs, Diana English, James White, Eva Hiripi, Catherine Roller White, Tamera Wiggins, and Kate Holmes, *Improving Family Foster Care: Findings from the Northwest Foster Care Alumni Study* (Seattle: Casey Family Programs, 2005), www.casey.org/Resources/Publications/NorthwestAlumniStudy.htm.

11. Press release, "Former Foster Children in Washington and Oregon Suffer Post Traumatic Stress Disorder at Twice the Rate of U.S. War Veterans, According to New Study," Casey Family Programs, April 6, 2005.

12. Testimony of William C. Bell, May 12, 2006.

13. Stukes Chipungu and Bent-Goodley, "Meeting the Challenges," 75.

14. Cheryl Wetzstein, "Child-Welfare System Flooded," A04.

15. Kathleen Kelley Reardon email interview with Robert Fellmeth, June 2008.

16. Reardon interview with Fellmeth.

17. Susan Kools, "Self-Protection in Adolescents in Foster Care," 139.

18. Data for 1980–2000 from Chipungu and Bent-Goodley, "Meeting the Challenges," 75, which cites U.S. House of Representatives, 2000 Green Book: Overview of Entitlement Programs (Washington, DC: Government Printing Office, 2000); U.S. Department of Health and Human Services, AFCARS Report #6 (Washington, DC: U.S. Government Printing Office, 2001); and U.S. Department of Health and Human Services. AFCARS Report #7 (Washington, DC: U.S. Government Printing Office, 2002); data for 2005 from AFCARS, www.childwelfare.gov/pubs/factsheets/foster.cfm.

19. Mitchell, L. B., Barth, R. P., Green, R., Wall, A., Biemer, P., ʃerrick, J. D., & Webb, M. B. (2005). Child Welfare Reform in the United States: Findings from Local Agency Survey. *Child Welfare, 84*(1), pp. 5–25.

20. Brooks, D., Jame, S., & Barth, R. P. Preferred Characteristics of Children in Need of Adoption: Is There a Demand for Available Foster Children? *Social Services Review* (December 2002).

21. Adapted from the AFCARS Report (Preliminary FY 2003 Estimates as of April 2005), in Grimm and Darwall, "Foster Parents," 2005.

22. Adapted from "Fostering the Future: Safety, Permanence and Well-Being for Children in Foster Care," paper presented to The Pew Commission on Children in Foster Care, Washington, DC (May 18, 2004), 4.

23. Ibid.

24. *The Foster Care Straight Jacket: Innovation, Federal Financing and Accountability in State Foster Care Reform,* (Urbana-Champaign: University of Illinois, Fostering Results/Children and Family Research Center, School of Social Work, 2004), 4.

25. "Foster-Care Funding Flows," *San Francisco Chronicle,* editorial, April 6, 2006, B8.

26. *The Foster Care Straight Jacket*, 1.

27. "Foster-Care Funding Flows," B8.

28. *The Foster Care Straight Jacket*, p. 1.

29. Ibid.

30. "Foster-Care Funding Flows," B8.

31. Karen De Sa, "Foster Care Targeted; Study Finds Health, Education Often Neglected," *San Jose Mercury News*, January 29, 2004, 1B.

32. Lucy D. Hadi, "Waiver Means Money Will Go to Family Services," letter to the editor, *Sun-Sentinel* (Ft. Lauderdale), April 17, 2006, 21A.

33. "Feds Abandon Foster-Care Plan," *San Francisco Chronicle*, editorial, February 27, 2006, B6.

34. Susan Kools, "Self-Protection in Adolescents in Foster Care," 139.

35. Ramona W. Denby and Carla M. Curtis, "Why Special Populations Are Not the Target of Family Preservation Services: A Case for Program Reform," *Journal of Sociology and Social Welfare, 3*, June 2003. http://findarticles.com/p/articles/mi_m0CYZ/is_2_30/ai_101762547/pg_1?tag=artBody;col1

36. David Fanshel and Eugene Shinn, *Children in foster care: A longitudinal investigation*, New York: Columbia University Press, 1978. J. Landsverk, I. David, W. Ganger, R. Newton and I. Johnson, "Impact of child psychosocial functioning on reunification from out-of-home care," *Children and Youth Services Review, 18*, 4/5, 1998, 447–462.

37. R. Newton, A. J. Litrownik, J. Landsverk, "Children and youth in foster care: Disentangling the relationship between problem behaviors and number of placements," *Child Abuse and Neglect, 24*, 2000, 1363–1374.

38. Kathleen Wells and Dale Whittington, "Characteristics of youth referred to residential treatment: Implications for program design," *Children and Youth Services Review, 15*:3, 1993. 195–217.

39. Chris Fusco, "1 In 4 Boys in Foster Care Get Charged With Crimes," *Chicago Sun-Times*, January 14, 2004, 31.

40. Sigrid James, "Why do foster care placements disrupt? An investigation of reasons for placement change in foster care," *Social Service Review, 78*, 2004, 601–627.

41. K. Proch and M. Taber, "Placement disruption: A review of research," Children and Youth Services Review, 7, 1985, 309–320. Ilene Staff and Edith Fein, "Stability and change: Initial findings in a study of treatment foster care placements," *Children and Youth Services Review, 17*:3, 1995, 379–389.

42. Tracie Troha, "Kept out of school: Group home threatens to file lawsuit against Apple Valley School District over long delays to get students enrolled," *Daily Press* (Victorville, CA), March 6, 2006.

43. Chipungu and Bent-Goodley, "Meeting the Challenges," 85.

44. Brenda Jones Hardin, "Safety and Stability for Foster Children: A Developmental Perspective," *The Future of Children: Children, Families, and Foster Care* 14(1)(Winter 2004): 43–44.

45. Gina Barton, "Picking Up the Pieces: Young Adults Who've 'Aged Out' of Foster Care Can Get Help Learning to Handle Life on Their Own," *Milwaukee Journal Sentinel,* November 6, 2005, www.jsonline.com/news/metro/nov05/368464.asp.

46. Martha Shirk and Gary Stangler, *On Their Own: What Happens to Kids When They Age Out of the Foster Care System* (Cambridge, MA: Westview Press, 2004), 245.

47. Gina Barton, "Picking Up the Pieces."

48. Ibid.

49. Ibid.

50. Ibid.

51. Ibid.

52. Ibid.

53. See Emerich Thoma, "If you lived here, You'd be home by now: The business of Foster Care," *IPT Journal* 10(1998), www.ipt-forensics.com/journal/volume10/j10_10.htm.

7

Caseworker and Police Challenges—Who You Gonna Call?

Caseworkers are involved at every level of decision making. They link families with needed services, and they can, when their job is done right, provide children with a sense of continuity, a person who cares, something "often lacking in their foster care experience."[1]

Yet, despite the critical nature of their job, caseworkers often carry huge caseloads, are burdened by exhaustive paperwork, function with minimal training and are supervised by people with not much more preparation. They make life-altering decisions on behalf of children, yet children in foster care and foster parents find themselves left with little support in so many states and around the world. They must learn to work within the political climates of their organizations—often at odds with serving children—and adapt their styles, without good advice, to highly political and even pathologically political bureaucracies.[2]

In this chapter, we look at inadequacies and hopeful solutions in the training, initial and ongoing, and support of caseworkers and police. They are the frontline protectors of children at risk who know that theory may be useful but outstanding practice and support are what save children's lives.

The Extent of Their Burden

Child welfare workers are supposed to have between 12 and 18 cases, but most have far more, even as many as 100. How can caseworkers give children who need them attention under such conditions? Efforts to decrease these caseloads have been largely unsuccessful. Add to this a growing number of families with drug and alcohol problems and children with special needs entering the child welfare system. The number and complexity of cases, concern for their own safety, and enormous amounts of paperwork often overwhelm caseworkers.[3]

Breakdowns in the system of child protection leading to the deaths of children who may well have been saved have been reported by a number of newspapers. James Barron and Al Baker of the *New York Times* told the tragic story of Nixzmary Brown, a seven-year-old girl beaten to death by her stepfather for eating a container of yogurt. New York City Mayor Michael Bloomberg ordered an investigation into the breakdown in protection efforts that could have saved her life. He wanted to determine whether communications were a problem between the city agencies that tried to follow Nixzmary and exchange information about her.

The child's school had alerted child welfare that she frequently missed school, appeared undernourished, and once showed up at school with a black eye. Two detectives from a child abuse squad and a children's services representative had visited the school. Caseworkers went to Nixzmary's house, but no one answered the door.[4] On the surface it seemed that most people who could have saved Nixzmary did what they thought was required. Yet the girl died.

On nearby Long Island, a story in *Newsday* headlined "Awash in Abuse" detailed evidence of inadequacies in the child welfare system, particularly with regard to abuse and neglect. Child welfare investigators in Nassau and Suffolk counties weren't looking into abuse and neglect allegations within the two months required by the state.[5]

Judge David Freundlich, chief of Suffolk County Family Court, told *Newsday* that judges were becoming exhausted from the number of cases they were seeing, including more severe abuse cases and instances where children were tied to beds or even kept in cages.

"I get letters every day from the public reporting something. I never used to get that, never," Judge Freundlich was quoted as saying. "My judges are exhausted. The judges are there right now on a regular basis late at night because of the amount of emergencies."[6]

County child welfare workers were staggering under loads as high as 48 cases, more than four times the number recommended by the Child Welfare League of America. Caseworkers complained of mountainous paperwork loads.

Across the country in Seattle, things weren't much better. Social workers were overburdened by an unresponsive system, according to a *Seattle Post-Intelligencer* report by Claudia Rowe: "In the past five months in King County, social workers and child-welfare officials have spent hours sitting in contempt-of-court hearings for repeatedly failing to arrange mandated weekly reunion visits between troubled parents and children who have been removed from their homes." The visits were key in trying to reestablish bonds between parents and neglected children. But a cut in payments to the outside counselors who ran the meetings meant social workers had to work nights and weekends to have the meetings in addition to their other caseload duties, "unless a parent's relatives, neighbors or friends agree—after a cursory background check—to monitor the visits for free." Hundreds of parents and children were missing out on valuable hours spent together.[7]

One mother, Gisella Del-Rosario, lost custody of her four-year-old daughter after being arrested for theft and subsequently admitting to a drug problem. A court visitation order promised her two visits a week with the little girl. Del-Rosario said the visits with her daughter kept her going through a drug detox program. But then she didn't see the little girl for six weeks. When they finally got a chance to meet for a few hours, the child burst into tears at the end of the visit. Del-Rosario, believing the problem had been fixed, promised her daughter they would meet again the following Sunday. But the next week, once again, the visit fell through. Del-Rosario had to take the county to court in order to reestablish visits with her four-year-old daughter.[8] Staggering under heavy caseloads, some caseworkers were even held in contempt of court for failing to do their regular work and spend the extra hours to oversee visits between parents and children. "There is no way you can honestly expect social workers to take care of all these visits," one attorney for a parent said, charging the problem was not with the overworked caseworkers but rather with the system.[9]

The Systemic Problem

Surprisingly, there are no federal requirements regarding specific activities that caseworkers must perform during visits with children in foster care.[10] The Administration for Children and Families (ACF) reviews caseworker visits as part of its Child and Family Service Reviews (CFSRs).

As part of its Federal oversight role, ACF conducts reviews to assess state compliance with Federal requirements. These reviews include Title IV-E Eligibility reviews, Adoption and Foster Care Analysis and Reporting System reviews, Statewide Automated Child Welfare Information System reviews, and CFSRs. Of those reviews, only the CFSRs address the frequency and content of caseworker visits.[11]

ACF reviewed all 50 states, the District of Columbia, and Puerto Rico between 2001 and 2004. For approximately 50 cases per state the frequency of caseworker visits with children was assessed to ensure adequate monitoring of their safety and well-being and to determine whether visits focused on issues pertinent to case planning, service delivery, and goal attainment. States received a positive assessment (a strength rating) if visits were frequent and substantive enough. ACF reported that a strength rating for caseworker visits is associated with positive outcomes of achieving permanency and ensuring child safety.

The summary by ACF for 35 states provided details about caseworker visitation for the child welfare cases reviewed, which included both children in foster care and those receiving in-home services. Fourteen states were cited as needing improvement in the content of caseworker visits. Of the states assessed, 41 reported implementing standards addressing the content of caseworker visits at the state level. Thirty-eight of these had written standards specific to caseworker visits. Three reported having written documents addressing the content of caseworker visits, but as a part of broader program areas such as case planning and family service plans.[12]

Federal oversight is insignificant given the extent of the problems involved in caring for children at risk. States must comply with federal regulations to receive federal funding, but each state determines how services are provided to children in foster care. The ways children are cared for therefore vary considerably from state to state. In other words, the state where a child is born or raised determines to a large extent whether he or she will survive abuse and neglect. Children are being served or underserved according to where they happen to live. Many are simply lost in the system.

Some states directly provide foster care services to children. Other states have county-administered systems in which the state retains responsibility for the safety and well-being of children in foster care, and counties provide the services. It doesn't take a rocket scientist to figure out that problems at the intersection of two such systems are almost inevitable, especially given that oversight is inadequate. Complexity alone, to say nothing of communication requirements, makes serving children's needs difficult and, for many, impossible. As if this weren't enough of a threat to children at risk, some state- and county-administered programs contract a portion of, or even all, foster care services to private agencies.

To be eligible for foster care payments, states must submit a plan to be approved by the HHS secretary. Section 471(a)(22) of the act requires that the plan include "standards to ensure that children in foster care placements in public or private agencies are provided quality services that protect the safety and health of the children." In addition, the state plan must provide for the development of a written case plan for each child and provide for a case review system. The case plan must include steps for ensuring that the child receives safe and proper care and that services are provided to the child, parents, and foster parents to address the needs of the child while in foster care. State case review systems must include procedures for ensuring that the status of each child is reviewed at least every six months either by a court or by administrative review.[13]

When reviews are undertaken, three categories of child welfare outcomes are observed: safety, permanency, and well-being. In addition, the reviews address systemic factors affecting the child welfare system. If states are not found to be in substantial conformity, they must submit to ACF within 90 days a Program Improvement Plan (PIP) outlining steps to correct deficiencies. All states not in substantial conformity in the first round of CFSRs begin a full review two years after approval of their PIP. In this study, none, including the District of Columbia and Puerto Rico, were in substantial conformity after the first round.

For example, a Child and Family Service Review of June 1, 2004 indicated that Nevada was not in substantial conformity with the seven child welfare outcomes CFSR assesses. Also, performance was low—less than 75% substantially achieved—on all outcomes assessed. Key CFSR findings indicated that the Department of Child and Family Services (DCFS) was not "consistent in responding to maltreatment reports in a timely manner or establishing face-to-face contact with an alleged child victim in a reasonable timeframe." Also DCFS was found inconsistent in "(1) providing services to children and families to ensure children's safety while they remain in the home, or (2) addressing risk of harm to children by monitoring case progress through ongoing safety and risk assessment" and DCFS "experiences challenges in preventing maltreatment recurrence within a 6-month period."[14]

Reading this report is startling. How can we let children suffer under such conditions? Understatement such as "experiencing challenges in preventing maltreatment recurrence" is deplorable. These are children who are being maltreated over and over again but the understated wording is more suited to the less than adequate performance of a bicycle. No wonder we're not seeing extraordinary anger and outrage over consistent failing of our children's needs. The system itself, wording of many such reports suggest, downplays the horror.

The report continues with a delineation of barriers with regard to timely permanency, including (1) the frequent practice of the courts and the agency to pursue reunification even when the prognosis is poor; (2) agency-related delays in preparing the paperwork necessary for termination of parental rights (TPR) or for transfer to the adoption unit; (3) a reluctance to seek TPR if the child is not in an adoptive home; (4) a lack of available services to promote reunification; and (5) a lack of understanding of concurrent planning by the agency workers, courts, biological parents, and foster parents.[15]

Also noted in the report were too few visits to maintain a strong relationship between parents and children as well as the lowest performance on well-being outcomes ensuring and responding to children's mental health needs. Training of social workers and need for a license varied. Nevada administrative code requires all social workers and CPS staff, including supervisors, to be licensed. This requires ongoing training of 30 hours every two years to maintain a license. According to a statewide assessment, however, access to training and quality of training were problematic.[16]

Similar reports for other states reinforce that where a child lives predicts the level of services and even likelihood of obtaining permanency. Children at risk, then, are at the mercy of geographic circumstance. In addition, where caseworkers are employed also dictates the extent to which they are adequately trained, supported, overburdened, and even protected from legal charges for not providing good care.

Assessing Training

Surely excellence and consistency in training is part of the solution equation. ACF also funded a 2004 initiative by the National Resource Center for Family Centered Practice and Permanency Planning to develop training materials for states to guide the content of caseworker visits.

The training materials state that caseworker visitation is "not a friendly visit or an opportunity to chat about how the kids are doing." Instead, the visit should be well planned, purposeful, and focused on children's safety, well-being, and permanency.[17] ACF emphasizes that the visits focus on content relevant to the safety and well-being of children. The performance of many states was decidedly poor.

Surely the United States can do better, especially considering what is at stake for the children and the country and the costs involved. The federal budget for the Foster Care program in fiscal year 2005 was $4.9 billion. The U.S. Department of Health and Human Services anticipated at that time that it would provide funding monthly for 233,000 children eligible for assistance under Title IV-E. States receive federal matching funds under Title IV-E for children in foster care whose families meet income requirements. Who's minding the store? In too many cases, the answer is people who care but are without power or people without enough concern for powerless children.

This conclusion is evident in the story of 12-year-old Kursti Adkins, whose two-year-old half-sister was separated from her, taken from Alaska, and placed with a grandmother in Maryland in 2006. It is a heart-wrenching story of family separation that could have been negotiated more effectively for all involved—even though everyone appears to have had good intentions.

As Lisa Demer reported in the *Anchorage Daily News*, Kursti's father had died when she was six.[18] Kursti was the oldest of four children, each with a different father. After her own father died, Kursti's mother became involved with drugs. One of the mother's subsequent partners was periodically violent. Kursti assumed much of the care for her little sister, Mary Jaine, feeding her, changing her diapers, and comforting her.

Over time, all the children went into foster care. Kursti's maternal grandmother, who lived nearby, saw the problems in the home and took Kursti and her brother in. Mary Jaine stayed with her parents, but after being brought to Alaska Regional hospital with suspicious injuries, was placed in a local foster home along with her newborn brother.

Kursti and Mary Jaine stayed in close touch with numerous visits, and Kursti was invited for sleepovers, parties, and special events. Mary Jaine thrived, but the foster parents had never cared for a newborn baby before, and when the baby lost weight from accidentally being bottle-fed with undersized nipples, the two children were again taken by the state.

Kursti learned from her mother that the state intended to send Mary Jaine to Maryland, where her paternal grandmother lived. Instead of being placed nearby—or even with Kursti and her brother, because Kursti's grandmother was willing to take in Mary Jaine to keep the siblings together—the child would be shipped thousands of miles away.

When social workers, attorneys, and the grandmothers (by telephone) met to determine where Mary Jaine should live, Kursti stayed home from school in hopes that they would let her give (also by telephone) a four-page speech she had written, asking the state to help keep Mary Jaine and Kursti in each other's lives. No state official ever asked her opinion, however.

Mary Jaine was sent to Maryland, and Kursti was reduced to keeping a log of their telephone calls to each other. Alaska State Representative John Coghill learned about the case and was considering legislation to more specifically urge that siblings be kept together. The state also planned to fly Kursti and her brother to Maryland for a visit, but Kursti felt that she was losing her little sister. "I wanted to teach her how to ride a bike," Kursti told the reporter. "I wanted to hug her—a ton—and if she's in Maryland how I am supposed to hug her? . . . Most likely she's going to forget about me and everybody that is really important to her."[19]

What's particularly interesting in Kursti Adkins' case is that Alaska is one of those states that has been trying to keep children with their siblings. Federal standards specify that this should be the case whenever possible. Reporter Demer reviewed the statistics for 23 foster care cases in 2002 and found that in 12 cases the child was in foster care with at least one sibling, but in eight others, the child had been separated from all siblings. Reasons for the separation were often related to the special treatment needed for one or more of the children. Alaska was deemed by the federal government to have done the right thing in 90% of cases. During the 12 previous months, though, about 7% of Alaska's children in foster care were placed out of state.[20] Again, each placement was made for very good reasons.

Kursti's loss, though, makes us once again ask if we are really doing enough. Is there something those who worked with her might have done to make sure Kursti's fear of her sister forgetting her doesn't become a reality? Surely if parents are allowed visitation rights and access even if they have caused children significant pain, then a caring older sister should be afforded even more accessibility.

What Can the Federal Government Do?

A Kind of ROTC for Caseworkers

The Packard Foundation report suggests a promising way to grow the number of qualified social workers and recruit people to enter critical professions needed to protect children:

> The [federal] government could consider creating a loan forgiveness program for social work students. Loan forgiveness programs are a useful means of attracting individuals to enter critical professions that lack qualified staff. Under such a program, students majoring in social work would be offered loans to support their academic work. Upon graduation, students who went on to employment in a child welfare agency for a specified period of time would have their loans forgiven. Several successful loan forgiveness programs are in operation. For example, to encourage health professionals to consider careers in such fields as clinical, pediatric, and health disparities research, the National Institute of Child Health and Human Development loan repayment program will repay loans associated with training costs, in exchange for a two-year commitment to work in the selected field of study.[21]

We desperately need the equivalent of a ROTC for social workers—a Caseworker Education and Training Corps (CWETC, possibly pronounced *sweets*) that would recruit and train students, paying their college tuition in trade for working as caseworkers. In addition, we need not only to raise the standards of professions working with children at risk, but also the respect given to those who do it well. They should be celebrated. Theirs is largely a thankless job yet one of the most important parts of our social safety net. If we help them do their jobs well and increase professional standards while also providing realistic training and support, many children's lives would be saved each year.

For those who don't participate in a program like CWETC, a non-college, rigorous certificate program with credits useable toward a possible future degree is an alternative. The Packard Report addresses federal assistance in training through private agencies. Another alternative would be contracting with local colleges and universities.

The federal government provides matching funds for staff training and development of up to 75% for public workers but only up to 50% for private workers. Given that private workers make up a large portion of the child welfare workforce, the government should consider equalizing the reimbursement rate to private agencies for training and development to aid in the recruitment and retention of these vitally important workers.[22]

Learning From Mistakes

The current climate in child protection encourages hiding mistakes rather than deriving some benefit from them.

The necessity of learning from mistakes and passing on wisdom is exactly the view of some in the trenches and those who represent them. Harry Spence, the Department of Social Services commissioner for Massachusetts, believes that instead of firing social workers when a child is neglected on their watch, the state should encourage them to be honest about their mistakes so that the system can learn from them, rather than to lie to protect their jobs.[23]

"Children who feel deeply betrayed by adult authority are not best helped by adults who expect to be betrayed by adult authority," Spence told the legislature's Joint Committee on Children and Families, according to the *Boston Globe*. Children, he believed, would be better served by moving from "a punitive culture to a learning culture." In a "system of blame and punishment" professionals will tend to act purely defensively. "Errors occur every day," he said. "The question is how quickly can we learn from them? What can we do to put in safety nets to ensure that when an error occurs its consequences are minimized?"[24]

Of course, a learning-from-our-mistakes approach cannot excuse incompetence. On-the-job learning can be too late when it comes to protecting children at risk for abuse and neglect. Some happy medium is required where as much learning as possible goes on before responsibility for the lives of children is handed over. This means that training for caseworkers must be outstanding everywhere. We would not consider sending a novice into a wood shop or onto a farm to work with massive machinery, and yet we often do send the inexperienced and inadequately trained into the field to work with children whose lives have already been turned upside down, often by horrific circumstances. We reason, for some unacceptable reason, that this problem is so massive, like dancing with a bear, that no one can take the lead and all evaluations must be watered down in accordance with reality. This is unacceptable. It is also more often than not unrelated to the commitment of caseworkers. They work with the tools they are given and those tools are, far too often, woefully inadequate. As just one example, caseworkers need training in the politics of working within bureaucracies so they can successfully initiate and sustain positive change.

What a Caring, Well-Trained, Supported Caseworker Can Do for a Child

This 2006 *Washington Post* article describes the type of impact caring adults can have on children's lives.[25] The hero is Ginnie Volkman, who took her job overseeing six-year-old Darryl's eye care very seriously. Volkman does this without pay, which is, of course, not what we recommend as the norm. Caseworkers should be paid and paid well for what is a very difficult job.

Keeping Watch Over Children in the System: CASA Volunteers Help Judges Decide What's Best for Kids in Troubled Families

By Jerry Markon

Darryl, 6, stares at his new glasses and slowly runs his fingers along the frames. He breathes on them, cleans them on his shirt and then does it again, and again.

He's stalling because he doesn't want to put them on.

But a visitor to his Alexandria home on this recent Monday morning is determined to make sure he wears them.

"Let me see your glasses," says Ginnie Volkman, a volunteer with the Court-Appointed Special Advocate, or CASA, program.

Darryl quickly puts the spectacles on his nose.

"You look pretty handsome," Volkman says to laughter from four of Darryl's siblings. "So, are you going to wear your glasses?"

"Yes," Darryl answers quietly.

The importance of Darryl's glasses goes far beyond a child's vanity. Darryl has a disorder called strabismus, and glasses are required to correct it. But his mother, a former substance abuser who receives public assistance, neglected to get Darryl's glasses for several months—landing her in Alexandria's juvenile court system for medical neglect.

Volkman can recite intimate details of Darryl's condition. That's because she interviewed his eye doctor and then researched the condition extensively.

(Continued)

(Continued)

She knows that Darryl almost never wears glasses at school. She talked to his teacher.

And Volkman does all of this, the visits to Darryl's house and school, the conversations with his doctors and social workers, in her spare time—without being paid.

She is one of 55 CASA volunteers who choose to immerse themselves in the lives of troubled children, those who have been neglected or abused by their parents or guardians. The program began in Alexandria in 1988 and is a fixture of the city's Juvenile and Domestic Relations District Court.

Volkman, 64, a former Fairfax County Spanish teacher, began volunteering last year because being retired "wasn't enough to keep me busy. When I volunteer to do something, I do it wholeheartedly. You can't just step into a child's life and then step out in a week. It's a cause."

Darryl's mother, whose last name is being withheld to protect Darryl's privacy, began to tear up when she discussed Volkman and the CASA program. "This is heaven-sent for me. It's just such a blessing," she said. "I think it's amazing that she does all this without getting paid, to have to go into people's homes and keep calling and making school visits. It's quite a job."

After 20 years of abusing alcohol and such drugs as crack cocaine, Darryl's mother said she has been drug-free for 14 months. "CASA gives me a sense that it's going to be okay, that the smoke has cleared," she said.

Volkman said the woman has made great progress in getting her life together and is "a poster child, one of our success stories."

Yet problems linger. Darryl didn't have glasses for months after losing them and got his newest pair only last month. At a recent eye appointment, his mother learned that the eye disorder—an imbalance in the muscles of the eyeball that can lead to functional blindness—had spread to his other eye.

It was her inability to care for the problem, along with a skin condition characterized by boils that afflicted Darryl's 8-year-old sister that landed her in juvenile court. A judge last year ordered the woman to take Darryl to an ophthalmologist and to take care of the condition.

On this recent Monday, Volkman enters the family's cramped living room to visit the mother and five of her seven children. Only Darryl and his sister are in the court system, but Volkman said the other children suffer from developmental delays and have problems in school.

The mother begins by saying she missed Darryl's follow-up eye appointment the previous week because she couldn't get a ride, and says she can't get another appointment until September. "I'm terribly upset," she says.

Volkman gently questions her, maintaining the air of an aunt or good friend. "I have some goodies," she says, toting a bag of Fourth of July glow sticks.

As the children gather, Volkman asks about summer school, camp and swimming, and gives an impromptu Spanish lesson. She asks repeatedly about Darryl's glasses and pays special attention to the 8-year-old sister, rubbing her back and running her hands through the girl's braids.

"Have you been drawing lately?" she asks the girl, whose skin condition has improved markedly. "You know what I want you to do? I'd like you to draw a picture of your whole family and give it to me, because I know you're good at art."

The girl agrees, and then happily volunteers that her birthday is coming up. "In this family, you probably have a birthday every month," Volkman says to laughter from the children.

Soon, the 15-minute visit is over, as is any chance that Darryl will keep his glasses on. It's time to go swimming.

"Yeah!" he yells.

"You all have a happy Fourth of July," Volkman says as she leaves. She will return within a few weeks. "It's going to take time," she says.

CASA volunteers are meant to be the system's eyes and ears when children are placed in the system. In Alexandria, Virginia, the volunteers work with the Department of Social Services on problems that range from physical abuse to parents not properly feeding their children or leaving them unattended. They start by going through the court file and then interview the child and every important person in the child's life, including parents, social workers and mental health therapists.

CASA volunteer compile all this information into a report for the judge, including what the volunteer thinks is best for the child. That may be putting or keeping children in foster care, returning them to their parents or even recommending adoption. The volunteer then follows the case, visiting the child at least monthly, until the child's life has stabilized to the point where the file is closed. In his article about Ginnie Volkman, Markon described his interactions with others who give of their time to help kids at risk:

> "I think children kind of get lost in the system," said Jennifer Marfino, 35, an Arlington boutique owner who began volunteering last year. "The social services people are amazing, but they are completely overworked. They might have 20 cases, and each one is really intense. We plug a gap in the system, and we give the child a voice."

Volunteers can stay on a case anywhere from six months to three years and can work as much as 15 to 20 hours a week. Cannon said one volunteer just finished a case in which she was the only person to stay with the child all three years—the social workers, lawyers and foster homes all changed, as did the child's school.

The volunteers include students and real estate agents, engineers and retirees. They must be at least 21, pass a series of background checks and be willing to undergo a six-week training course. CASA officials said they have no problem finding volunteers through the Internet, ads in newspapers and word of mouth.

(Continued)

(Continued)

"It's amazing that the state puts their faith in volunteers and allows them to do this and that people are willing to do it," Marfino said. "I think all volunteer work is important, but you are really putting your mind to use here, and it's so intense."

Sometimes, the intensity can make the work difficult. "These children have suffered tremendous pain," said Tim Stock, 67, a retired corporate lawyer who began volunteering seven years ago. "They are being separated from their parents, who may well have been abusive toward them, but they're still the parents and they love them. It's painful to see a child go through that."

But Stock and other volunteers said the benefits are worth any emotional toll. "The satisfaction of knowing that you've done something for these kids is beyond price," Stock said. "There was tremendous intellectual and professional satisfaction doing what I did as an attorney, but this is human, this is real. It's a different order of satisfaction."

Challenges of Police Involvement

CPS workers and police officers come from different professional cultures. Police officers are used to making quick, often life-and-death decisions in their jobs. CPS workers are frequently involved in shared, often protracted decision making involving supervisors and other officials.

Yet, as Nixzmary Brown's death reminds us, collaborative teams are usually needed to investigate cases. Problems, beyond those relating to cooperation in police or CPS collaboration, may thwart even the best intentions regarding cross referrals. First, people are more reluctant to report child abuse to the police. Reporting an incident to CPS may seem more reasonable and less harsh. Furthermore, citizens may receive explicit or implicit messages that abuse and neglect are family matters. People may believe that most police stations or departments are not set up to deal with child abuse; they may also feel some embarrassment or shame in calling the police. In late 1999, the U.S. Justice Department reported that only 28% of all violent crimes against children were reported to the police, compared with 48% of crimes against adults.[26]

Second, the experience of those in the field is that CPS continues to be perceived by both agencies as the lead agency for child abuse and neglect cases. CPS agencies across the country certainly have an interest in protecting the funding they already receive. Giving away turf to a separate governmental entity might allow political enemies of CPS to argue for vast reductions in funding for CPS.

Many police officers are wary of intervening in domestic calls because of the perceived heightened threat of violence when intervening in family disputes. But again, as Nixzmary Brown's case demonstrates, police involvement is often necessary to exert the force of law in protecting children.

Child advocates in the field believe that even where joint agreements between CPS and the police are in place, CPS still ends up handling the brunt of the investigatory work. And because most CPS workers are not trained in specific law-enforcement investigatory techniques, the evidence turned over to the police is often insufficient or not credible. By the time police department experts get involved in child abuse and neglect crimes, crucial evidence has been lost, destroyed, or spoiled.

Ways to overcome these challenges need to be sorted out if we are to better protect children from abuse and neglect. First Star's Multidisciplinary Centers of Excellence are an opportunity for training in collaboration among all those working within the same regions. It is important to deal with common wisdom such as "It's better not to interfere with families" or turf divisions that aren't conducive to helping children at risk. The only way to do that effectively is to get the people such children depend on together for training and to assist them in developing protocols to which they can turn so that no child falls through a gap to become a statistic.

Summary

Good people with exemplary intentions are not enough to save children from abuse and neglect. Every day we ask caseworkers and police to be courageous—to step out from under the radar, the tendency to do only what the system requires, and to rock the boat—without providing them with the support they need to do so. Courage is a tall order under even the best of circumstances. To be courageous, to do the best and right thing, those who work with children need to be well prepared and supported (this, of course, also increases the odds of their success). Potential heroes for children at risk need the support of the federal and state governments. They can't be expected to go it alone. Just as important, excellent support in one area of the country shouldn't be offset by meager support in another area. If we develop a highly supportive system, the need for courage—going beyond the expected to do the right thing for children at risk—would become more rare as acting courageously becomes the norm. Until we get that far, there will continue to be cases like that of Nixzmary Brown and innocent lives will continue to be lost because people who could make a difference decided it was simply beyond them.

Endnotes

1. Sandra Bass, Margie Shields, and Richard Behrman, "Children, Families and Foster Care," *The Future of Children* 14(1)(Winter 2004): 5–29.

2. See Chapter 8 and Kathleen Kelley Reardon, *The Secret Handshake: Mastering the Politics of the Business Inner Circle* (New York: Doubleday, 2002) and *It's All Politics: Winning in a World Where Hard Work and Talent Aren't Enough* (New York: Doubleday, 2005).

3. Reardon, *The Secret Handshake* and *It's All Politics*.

4. James Baron and Al Baker, "Bloomberg Orders Inquiry in Death of Abused Girl, 7," *New York Times*, January 14, 2006.

5. Lauren Terrazzano, "Awash in Abuse: Child Welfare Caseworkers Unable to Keep Up with Surge in Abuse Reports," Newsday.com, February 28, 2006.

6. Ibid.

7. Claudia Rowe, "Social workers can't keep up with child-welfare visits," *Seattle Post-Intelligencer*, November 22, 2005, http://seattlepi.nwsource.com/local/249280_visitation22.html.

8. Ibid.

9. Ibid.

10. Office of Inspector General, *State Standards and Practices for Content of Caseworker Visits with Children in Foster Care*, OEI-04-03-00351 (Washington, DC: U.S. Department of Health and Human Services, 2005).

11. Ibid.

12. The difference between the CFSRs and this Office of Inspector General (OIG) evaluation is that the CFSRs include a detailed review of approximately 50 child welfare cases per state (a combination of foster care cases and those receiving in-home services), whereas the OIG evaluation focused exclusively on state standards for children in foster care. OIG's report provides an analysis of states' written standards for the content of visits, as well as reported content activities for states without standards.

13. From page 4 of the OIG report: "This report is the second in a series of three about caseworker visits with children in foster care. In the first, *State Standards and Capacity to Track Frequency of Caseworker Visits with Children in Foster Care*, OEI-04-03-00350 (Washington, DC: U.S. Department of Health and Human Services, 2005), OIG examined standards states have established related to the frequency of caseworker visits. The third, *Compendium of State*

Standards: Content of Caseworker Visits with Children in Foster Care, OEI-04-03-00353 (Washington, DC: U.S. Department of Health and Human Services, 2005), provides state written standards guiding the content of caseworker visits with children in foster care. The compendium includes standards provided by 38 states. In addition to OIG work, the Government Accountability Office examined the CFSRs in a 2004 evaluation and found that ACF and states viewed the CFSRs as a valuable process. The report offered several recommendations to further improve the CFSRs."

14. Administration for Children and Families, *Final Report, Nevada Child and Family Services Review* (Washington, DC: U.S. Department of Health and Human Services, 2004).

15. Ibid.

16. Ibid., 73.

17. Office of Inspector General, *State Standards and Practices for Content of Caseworker Visits with Children in Foster Care*, OEI-04-03-00351 (Washington, DC: U.S. Department of Health and Human Services, 2005), 4.

18. Lisa Demer, "A Sister's Love, The State's Call," *Anchorage Daily News*, February 4, 2007.

19. Ibid.

20. Ibid.

21. Packard Foundation Report, winter, 2004.

22. Ibid.

23. Janette Neuwahl, "DSS commissioner urges end to 'punitive culture' for social workers," *Boston Globe*, May 10, 2005, www.boston.com/news/local/articles/2005/05/10/dss_commissioner_urges_end_to_punitive_culture_for_social_workers.

24. Ibid.

25. Jerry Markon, "Keeping watch over children in the system: CASA volunteers help judges decide what's best for kids in troubled families," *Washington Post*, July 13, 2006, VA 14.

26. David Finkelhor and Richard Ormrod, *Reporting Crimes Against Juveniles* (Washington, DC: U.S. Department of Justice, Office of Juvenile Justice and Delinquency Prevention 1999), 3, www.ncjrs.org/html/ojjdp/jjbul9911-3/contents.html.

8

The Politics of Child Abuse and Neglect

"They couldn't be more alone. They are no one's natural constituency."

—Bob Herbert, *New York Times*

In our post–9-11 world, terrorism for those living in the United States is a very real and immediate threat. Yet for the vast majority of us, even this closer proximity to the reality of terrorism is not nearly as imminent and personally threatening as domestic violence is for children. Children can't come together to determine a strategy for mutual defense. Children can't benefit from red, yellow, or green alert levels. Their terrorists strike without warning, largely without media coverage and—worse—without causing an outraged national response.

Of course, those few children who wind up in the media spotlight of a Bob Herbert column or a television news human-interest story claw at the hearts of Americans. But what about the 15,000 who have died in the last decade from domestic violence? The 2008 Children's Advocacy Institute and First Star report on state secrecy and child deaths reveals that approximately 1,500 children are still dying each year from abuse and neglect.

At least four American children die from abuse and neglect every day. According to the watchdog group Children's Rights, the actual number is higher due to reporting deficiencies. Nearly half of those dead American children are less than one year old when their hearts stop forever. Three in four are toddlers—under four years. Just as heartrending, one in three are the subjects of an open child welfare case in their locality.[1]

Moreover, the situation is getting worse. In 1999, child fatalities were at a rate of 1.62 per 100,000 population. By 2,000, the rate was 2.0. That is, two children die each year from abuse and neglect in American cities the size of Stamford, Connecticut.

So, what about the 15,000 American children who have perished at the hands of their own private terrorists in the last decade? These children didn't die from smoking, auto accidents, cancer, or coronary disease—as many adults fear doing. All died at the hands of people living in the United States. The U.S. child homicide rate makes this the most deadly country among the developed nations for children. The American rate is more than twice that of the second most deadly, Australia. For citizens of the United States, that particular first place award should be a source of shame and a strong impetus to change.

Beyond those children who die, we ask millions more to do what we would never ask ourselves: to endure pain, suffering, and unspeakable acts at the hands of people in their own homes. Incidents of child abuse and neglect in the United States run at more than double the rate in Canada or the United Kingdom. Is that truly a leadership role?

How Bad Is the Situation?

A 2007 UNICEF study covering 19 countries in Europe as well as Canada and the United States, found the United States in the bottom third of 21 developed countries on five dimensions of children's well-being.

Our report card is abysmal:

Material Well-Being	17
Health and Safety	21
Educational Well-Being	12
Family and Peer Relationships	20
Behaviors and Risks	20

Child abuse and neglect could not be measured directly because of differences in definition and measurement in various countries. However, the organization's earlier 2003 report found that a small group of OECD countries—Spain, Greece, Italy, Ireland, and Norway—have the lowest rates of child death from maltreatment. Once again, the risk factors most closely and consistently associated with child abuse and neglect are poverty, stress, and parental drug and alcohol abuse. In total, approximately 3,500 children (under the age of 15) die every year in the OECD countries from maltreatment, physical abuse, and neglect . . . such figures need to be read in the light of the unimaginable anguish and grief of the families concerned, and of the fact that the number of deaths is but the tip of an iceberg of trauma and disability.[2]

It is telling that the United States fell last on child health and safety as measured by infant mortality, low birth weights, immunization, and deaths from accidents and injuries. It is also telling that the study found "no obvious relationship" between levels of child well-being and national income. The United States placed below Hungary, the Czech Republic, Poland, Portugal, Spain, Italy, and Greece on measures of child well-being.[3]

Beyond its portrayal of each country's strength and weaknesses, why is this research important? The authors explained it this way: "It shows what is achievable in practice and provides both government and civil society with the information to argue for and work towards the fulfillment of children's rights and the improvement of their lives. Above all, such comparisons demonstrate that given levels of child well-being are not inevitable but policy-susceptible. The wide differences in child well-being seen throughout this report card can therefore be interpreted as a broad and realistic guide to the potential for improvement in all OECD countries."[4]

Why Haven't We Fixed It?

The authors of *The Politics of Child Abuse in America*—Lela Costin, Howard Karger, and David Stoesz—marvel at the inadequacies of American public policy in protecting children at risk: "How can a society that is health conscious enough to require air bags in automobiles, limits on advertising for cigarettes, and warnings about alcohol consumption during pregnancy be so ineffectual about the neglect, abuse, and murder of its children?"[5]

Laws have been passed with great seeming potential, only to languish and wither in ignominy. As child advocate lawyer Lewis Pitts has said,

> As a nation we have made written promises (laws) that we will provide health care, education, and speedy, safe, permanent placement for abused and neglected children. . . . Yet in every state we break these promises daily with catastrophic results to the children requiring costly

measures later. Our broken promises lead to delinquency and crime; pain and suffering of children victims who often then victimize other innocent people. We break these promises not because we do not know what these children need or how to deliver the services but due to inadequate federal and state appropriations of the funds to get the job done. In other words, our elected officials are spending our tax money on something other than these children.[6]

Secrecy shrouds the handling of child protection cases. Champions for children are paralyzed by misinformation, lack of information, and downright disinformation. The president, the legislators, and the courts are always, we're told, taking care of the children. No child left behind, and so on. Such myths prevail because skilled politicians and their allies know how to keep the rest of us from knowing who is really doing what to whom.

> "Mirrors and blue smoke, beautiful blue smoke rolling over the surface of highly polished mirrors, first a thin veil of blue smoke, then a thick cloud that suddenly dissolves into wisps of blue smoke, the mirrors catching it all, bouncing it back and forth."[7]
>
> —Columnist Jimmy Breslin, 1975

Great castles and kingdoms in child protection have been promised. When it comes to children's lives, smoke and mirrors should be intolerable. Yet they are what have largely been passed off as accomplishment by the child-protection myth-manufacturing industry. Even some well-intentioned people have fallen for the side stories, overstatements, and understatements characteristic of what today passes for political conversation. As Franklin Roosevelt once said, "nothing in politics is accidental." And neither is placing abuse and neglect of children on the back burner of U.S. government concerns.

Polarization and the Damage Done

"In the traditional political world, there is a disconnect between 'pro-child' liberalism and 'anti-crime' conservatism," said Grier Weeks, a founder of Protect and ProtectPAC, the political action committee for child protection. Weeks learned a great deal about politics as he led the effort to eliminate the incest exception to child sexual abuse law in North Carolina. He has described the politics of child abuse as follows:

> Anti-crime politics is a bread and butter issue for most traditional conservatives. But when it comes to crimes against children, a strong "pro-family" lobby keeps many conservatives soft and confused about just exactly who the real victim is in child sexual abuse cases—the child or the parents who are besieged by DSS and law enforcement. And, of course, they're first to cut crucial programs for children.
>
> Traditional liberals, on the other hand, see themselves as "pro-child" and tend to think tough-on-crime politics is demagoguery. They may not be opposed in theory to getting tough on crimes, especially against children, but they simply don't have a lot of appetite for it. On the other hand, they love children—just ask them. They're natural allies when it comes to funding services that help children and families.
>
> But none of this goes very deep. This great political ambivalence, silliness and apathy in the face of rampant child abuse would dissolve overnight if an organized constituency demanded both a pro-child and anti-crime response. Senator Steve Metcalf's legislation to criminalize incest in North Carolina was a perfect prototype of smart, nonpartisan legislation to protect children.
>
> It languished for over a year because he had fewer than a dozen committed supporters behind him. It passed in two weeks because political will became focused on it overnight.[8]

This polarization is among the factors that David Stoesz, professor of social policy at Virginia Commonwealth University and co-author of *The Politics of Child Abuse in America*, believes account for how Americans have become negligent in responding to abused and neglected children. It is an "ideological polemic (that) has impeded advocates of parents' vs. children's rights from crafting a pragmatic middle ground that would protect maltreated children.[9]

Michael Petit has done a great deal of research and thinking about the myths and reality of child abuse and neglect in America. As a result, Petit, president of the Every Child Matters Education Fund, issued a major report in 2007 titled *Homeland Insecurity . . . American Children at Risk*.[10] Petit holds that the progress in children's health and safety made during the 20th century came from the widespread public support of federal spending on maternal and child health services, hospitals, medical research, higher education for doctors and nurses and other public health measures.

"Many of these social gains are now stalled or at risk of being reversed thanks to two myths underpinning conservative political ideology dominant since the early 1980's," Petit wrote. "First, that the federal government can't do anything right, and second, that taxes are akin to outright thievery."[11]

Proven programs and policies that could actually reduce abuse and neglect have been attacked since the 1980s, and the attacks have grown under the George W. Bush administration, according to Petit. "Cuts in federal taxes and their impact on state revenues forced many cuts in childcare programs, child support enforcement, health care assistance, Head Start, and more, ignoring decades of documentation showing that more, not less, federal spending on children was needed. The result is a huge investment gap, one producing much worse outcomes for U.S. children and families than found in other rich democracies."[12]

Child abuse and neglect costs the citizens of the United States $258 million every day.[13] Yet, as Petit has pointed out, rather than focusing on services that would protect abused children (and hence could save billions each year), Republican conservatives when in control of the administration and Congress preferred to devote their attention and hearings "to debate such 'family values' issues as same-sex marriage, flag-burning and whether to allow the national anthem to be sung in Spanish." Petit warned that "unless a new Congress makes greater investments, child abuse and neglect will continue at epidemic proportions in the richest of the rich democracies."[14]

As bitterly disappointing as the disparity between the United States and other developed countries, so are those between the states on such measures as deaths from child abuse. Children in the bottom 10 states are seven times more likely to die from abuse and neglect than those in the top 10 states.[15] The comparisons Petit makes between blue and red states are compelling evidence of a relationship between the willingness to support social services and the actual human consequences. He offered President George W. Bush's home state of Texas—a "classic low tax, low service state"—as a prime example of the effect of political ideology on people's lives. Texas ranks

- first in child abuse deaths
- first in the percentage of uninsured children
- first in food insecurity

- first in the number of incarcerated adults
- second in the percentage of the population that goes hungry
- first in teen pregnancy
- fifth in the overall poverty rate
- sixth in crime
- 47th in income and food stamps benefits for the neediest
- 50th in the percentage of fully immunized two-year-olds

"Yet," Petit wrote, "the politicians whose harsh policies produce these outcomes stubbornly insist that more tax breaks and more cuts in programs are good for America's children."[16] Using official data to develop statistically based rankings of child well-being, Petit found that states with the best outcomes tend to tax themselves to make the necessary investments in programs for children. In those states, abused children are more likely to be helped, to be covered for health, and to participate in after-school programs than in the low-tax states.

The Great Society initiatives of the mid-1960s "helped knock back child poverty to a record-low 14 percent by 1969," Petit observed, but the story does not end there:

> Conservative ideologues have taken pains to misrepresent the effectiveness of government poverty programs, loudly proclaiming that only the private sector could help the poor while ignoring evidence that the much lower child poverty rates in other countries are the direct result of public, not private, policies. Most telling, government data show that since the latest round of conservative tax and budget dogma was imposed in 2001, household income has dropped, poverty has increased and health coverage has declined. . . . Earlier generations of Americans understood that progressive taxes are essential to democracy and its commitment to equal opportunity for all children. The current generation of anti-tax conservatives seems determined to prove our ancestors wrong.[17]

The Bush administration issued a proposed 2008 budget that froze funding for most child welfare programs at the 2007 levels, even as inflation caused the cost of maintaining critical programs for children to rise. The Child Abuse Prevention and Treatment Act was one exception, however, with the President's budget directing an additional $10 million in discretionary funding to nurse home visits for at-risk families. But the budget also proposed reductions in Head Start and several other key discretionary programs and included cuts to some mandatory programs, such as the Social Services Block Grant that provides funds to states for basic services to vulnerable low-income children.[18]

The Realities on the Ground

In the current situation, politics has proven more destructive than constructive in improving the lot of American children at risk. Experience has taught us the harsh lesson that no single solution will work for everyone. Why must we see children in terms of our political party preferences? Why can't we think of all the hundreds upon hundreds of children who are harmed every day in the United States because for decades we've failed to get our values aligned and our priorities in order?

The Annie E. Casey Foundation study in 2008 was the first to analyze 2006 Census Bureau data, the most recent available, for a detailed look at foster parents. Foster households have a lower average income ($56,364) than all households with children ($74,301), even though they care for more children. Approximately 50% of foster households have three or more children, but only 21% of all other households have as many. The study also finds that foster parents are more likely than others to be unemployed and to lack a high school diploma.[19] Well-meaning people without much support are trying to help children at risk. Surely the government can do more.

Values compete—it's a fact of life. Instead of simply crying "Foul!" when one pet agenda might be compromised by the advance of another, we all need to consider carefully how and when values collide when it comes to children. In large part, widely shared political views across our nation actually cause inadequate attention to children at risk. Take family preservation, for example. Keeping families together sounds like a good priority and it is good—when it suits the situation at hand. But we must not sacrifice vulnerable children at the altar of the intact family. Indeed, can we even consider a family intact whose children are abused or neglected?

As a group, neither Republicans nor Democrats dislike children nor advocate ignoring their needs. Their actions, though, ought to speak louder than their words. Despite some gains, American children at risk have largely been ill served by both major political parties. We need to find ways to help people listen past the loudest voices in debates on these issues. When those voices belong to people who profit from the ever-increasing tax dollars thrown at the disasters that result from child abuse—then it needs to be pointed out.

Why Is This the Case and How Do We Change It?

At its best, politics helps different kinds of people come together and achieve a task—even if they compete in the doing. But when the who gets ahead or the how of doing something becomes more important than actually accomplishing a goal, politics has ceased to help. The first thing to keep in mind, then, is that the prime issue isn't whether somebody's project, company, career, or party is advanced; it's whether the youngsters in the care of our society get their due.

Second, if politics is inevitable and the laws already passed can't be trusted to deliver, should we throw up our hands and quit? Not if we understand the bear that is democratic politics—both its friendly and vicious sides. Very little gets done without politics—knowing with whom to talk and how to speak so that key people will listen. In a democracy, of necessity, all views must be considered and all parties heard. But rather than despairing at the inevitable shortcomings in policy that proceed from politics, and being intelligent, honorable and caring people, we need to help make politics work for children. We can't rid human dealings of politics, but we can press our politicians to open the windows, let in some fresh ideas, and keep another child from dying in despair and agony tonight.

Getting a share of the politician's mind is no easy task. How can we help ensure that officials and opinion leaders understand and view the problems of child protection as objectively as possible? Let's start by looking at some of the reasons why so little understanding and priority are attached to at-risk children. Why don't most politicians hear their cries?

Children Don't Vote

Poor children are especially underrepresented in Congress because they do not vote, do not attend fund raising dinners, and are sorely lacking in political clout.

It's time we faced how we frame children at risk for abuse and neglect in our society. If we see them as passive victims—or worse, just not see them at all—then their stories become fabricated. In other words, we make them up. The media play a huge role in how the public sees abused and at-risk children by not showing us their lives. And, with their ready access to the media, elected politicians and appointed officials in federal, state, and local governments influence those perceptions as well—by what they say and what they fail to say.

Our own interest in the plight of abused and neglected children, then, rises and falls with the limited attention spans of the media and public officials. Politicians, especially, pay attention to issues that affect their electability. This is why laws protecting women and men are better than those to protect children. It is also why more money goes to pay for such protection.

In 2006, *New York Times* columnist Bob Herbert described several gut-wrenching deaths from child abuse in an op-ed article. Of his near despair at the situation, Herbert wrote that terrible stories of child abuse appear periodically, and then, following a public outcry and calls for reforming the child welfare system, the story disappears and the public goes about its business as if the problem has been solved. Yet children remain "trapped in the torture chambers of their own homes," Herbert wrote:

> The kids who are most frequently the victims of abuse are from the lower economic classes. They are not from families that make a habit of voting. There is no real incentive for government officials to make the protection of these kids a priority.[20]

When roads and bridges show signs of disrepair, the relevant agencies generally do something about it, and most states provide adequate funding to at least keep the system functioning. And when it fails catastrophically—say, a highway overpass collapses on a dark night causing a motorist to fly off the road—the results are newsworthy enough to top the front page, photos included, and the evening news, prompting a sustained outcry and prompt government action.

Sexy Stories Give Cover to Cowardly News Hounds

Every time that a child in the child welfare system dies of abuse or neglect is a catastrophic failure. Just like a highway bridge collapse or a midnight mudslide on a family home, each such death tends to be terrifyingly unique. Yet how often do deaths and injuries from child abuse become the lead news story of the day? What is the problem with journalists here, particularly those in television and radio? Where many reporters will gladly go into gruesome detail about celebrity murders and suicides, co-ed kidnappings, or serial killers' twisted methodologies, what of America's own dead and dying children?

Do news editors think our sensibilities are too delicate to show us the real stories of child abuse tragedies? Even when they are covered, sanitized visuals and neutered news copy hobble such stories' ability to capture a share of the audience's mind. Editors also know very well that capturing that share is the only way to prompt the righteous indignation of the American public—the flood of letters, phone calls, and e-mails to officialdom—that actually gets things done.

We all know the ability of graphic visual evidence to capture the public mind. Think of Saddam Hussein's execution, the Abu Ghraib photos, Princess Diana in the wrecked Mercedes, the shooting of Lee Harvey Oswald, Robert Kennedy lying stricken, or the balcony photograph after Martin Luther King was assassinated. Such images drill into the individual minds of citizens—even if they only hear about it. This is exactly why child abuse and neglect needs its graphic moment—or indeed hours.

How long would Americans let thousands of children each day suffer beatings, torture, scalding, malnutrition, sensory deprivation, and even starvation if the media actually covered the issue with the priority it deserves. News networks will happily show several minutes of video about teachers becoming intimate with students over the voice of a sanctimonious news anchor bemoaning the decline of American morals. Why don't more news organizations instead have the guts to present the public with at least a glimpse of the devastation wrought by child abuse or neglect? Faced with graphic representations of actual reality, how many citizens would get off their couches and demand real, unshakeable efforts to improve the safety of America's children? We think many would—and quickly!

Is there a photojournalist willing to compile a traveling exhibition of photos depicting the terrible conditions that prevail in tragedies of child abuse and neglect—and the horrific aftermaths? Is there an institution or corporation willing to support such a project? Or a news magazine willing to print such a photo spread? The impact would be an international furor. The odds are very good that it would save lives. It would certainly sell copies. Isn't that the real job of journalists—to print the news and raise issues to a level lawmakers cannot ignore? Okay, so children don't vote—but voters do. When will newspapers, magazines, television, and radio networks turn around and help American voters do the right thing for our nation's children?

More attention from major media is critical to raising the priority of child abuse and neglect among politicians and the public. Bill O'Reilly, the outspoken and controversial host of The O'Reilly Factor on Fox News, has long made a priority of featuring child abuse cases among the news stories his show develops. He is perhaps unique among major newscasters in that regard. O'Reilly spoke with Kathleen Reardon in early 2006 about the reasons for his strong interest in the issue.

Reardon:	Why has the issue of child abuse affected you so deeply that you've made it a continuing part of *The O'Reilly Factor*?
O'Reilly:	I was a high school teacher and I was always interested in how kids are protected by society and how they're dealt with on educational and social levels. When I became a journalist it was clear to me that there were just huge holes in American society dealing with kids, especially when they left the school grounds. There are no advocacy groups for kids. There's no ACLU for kids. And the child advocates that exist, some of them are good and some of them are in it for the wrong reasons—and they don't have a lot of power. So I decided that if I ever had a chance I would move forward on issues that would raise the consciousness of what children face in this society. So we started on *Inside Edition* when I anchored that show, and then just brought it over here to Fox. Basically we're trying to be watchdogs. We're trying to [ensure] certain protections. There's really nobody lobbying for those protections and we're going to put a lot of heat on politicians to do the right thing. They won't do it without that heat.
	Everything I read indicates that nothing will get done unless people in the press like you move things along.
Reardon:	Yes, because kids don't vote. There's no self-interest for politicians to do the right thing. And as we see in Vermont now, there are a lot of hidden agendas when it comes to protecting children. We're peeling them back but, you know, they're there. We just have to push back.
O'Reilly:	Yesterday . . . I was wondering if your people had begun to peel that [politics in child abuse] back.
Reardon:	Yeah. We're making some good progress up there. We understand that there's nobody in Vermont willing to put themselves out. We've been looking for a hero and none has emerged in the whole state. The media is disgraceful. The politicians are cowardly and this little girl, we haven't identified her, but we know who she is and where she is, we know her circumstances. She's just poor. Her parents are largely uneducated. She has nobody looking out for her. And they know this. If this were Kennedy's or Howard Dean's children, I mean, this is the trip. So we're bringing all of that to the table and it's a shame we have to hurt the state of Vermont in the process. But something has to give up there. They can't be doing this kind of thing.
O'Reilly:	This is likely the tip of the iceberg.
Reardon:	Yeah, I mean, I hate to think that, but you're probably right. But I only go as far as the evidence takes me. We had a horrible situation in Florida, [convicted sex offender] John Couey killing this nine-year-old girl. The legislature was forced to pass Jessica's law.

And that started the ball rolling and now we have, I think, twelve states. By the end of the year we hope to have 40 of the 50 states pass some semblance of Jessica's law. Some states, like Oregon, are just hopeless and won't do it. [Oregon has since passed the law.] And, you're right; it all comes down to politics and who is running the legislature. But there are certainly very few heroes, especially in the liberal press where you would think they'd be trying to protect the downtrodden. They're just MIA. They're just not around because they can't get any political currency with this kind of stuff because it is a bi-level issue. It's not a liberal or conservative issue. There are abuses on both sides.

O'Reilly: Do you think the liberal press has done fairly well in terms of child abuse?

Reardon: No. I mean child abuse is out of control in this country.

O'Reilly: I mean has the liberal press done as well as the conservative press on this?

Reardon: There is no conservative press [on this issue]. That doesn't exist in America right now. And if I didn't do it on Fox I don't think Fox would be in the forefront of doing this because it's messy work. The *Wall Street Journal* doesn't do it and that's probably the most powerful conservative voice in the country. So, there's no conservative press to speak of.

But talking to me you come across as really concerned about this little girl.

O'Reilly: Yeah. We're populist on this program no matter what. But, I'm getting increasingly angry not only at the cowardly politicians who refuse to do the right thing but at the hypocritical media who every two minutes are parading around about the human rights violations against Guantanamo Bay terrorists, but when you get a human rights violation against a little girl in Vermont, they can't be bothered.

As I'm sure you know we have human rights violations against children constantly. A child dies in New York of abuse every couple of weeks.

Reardon: Absolutely. And not only in New York, but everywhere.

With regard to politics, the people who do work with kids at risk find there are so many players in the system—people who have their own theories and, as you mentioned, their own agendas. Do you hope ultimately to unearth that so people realize . . . .

(Continued)

(Continued)

O'Reilly: Well, we're going to take the bad guys down on a case-by-case basis. I don't have the time or the resources to take on the big picture of why the political system in America doesn't honor children. They don't honor the elderly either. I mean it's just too big and I can't do it. But what I can do is take cases like Vermont, like Florida, and the cases in Minnesota, and Idaho where they let that guy out and he wiped out the kids. I can take on those and bring them to the attention of the public and then I can take on Jessica's law, because they're so clear, and I can get that done as an advocate and a watchdog. But once I get into the theoretical, I can't. I have to go case by case on something the audience is going to react to. That's just the way television news is.

Reardon: If there are players in those particular systems then you'll take them down?

O'Reilly: Yes. We're committed to protecting children here when we find abuses of children, no matter where they lie. Some stories are bigger than others. This Vermont thing is just a horror, so we've latched on to that. But we will continue to do this reporting.

Reardon: Do you have any intention down the line to take on all situations for example where children come very close—after being abused and neglected and being in the system for a while—to being placed (in a family) and they experience something like what was described to me today—the judge decides that the family is just not right—the people are fat and they might make the kid fat?

O'Reilly: That's a tough one, because there's a lot of "he said, she said" in those kinds of situations. My responsibility is to be right. We get tons of stories that I can't do because I really don't know what the judge's intention was and why he made the ruling—and sometimes there's powerful evidence on both sides. I have to be very, very careful not to go on a witch hunt and not to demonize people who just make mistakes or make an honest judgment that didn't turn out correct—you know what I'm talking about. So, it has to be something that's so egregious, like a woman in Florida handing a bus ticket to flee the state to a man who she knows may have killed a nine-year-old and that woman isn't charged by the state attorney. There it is—there are no two sides to the story. And those are the things (where) I go in with a big hammer. We raise awareness to the system and why the system doesn't work. So you get the bigger picture based on these snapshot stories.

Reardon: I know how angry you're getting. You told me and I can see it on your show. I'm a registered independent but I blog on the *Huffington Post* so you know that sometimes I can get Republicans as well as liberals mad at me, but at the same time making children one side or the other is a bit troubling. The children's issue—claiming the liberal press isn't doing what they should—and they also come after you for. . . .

O'Reilly: We press issues beyond the children. We think the press is gen-uinely deteriorating and basically dishonest as it stands now in the country. You can see it with the *Los Angeles Times*. At least they're trying to do something out there but it reached a nadir about a year ago and they had to fire everybody because it was so corrupt, and the *New York Times* is at that point now. So the press is a separate issue. But there's no excuse, you know, for left-wing Americans who say they're for human rights and protecting the downtrodden to continually dismiss and ignore these abuses (of children). And they do. When's the last time you saw the ACLU go in and try to help one of these kids? Because their agenda is to pro-mote their secular, progressive issues—not to be a watchdog and protect the children. That's not even on their radar screen.

Reardon: I do have to admit that one of the blogs I did on children and this issue—while I may get an awful lot of responses on something that's more critical of the government or the way Katrina's being handled—on children's issues there's just no tread there.

O'Reilly: No, because it doesn't fit into their hatred of conservatives and on the other hand the conservatives' hatred of liberals. The real telling point here, professor, when you look at the states that are considering Jessica's Law, is how the conservative community and the liberal com-munity look at Jessica's Law. The conservative community almost always supports the tough mandatories. The liberal community does not. It wants to water the law down. It wants the emphasis on reha-bilitation rather than punitive. It doesn't believe the punishment should fit the crime. If you have a full-grown woman raped, you could never sentence the rapist to 60 days in jail. NOW would be standing there, screaming. And you'd have every liberal newspaper in the world coming down on you. If the little girl were black or Hispanic or Native American, they'd be there at the door kicking it in, the left-wing press. But the little white girl of no means, means nothing. They cannot fur-ther their agenda by taking up that little white girl's cause. So it is interconnected. But the problem in the left community, the liberal community, is that it refuses to make judgments about how to punish people who destroy little children. It will not make the judgment that these people deserve to be sentenced to 20 or 25 years, whatever it may be. And so you get a culture war over that. And I've got to tell you that the Left in this country is damaging themselves tremendously by not advocating protections for children. I mean every state, Oregon, New York state, it's all held up in Vermont as well by left-wing politi-cians. They're always the ones who hold it up. It's irrefutable.

(Continued)

(Continued)

Reardon: But as you know, on the ground, there are both [liberal and conservative people] working for and caring about kids.

O'Reilly: Yeah, but I only go where the evidence takes me. And I've got 16
stories on the board and 16 stories are being inhibited by left-
wingers. None are being inhibited by the Right. I will grant you
that the Right is very apathetic about this as well.

Reardon: Yes.

O'Reilly: Particularly in the right-wing press, but they don't obstruct solutions to the problem. The left does, consistently.

Reardon: Where are you taking this? You're going to keep at this, right?

O'Reilly: Well, Vermont is going to have to right the wrong, or they're going
to get punished economically. It's as simple as that.

Reardon: And this notion that you're after Vermont?

O'Reilly: No. Vermont is a state that just came across my desk. I love Vermont.
I've been going there since I was five years old. But they're going to
have to right the wrong or we're going to have to suggest that people
not go to Vermont. I haven't done that yet, but we will.

Reardon: And the American Bar Association? You've had representatives on
(the show). They protect each other as well?

O'Reilly: Yeah. They're not interested. The American bar is interested in making money. They're not interested in pro bono cases about a little
girl in Vermont who got raped. Where are the pro bono attorneys up
there filing suits on her behalf? You know, they don't exist.

Look, you know what the system is, professor. I'm not telling you
anything you don't know. Kids in America don't have advocates. They
don't have heroes. They can't vote. Poor kids in America . . . don't
have anybody looking out for them at all. Nobody. And it's such a
messy thing because a lot of these parents are drug addicted, mentally disabled, they're incompetent. They're as much of the problem
as anyone else. So, when you get into abuse situations the parents
are either responsible or allowing it to happen. I mean there are all
kinds of horrible things going on and most people in polite society
don't want to get their hands dirty. They don't want to deal with it.
And what our job here is, when the most egregious cases come
across our desks, we are going to go after the people who do not
do the right thing. We don't care whether they're Republicans or
Democrats, liberals or conservatives. We don't care.

Reardon: That's good.

O'Reilly: But I'm just laying out the landscape to you about what's happening and who's doing what at this juncture as far as I can tell, and
we have pretty good information.

Reardon: I'm coming at this subject not as liberal or conservative. There are those who would say, "You're talking with Bill O'Reilly? Do you agree with him on everything?" Probably no one agrees with you on everything.

O'Reilly: Not even my mother.

Reardon: But on this issue I think you're doing a terrific job . . . .

O'Reilly: Well, thank you. But believe me, it will not be recognized by the journalistic community.

Reardon: I'm going to write about it.

O'Reilly: Yeah, I know you are, and I'm looking forward to reading your book. But will I win a journalistic prize for any of this? No. It's just not important to these people. What's important to most journalists in power, editors, and television producers is advancing whatever social agenda is on their mind whether it's conservative or liberal. That's what they're in the business to do. And to make money.

Reardon: There might be a prize out there for champions for kids.

O'Reilly: I don't think so. I've never seen it. I'd be stunned. But that's okay. If we can get Jessica's Law this time next year passed in 40 out of the 50 states, then we'll have done God's work, I think.

Note: As of February 2007, 21 states and the District of Columbia had passed laws similar to Jessica's Law.

Race and Class

"Our national failure carries a haunting class and racial bias," Judge Charles Schudsen of Wisconsin has said time and again regarding the lack of protection of children:

As long as the homeless, the neglected, and the abused are poor or black, many policymakers will tolerate governmental acquiescence and inaction. That attitude, unspoken yet strong, often permeates even the most apparently benign legislative evaluations of prevention programs.

Where are your studies to show that this prevention proposal will work? Where is your statistical validation?' they ask as they scrutinize every meager allocation for services to children. They choose to forget how often they failed to ask comparable questions of other proposals, such as tax incentives for the rich. They choose to forget how often they otherwise accept that common sense, not statistical validation, forms the basis for many human actions—actions as important as going to war, or hugging a child, or praying.[21]

A recipient of the National Human Rights Leadership award, Judge Schudsen first made that charge against legislators in 1991. Unfortunately, it remains chillingly true today. How do we overcome such latent and not-so-latent biases? In an era of media adulation for the heroes in our society, people need to see motivating stories of courageous children who have fought and prevailed against their own destruction and refused to accept assaults on their human dignity.

As Americans, we pride ourselves on the absorption of millions of poor immigrants and the achievements of many minority families in joining the great middle class, as well as people who have dragged themselves out of poverty to become success stories, sometimes famous ones. Sports, business, and political heroes become subjects of mass admiration, even adulation. Think of Jackie Robinson, Mohammed Ali, Cesar Chavez, and Jaime Escalante. Their time in the spotlight has lasted for not 10 minutes, but for years and even decades. To involve people who do vote, to garner their attention, and to enlist them in protecting abused and neglected children, stories about at-risk and abused children in contemporary America must be told, preferably by the children. Why would a media, sports, or business celebrity step forward to tell such a story? Because their stories, if effectively told and tied to the issues of abuse and neglect, would have huge persuasive power, and could help weaken the political power of those who consistently deflect attention away from the needs of children at risk.

Which major American personality will be brave enough to get his or her story out? Not to have it whispered about in gossip columns or hinted at in interviews and news stories, but to address it forthrightly and on behalf of others who still suffer. Who is willing to make it a part of the national psyche and to help put their story—like the story of Anne Frank— into the memory bank of a nation's much regretted past? To be effective, of course, it would also require an active involvement in the issue, and a desire to make sure the stories of children still alive and still suffering are heard and felt deeply by those who can make a difference. And by politicians who, when they try to turn away, will be turned back on pain of losing votes.

Breaking Through Political Barriers

Politics is an inseparable part of every organization and every human endeavor where people are competing for clients, money, votes, positive regard, reinforcement of their own views, power, or even just to be seen as being right.[22] When it comes to the protection of children, we adults must understand that today's politics often stand in the way of protecting the innocent and that it's up to us to change that, no matter the risk of personal cost, loss of votes, being wrong, relinquishing some power, or whatever it takes.

Strength Through Cooperation

Advocacy groups like the Children's Defense Fund and professional organizations like the American Academy of Pediatrics have attempted to provide poor children with a political voice.

One example of the potential efficacy of such cooperation is First Star, which, along with Stop the Silence and the Child Abuse and Interpersonal Violence Initiative, as well as representatives from academia and the bar, is pressing federal legislators to pass a bill that would create an institute on child abuse and interpersonal violence within the National Institutes of Health.

Part of the incoherence in the federal approach to child abuse and neglect undoubtedly results from the fact that federally funded research consists of a patchwork of initiatives across several independent federal entities. The proposed institute would establish a primary base for what are currently fragmented research efforts and would "galvanize resources to focus public attention on this horrifying tragedy," the backers have pointed out. As of early 2007, they were pressing for development of a bill and a congressional hearing on the initiative.

In collaboration with leading law schools, First Star is planning multidisciplinary centers of excellence (MCEs) to offer comprehensive training to professionals responsible for the welfare of abused and neglected children across the United States. Those will include doctors, judges, lawyers, nurses, social workers, teachers, psychologists, and police officers. The curriculum will incorporate coursework from leading schools of law, social work, nursing, psychology, and public health. Attendees will learn to apply a holistic, collaborative approach to each child's situation, needs, and interests.

Publicize Best Practices

"States rights are terrific for freedom and innovation," said Peter Samuelson, co-founder of First Star, "But the failure of the 50 states to productively share successful legislation and techniques with each other has proven lousy for protecting children."

> Every scintilla of best practice with regard to child safety was worked out years ago. Self-invented methods for dealing with abuse and neglect have been successfully implemented somewhere among the 2,200 independent jurisdictions throughout the nation. But at least 80 percent

of the country has never heard or learned those lessons. That leaves over three-fourths of the country in a Dark Ages of inept, broken, shambling, bureaucratic ineptitude.

In most states, we fail to adequately train the grownups through whose hands pass the abused and neglected children. In Texas it takes more weeks of training to become a state-certified manicurist than it does to become an investigating social worker.[23]

Samuelson is working to convince states and agencies to share and implement best standards nationally through "peer pressure, public pressure and the federal government revising the levers inherent in block grants, which pay about half the cost of the state systems." He cited First Star's four-year study on legal representation for children, which found that children who are represented by well-trained, client-directed attorneys in dependency hearings receive the best care, and are moved more quickly to nurturing and permanent homes. The report card, Samuelson stated, "shows exactly that when the laws and procedures are better, the outcomes are better."[24]

In April 2007, First Star released its published findings in the first *National Report Card on Legal Representation for Children*. In the months following, First Star began meeting with state policymakers and stakeholders to provide each state with constructive recommendations, including model legislation, on how to make laws better for children within their jurisdiction.[25]

Moreover, Samuelson believes that we would do well to study other advanced nations' practices and look at the statistical outcomes they are obtaining, then adapt the most successful methods to our own use here in America. "We should be among the top 10 percent of first world nations in child safety. Why would we tolerate anything else?"[26]

Sue the Laggards

"We won't rest until every state in the U.S. lives up to its constitutional and statutory obligation to provide basic services, care and protection to abused and neglected children," proclaimed Children's Rights, the child advocacy group, which holds state-run child welfare agencies accountable for their action—or inaction.[27] The group filed its first lawsuit in 1980, and in the last two years alone has sued New Jersey, Missouri, Michigan, and Mississippi. Its lawsuits have prompted child protection reforms in 13 states.[28]

"We don't go away until we know that states are in compliance with court orders, and that children are being fully protected while in state custody," declared associate director Susan Lambiase, citing long-standing cases in New Jersey and New Mexico where that is now happening.

When it sues an agency, Children's Rights stays involved from the decision to file a lawsuit until the day court oversight finally ends. In cases like Connecticut's child welfare system, which it first sued in 1989, the effort can span decades.[29] A Children's Rights lawsuit against New Mexico ended in 2005 after 23 years of federal court oversight of the state's foster care system.

Such tactics have certainly caught the attention of other states. When Children's Rights announced it would sue Michigan to improve its efforts to find permanent homes for foster children, state officials immediately offered to discuss the possibility of an out-of-court settlement. Of course, there had already been talks. "We're going to be asking for the end of violations of children's rights," executive director Marcia Robinson Lowry said at the time. "We're going to ask that the state, in fact, stop violating children's rights and both develop and put in place a plan under which children are protected and receive the services to which they are entitled and the protection to which they are entitled."[30]

Challenge the Secrecy Laws

In the latter half of the 20th century, what we refer to as sunshine laws opened up many aspects of government to media and public scrutiny. To those who believe an informed public is crucial to sustaining democracy, and that open government equates with effective government, this was a healthy development. It has been countered, though by a growing trend toward secretiveness in the federal executive branch, especially since the turn of the century.

In the interest of America's children—and that of the U.S. taxpayer who foots the bills for both child welfare and the costly consequences when government fails to look after the best interests of our children— it's time for a counterforce.

In the 14 states with open hearings and guidelines to protect the child's identity, errors are corrected because Americans, once they know the facts, demand no less. But in 36 states, there is a presumption of governmental secrecy, regardless of whether it's necessary for the child's protection. This hood of secrecy—which frequently remains intact even after a child's violent death—allows patterns of ineptitude and bureaucratic misfeasance to roll on endlessly. We need the light of day holding the responsible parties to press and public account.[31]

Reverse the DeShaney Decision

Peter Samuelson has pointed out that unlike all other Americans, children who have been harmed by state decisions and actions—neglected and abused children—have no right to seek redress or damages. "As a result, the agencies mandated to protect children are not required to protect them. These agencies face no legal consequences for repetitive failures, even if they come to light."[32] To change this reprehensible condition, we advocate the reversal of the U.S. Supreme Court's DeShaney ruling either by legislation or by finding an appropriate case and challenging its effects back up to the Supreme Court.

Joshua DeShaney was a Wisconsin child who had been repeatedly beaten by his father. Complaints were made to social workers at the Winnebago County Department of Social Services, which decided to allow the child to remain in his father's custody. When more beatings finally resulted in severe, permanent brain damage that left him profoundly retarded, Joshua and his mother sued the department, arguing that by failing to protect him from his father's attacks, they had deprived Joshua of his 14th Amendment right. The case ultimately came before the U.S. Supreme Court, which supported lower courts' rulings in favor of the county.

The majority opinion by Chief Justice William Rehnquist said the state's failure to protect Joshua did not violate the due process clause of the 14th Amendment because the clause "imposes no duty on the state to provide members of the general public with adequate protective services."[33] It held that the clause protects people against state action only, and given that Joshua's father had damaged him, it was not the DSS's responsibility:

> While the state may have been aware of the dangers that he faced, it played no part in their creation, nor did it do anything to render him more vulnerable to them. Under these circumstances, the Due Process Clause did not impose upon the state an affirmative duty to provide the petitioner with adequate protection.

Dissenting Justice William Brennan, however, wrote that

> It simply belies reality . . . to contend that the state "stood by and did nothing" with respect to Joshua . . . Through its child-protection program, the state actively intervened in Joshua's life and, by virtue of this intervention, acquired ever more certain knowledge that Joshua was in grave danger. . . .
>
> My disagreement with the Court arises from its failure to see that inaction can be every bit as abusive of power as action, that oppression can result when a State undertakes a vital duty and then ignores it. Today's opinion construes the Due Process Clause to permit a state to displace private sources of protection and then, at the critical moment, to shrug its shoulders and turn away from the harm that it has

promised to try to prevent. Because I cannot agree that our Constitution is indifferent to such indifference, I respectfully dissent.

In his own famous dissent, Justice Harry Blackmun wrote that

Today, the Court purports to be the dispassionate oracle of the law, unmoved by "natural sympathy" . . . . But, in this pretense, the Court itself retreats into a sterile formalism which prevents it from recognizing either the facts of the case before it or the legal norms that should apply to those facts. As Justice Brennan demonstrates, the facts here involve not mere passivity, but active state intervention in the life of Joshua DeShaney—intervention that triggered a fundamental duty to aid the boy once the State learned of the severe danger to which he was exposed.

The Court fails to recognize this duty because it attempts to draw a sharp and rigid line between action and inaction. But such formalistic reasoning has no place in the interpretation of the broad and stirring clauses of the Fourteenth Amendment. Indeed, I submit that these clauses were designed, at least in part, to undo the formalistic legal reasoning that infected antebellum jurisprudence . . .

Like the antebellum judges who denied relief to fugitive slaves . . . the Court today claims that its decision, however harsh, is compelled by existing legal doctrine. On the contrary, the question presented by this case is an open one, and our Fourteenth Amendment precedents may be read more broadly or narrowly depending upon how one chooses to read them. Faced with the choice, I would adopt a "sympathetic" reading, one which comports with dictates of fundamental justice and recognizes that compassion need not be exiled from the province of judging . . .

Poor Joshua! Victim of repeated attacks by an irresponsible, bullying, cowardly, and intemperate father, and abandoned by respondents who placed him in a dangerous predicament and who knew or learned what was going on, and yet did essentially nothing except, as the Court revealingly observes . . . "dutifully recorded these incidents in [their] files." It is a sad commentary upon American life, and constitutional principles—so full of late of patriotic fervor and proud proclamations about "liberty and justice for all"—that this child, Joshua DeShaney, now is assigned to live out the remainder of his life profoundly retarded. Joshua and his mother, as petitioners here, deserve—but now are denied by this Court.[34]

Amend the U.S. Constitution

This reprehensible situation leads inevitably to the issue of providing protection for children in our nation's constitution. Children are offered specific protection by the constitutions of more than 100 sovereign nations—including Iraq but not the United States of America. In those nations that ignore their constitutions, such protections aren't worth the paper they're printed on. But our U.S. Constitution has teeth. For that reason, an amendment protecting the rights of children would meet opposition from certain quarters. For that reason, a drive to enact such an amendment would also help put our children front and center now and for many years into the future.

The ensuing debate would help highlight the awful fact that more than half of American children have no lawyer when they appear in court hearings at which their interests and futures are at stake. The public argument would bring to the fore the dire situation—which any rational adult would find horrifying and totalitarian—that most official consideration of American children's best interests in abuse, neglect, and dependency determinations takes place without the child even being heard, without the necessary resources, and without the trained, qualified investigation and deliberation that would best serve the child.

Ratify the UN Convention on Children's Rights

More than 170 nations have ratified the United Nations Convention on the Rights of the Child. Only two have failed to do so: the United States of America and Somalia.

Somalia doesn't have a functioning government. What is our excuse? It can't be because when something emanates from the cooperative action of the UN member states—including our many friends and allies in Europe, Asia, and Latin America—it is automatically suspect, can it? Such dysfunctional political knee-jerkism only damages American interests at home and abroad.

We need to do much more for American children and children around the world who have grown up in the care of deficient systems. A recent study by the Pew Charitable Trust found that an increasing number of young people are aging out of foster care, even as research shows that many are ill-prepared for life after the system. Many have not finished high school or college and have limited employment and job skills.[35] A 2005 study by researchers at the University of Chicago found they have higher rates of homelessness and incarceration than their peers.[36]

Some children beat the odds of being lost once foster care is no longer available to them. But without our help, far more are never given a chance to succeed as their talents would allow.[37]

A Statement of Principles

Politics, as mentioned earlier, is a part of every organization and every human endeavor where people are competing for votes, positive regard, reinforcement of their own views, power, or even just to be seen as right. When it comes to the protection of children, we adults must know that politics often stands in the way of protecting the innocent and it's up to us to change that, no matter the personal cost, the loss of some votes, being wrong, relinquishing some power, or whatever it takes. Instead of demonstrating how "tough" a maverick nation the US is, we need to adopt a principled stance on behalf of America's children that overrides selfish political inclinations:

- Protecting the rights of children cannot be viewed in any way other than non-partisan. No political party owns the issue of children's rights, and none should be allowed to use it as a political football.
- Every key government post connected with the protection of children must be held by a person who knows and cares enough about the issues to be a tireless advocate. If such a person becomes focused on advancing the views of one party to the detriment of children, he or she should no longer serve in the post.
- Judges presiding over children's cases must be extensively trained and possess suitable experience. Ongoing training should be required of all judges whose work involves children.
- Attorneys assigned to represent children must also be extensively trained and possess suitable experience. Ongoing training should be required to continue working with children.
- No assignments to government positions involving the protection of children will be in any way influenced by cronyism, partisanship, or favor-granting. Where children are concerned, meritocracy must prevail.
- The needs of children should be one of the top three national priorities—thus making all American children our children.
- Laws already on the books should be implemented, not ignored.
- As a society, we must insist that theories of child protection (psychoanalytic, economic, etc.) not be allowed a lock on our thinking without significant and long-term study.
- Child-friendly courtrooms and laws need to be a major focus of every state and of the federal administration. This includes assuring that confidentiality concerns don't hurt any children more than they help them.
- Give children a voice by bringing their concerns into the fabric of our legal system.
- Every state should pass laws similar to Jessica's Law to protect children from predators.
- Jail sentences for child predators should be significant and surveillance consistent when people dangerous to children are living near where children live and play.

We're out of excuses if there ever were any good excuses for allowing children to be harmed day in and day out. What kind of society does that? Not the kind we think we are—not by a long shot. Children at risk need us not for our sympathy alone or even the help provided by foster and group care. They need us as a political force, at the lead, covering their backs. Years from now won't future generations ask, "What were they thinking?" or, more likely, "Why weren't they thinking?" "Why didn't more people care?"

We can't let one more child struggle without our help and call ourselves civilized. We need to bring their stories to the public. We need to incite outrage, because children's lives depend on us to do so. There isn't more time. The time is now to dance with this bear that is nation-wide neglect of children at risk until it drops. Then our children, as they certainly are, can take the floor, dance without fear, experience love with consistent, constant protection, and live the lives and experience the joys all children richly deserve.

Endnotes

1. Children's Rights, "Child Fatalities," www.childrensrights.org/site/PageServer?pagename=Issues_ChildFatalities.

2. UNICEF, "A League Table of Child Maltreatment Deaths in Rich Nations," Innocenti Report Card 5 (Florence UNICEF Innocenti Research Center, 2003) www.unicef-irc.org/cgi-bin/unicef/lunga.sql?ProductID=353

3. Indicators of material relative well-being included the percentages of children living in homes with incomes below 50 percent of the national median and in households without jobs, and the percentages of children reporting low family affluence, few educational resources, and fewer than 10 books in the home.

4. UNICEF, "Child poverty in perspective: An overview of child well-being in rich countries," *Innocenti* Report Card 7 (Florence: UNICEF Innocenti Research Centre, 2007) www.unicef.org/media/files/ChildPovertyReport.pdf

5. Lela Costin, Howard Karger, and David Stoesz, *The Politics of Child Abuse in America* (New York: Oxford University Press, 1996), 5.

6. Lewis Pitts, "Suggested Core Message or Thematic for First Star Work," unpublished, March 15, 2005, 1.

7. Jimmy Breslin, *How the Good Guys Finally Won: Notes from an Impeachment Summer* (New York: Viking Press, 1975), 33.

8. Grier Weeks, "The North Carolina Experience," *National Association to Protect Children*, October 16, 2002, www.protect.org/articles/nc_law.shtml

9. David Stoesz, "A Memorial For Sierra Osborne," *Richmond Times Dispatch*, A11, February 8, 2001.

10. Michael R. Petit, *Homeland Insecurity . . . American Children at Risk* (Washington, DC: Every Child Matters Education Fund, 2006), www .everychildmatters.org.

11. Ibid., 79

12. Ibid., Michael Petit, "Our Children's Homeland Insecurity." Tom Paine, Common Sense, February 6, 2007. www.tompaine.com/articles/2007/02/06/our_childrens_homeland_insecurity.php

13. Prevent Child Abuse Georgia, "Cost of Child Abuse & Neglect in U.S. Estimated at $258 Million Per Day," cited in Petit, *Homeland Insecurity . . . American Children at Risk*, 42.

14. Petit, *Our Children's Homeland Insecurity. . . . American Children at Risk*, 4.

15. Ibid., 44

16. Ibid., 1

17. Ibid.

18. First Star, "President's FY08 Budget Freezes Funding for Child Welfare Programs," *First Star Review*, February 2007.

19. wwwacef.org, May 2008

20. Bob Herbert, "Children in Torment," *New York Times*, op-ed, March 9, 2006.

21. Charles B. Schudsen, "Violence Against Children," remarks to Attorney General's Summit on Law Enforcement Responses to Violent Crime: Public Safety in the Nineties, Washington DC (March 4, 1991).

22. Kathleen K. Reardon, *The Secret Handshake: Mastering the Politics of the Business Inner Circle* (New York: Currency/Doubleday, 2000); *It's All Politics* (New York: Currency/Doubleday, 2005).

23. www.petersamuelson.blogspot.com

24. Ibid.

25. http://www.firststar.org/news/reportcardpressrelease.asp

26. www.petersamuelson.blogspot.com

27. Children's Rights, "Who We Are," see Google cache of www.childrens rights.org/site/Page Server?pagename=aboutus.

28. Jack Kresnak, "Child advocates to sue state over care; group seeks to prod officials to find homes for foster kids," *Detroit Free Press*, August 8, 2006.

29. From the Children's Rights website case summary on Juan F. v. Rell, No. H-89-859 (AHN), U.S. District Court, District of Connecticut: "In 1989, Children's Rights filed a class-action lawsuit to overhaul Connecticut's child welfare system, which routinely failed to provide basic protection and services for children. Under a Consent Decree reached in 1991, there were significant infrastructure improvements to the Department of Children and Families (DCF). However, after repeated failures to comply with other court-ordered changes, Children's Rights obtained an extraordinary court order in 2003 where, for the first time nationally, management authority over a state child welfare system was voluntarily transferred to a federal court. A comprehensive 'exit plan' was developed in early 2004. Since then, DCF has finally achieved full compliance with caseload requirements, and other practice improvements have followed. Management authority was returned to the state in the fall of 2005. While many

system-wide reforms have taken place, several very significant problems remain. Children's Rights continues to serve as a watchdog to ensure state compliance with the court-ordered Exit Plan." (See Google cache of www.childrensrights.org/pdfs/Juan% 2010.06%20Web%20Update.pdf)

30. Jack Kresnak, "Child advocates to sue state over care; group seeks to prod officials to find homes for foster kids," *Detroit Free Press*, August 8, 2006.

31. First Star, "Legal Research: Public Access to Abuse/Neglect Proceedings," July 2006, www.firststar.org/research/hearings.asp

32. Peter Samuelson, "Whose Future?" http://petersamuelson.blogspot.com

33. U.S. Supreme Court, DeShaney V. Winnebago Cty. Soc. Servs. Dept., 489 U.S. 189 (1989), http://laws.findlaw.com/us/489/189.html.

34. Ibid.

35. Pew Charitable Trusts, "Time for Reform: Aging Out and On their Own," 2007, 1. http://www.kidsarewaiting.org/tools/reports/files/0006.pdf

36. News Advisory, "Study Shows Broad Challenges for Young Adults Leaving Foster Care," Chapin Hall Center for Children, University of Chicago, May 19, 2005. www.About.chapinhall.org/press/newsalerts/2005/AgingOutStudy.html

37. Chris L. Jenkins, "A Foster Child Comes of Age," *Washington Post*, May 8, 2008, B01.

Appendix

First Star sent these Sense of Congress letters to the U.S. Department of Health and Human Services to ensure that the HIPAA legislation would be correctly interpreted across the country and those representing children would not be prevented from accessing their child clients' health care records.

February 13, 2004

Dear Colleague:

America's children are suffering at the hands of a failing system. In 2001, 903,000 children were victims of child abuse and neglect, and 275,000 of those cases were placed in foster care. Tragically, 1,300 children died from the abuse they suffered.

As Members of Congress who are dedicated to the protection of our nation's most vulnerable children, we would like to inform you of two separate sign-on letters, addressed to Secretary Tommy G. Thompson of the U.S. Department of Health and Human Services (HHS), which requests a clarification of language used in two pieces of legislation passed by Congress: the Keeping Children and Families Safe Act of 2003 and the Health Insurance Portability and Accountability Act (HIPAA).

More specifically, we ask that HHS elaborate, with instructional guidance, on Sections (b)(2)(A)(viii) and (xii) of the Keeping Children and Families Safe Act of 2003. Clarification is needed on the former section's requirements for the disclosure of confidential information among those with "a need for such information in order to carry out its responsibilities under law to protect children from abuse and neglect." Meanwhile, we request HHS elaboration on the latter section's definition of "training appropriate to the role" to any individual appointed by any court to represent a child in a dependency hearing. A second letter to Secretary Thompson addresses the effect of the Health Insurance Portability and Accountability Act (HIPAA) on child abuse and neglect victims and the systems designed to protect them.

Should you need more information, please feel free to contact Rosalea Orozco in Rep. Sanchez's office at x52965 or Tony Eberhard in Rep. Emerson's office at x54404.

Sincerely,
U.S. Representative Loretta Sanchez
U.S. Representative JoAnn Emerson

The Honorable Tommy G. Thompson, Secretary
U.S. Department of Health and Human Services
200 Independence Avenue, S.W.
Washington, D.C. 20201

Dear Secretary Thompson:

We, the undersigned Members of Congress, write to express our desire for important clarification with regard to policy implementation at the state level as it relates to certain provisions of the recently amended Child Abuse Prevention and Treatment Act (CAPTA).

Specifically, we ask that the Department of Health and Human Services elaborate, with instructional guidance, on Sections (b)(2)(A)(viii) and (xii) of the Keeping Children and Families Safe Act of 2003 ("the Act"), addressing respectively the disclosure of confidential information among those with "a need for such information in order to carry out its responsibilities under law to protect children from abuse and neglect," and the provision of "training appropriate to the role" to any individual appointed by any court to represent a child in a dependency hearing.

Section (b)(2)(A)(viii): We understand that abused and neglected children, as well as the nation's health on the whole, benefit from an environment of openness and a system that provides for thorough sharing of all information potentially relevant to the child or case at issue, including but not limited to records that might otherwise be considered confidential. Adopted in 2003, the Act requires state Child Protective Services (CPS) to "disclose confidential information to any Federal, State, or local government entity, or any agent of such entity," that has a legal responsibility to protect children. There is an immediate need for HHS, through policy guidance or regulations, to clarify standards for the states regarding (a) the types of agencies and agents that need to receive information; and (b) the scope of information to be provided. We hope that HHS will act quickly to ensure that such information sharing begins and is enforced with the strength the nation's children deserve.

Section (b)(2)(A)(xii): Additionally, the Act amended CAPTA by requiring that states receiving CAPTA grants provide "training appropriate to the role" to any individual appointed by the court to represent children in abuse, neglect and dependency hearings. We wish to clarify to HHS that by including this language it was our intent to ensure that every person, attorney or non-attorney, appointed by the court receives adequate and significant training, and that failure to provide for such training or the appointment of any individual lacking such training would be a violation of CAPTA and result in the forfeit of CAPTA funds. We hope that HHS will act quickly to alert the states, through policy guidance and regulations, that no court in any state receiving CAPTA funds may appoint a person (Attorney Ad Litem, Guardian Ad Litem, Court Appointed Special Advocate, or other) to represent a child without that person having first received training appropriate to the role.

We further request for an underscore of the importance of the training itself. We urge HHS to encourage states to adopt policy guidelines and regulations, and offer to the states technical assistance in determining what degree of training meets the substantial caliber of professionalism envisioned by Congress in crafting this legislation to protect our most vulnerable constituency, our children.

Thank you for your time and consideration of this important request.

Sincerely,

The Honorable Tommy G. Thompson, Secretary
U.S. Department of Health and Human Services, Office for Civil Rights
200 Independence Avenue, S.W.
Room 509F, HHH Building
Washington, D.C. 20201

Dear Secretary Thompson:

We, the undersigned Members of Congress, write to express our desire for improved clarification with regard to the effect of the Health Insurance Portability and Accountability Act (HIPAA) on child abuse and neglect victims and the systems designed to protect them. Regulations promulgated under HIPAA have resulted in inconsistent and uncertain results for abused and neglected children across the United States.

Of key concern to us is the conflict between HIPAA and the Child Abuse Prevention and Treatment Act (CAPTA). This summer, the Keeping Children and Families Safe Act of 2003 amended CAPTA by requiring state agencies to "disclose confidential information to any Federal, State, or local entity, or any agent of such entity, that has a need for such information in order to carry out its responsibilities under law to protect children from abuse and neglect." Recognizing that children in abuse and neglect cases benefit when those working on their behalf have a more thorough understanding of their health (including mental health), educational and social services histories, the amendment reversed previous policy that cautioned against sharing such information. The inconsistency between this recent policy and HIPAA regulations raises questions concerning the basic access of state Child Protective Services (CPS) to health information and the access of others to information contained within CPS files.

Insofar as this conflict frustrates efforts to protect children already at risk in the child welfare system, we ask that the Office for Civil Rights act with due speed to clarify HIPAA and recognize the Congressional intent of the Keeping Children and Families Safe Act. Ideally, such guidance from the Office will instruct that nothing in HIPAA be construed to impose barriers to the exchange of information afforded by CAPTA or other legislation. It is our opinion that child abuse-related health information must be freely shared with those working to protect, to diagnose, and to treat abused and neglected children. The privacy regulations must not endanger these efforts.

Thank you for your attention to this important request.

Sincerely,

Index

About the Authors

Kathleen Kelley Reardon is professor of management at the University of Southern California's Marshall School of Business, where she has served on the preventive medicine faculty. She is the author of seven books, including the Amazon best-seller *The Secret Handshake* and *It's All Politics*, which addresses the impact of politics on the careers of individuals and missions of organizations. She is the author of *Persuasion in Practice* (SAGE) and is a three-time *Harvard Business Review* author; her latest article was "Courage at Work." She was co-principal investigator and author on the feasibility study that launched Starbright, later chaired by Steven Spielberg and conjoined with Starlight. Dr. Reardon was inducted into Phi Beta Kappa, Phi Kappa Phi, and Mortar Board; received her PhD from the University of Massachusetts, Amherst; and has been a political analyst with the *Huffington Post* (www.huffingtonpost.com).

Christopher T. Noblet is a professional writer and editor. He is currently co-authoring a book on strategies for patients to obtain excellent health care. He has worked as journalist, newspaper editor, speechwriter for the chairman of Transamerica Life Companies, book editor, and in public affairs, marketing, and public relations. His BA and MA degrees are from the University of Connecticut, and his MBA degree is from the Marshall School of Business at the University of Southern California.